A Year with C. S. Lewis

A Year with C. S. Lewis

Daily Readings from His Classic Works

C. S. LEWIS

Edited by Patricia S. Klein

HarperSanFrancisco

A Division of HarperCollins*Publishers*

A YEAR WITH C. S. LEWIS: *Daily Readings from His Classic Works.* Copyright © 2003 by C. S. Lewis Pte. Ltd. All rights reserved. Printed in the United States of America. No part of this book may be used or reproduced in any manner whatsoever without written permission except in the case of brief quotations embodied in critical articles and reviews. For information address HarperCollins Publishers, Inc., 10 East 53rd Street, New York, NY 10022.

HarperCollins books may be purchased for educational, business, or sales promotional use. For information please write: Special Markets Department, HarperCollins Publishers, Inc., 10 East 53rd Street, New York, NY 10022.

HarperCollins Web site: http://www.harpercollins.com

HarperCollins®, ®, and HarperSanFrancisco™ are trademarks of HarperCollins Publishers, Inc.

FIRST EDITION

Library of Congress Cataloging-in-Publication Data
Lewis, C. S. (Clive Staples), 1898–1963. Edited by Patricia S. Klein.
    A year with C. S. Lewis : daily readings from his classic works / C. S. Lewis.—1st ed.
    p.   cm.
    ISBN 0-06-056616-7 (hardcover)
    1. Devotional calendars. I. Title.
BV4811.L48 2003
242'.2—dc21   2003056584

05 06 07 Quebecor 20 19 18 17 16 15 14 13 12 11

Contents

JANUARY

Supposing We Really Found Him?

It is always shocking to meet life where we thought we were alone. 'Look out!' we cry, 'it's *alive*'. And therefore this is the very point at which so many draw back—I would have done so myself if I could—and proceed no further with Christianity. An 'impersonal God'—well and good. A subjective God of beauty, truth and goodness, inside our own heads—better still. A formless life-force surging through us, a vast power which we can tap—best of all. But God Himself, alive, pulling at the other end of the cord, perhaps approaching at an infinite speed, the hunter, king, husband—that is quite another matter. There comes a moment when the children who have been playing at burglars hush suddenly: was that a *real* footstep in the hall? There comes a moment when people who have been dabbling in religion ('Man's search for God!') suddenly draw back. Supposing we really found Him? We never meant it to come to *that!* Worse still, supposing He had found us?

—from *Miracles*

January 1911 Lewis (age twelve) enrolls at Cherbourg Preparatory School in Malvern.

Imagine a Mystical Limpet

Why are many people prepared in advance to maintain that, whatever else God may be, He is not the concrete, living, willing, and acting God of Christian theology? I think the reason is as follows. Let us suppose a mystical limpet, a sage among limpets, who (rapt in vision) catches a glimpse of what Man is like. In reporting it to his disciples, who have some vision themselves (though less than he) he will have to use many negatives. He will have to tell them that Man has no shell, is not attached to a rock, is not surrounded by water. And his disciples, having a little vision of their own to help them, do get some idea of Man. But then there come erudite limpets, limpets who write histories of philosophy and give lectures on comparative religion, and who have never had any vision of their own. What they get out of the prophetic limpet's words is simply and solely the negatives. From these, uncorrected by any positive insight, they build up a picture of Man as a sort of amorphous jelly (he has no shell) existing nowhere in particular (he is not attached to a rock) and never taking nourishment (there is no water to drift it towards him). And having a traditional reverence for Man they conclude that to be a famished jelly in a dimensionless void is the supreme mode of existence, and reject as crude, materialistic superstition any doctrine which would attribute to Man a definite shape, a structure, and organs.

—from *Miracles*

January 1914 Lewis and childhood Belfast friend Arthur Greeves begin what would be a lifelong correspondence.

Not Naked but Reclothed

Our own situation is much like that of the erudite limpets. Great prophets and saints have an intuition of God which is positive and concrete in the highest degree. Because, just touching the fringes of His being, they have seen that He is plenitude of life and energy and joy, therefore (and for no other reason) they have to pronounce that He transcends those limitations which we call personality, passion, change, materiality, and the like. The positive quality in Him which repels these limitations is their only ground for all the negatives. But when we come limping after and try to construct an intellectual or 'enlightened' religion, we take over these negatives (infinite, immaterial, impassible, immutable, etc.) and use them unchecked by any positive intuition. At each step we have to strip off from our idea of God some human attribute. But the only real reason for stripping off the human attribute is to make room for putting in some positive divine attribute. In St Paul's language, the purpose of all this unclothing is not that our idea of God should reach nakedness but that it should be reclothed. But unhappily we have no means of doing the reclothing. When we have removed from our idea of God some puny human characteristic, we (as merely erudite or intelligent enquirers) have no resources from which to supply that blindingly real and concrete attribute of Deity which ought to replace it. Thus at each step in the process of refinement our idea of God contains less, and the fatal pictures come in (an endless, silent sea, an empty sky beyond all stars, a dome of white radiance) and we reach at last mere zero and worship a nonentity.

—from *Miracles*

1892 J. R. R. Tolkien, Lewis's longtime friend, colleague, and fellow Inkling (a group of friends who meet regularly from about 1930 to 1963 to share writings, good conversation, and the odd pint), is born in Bloemfontein, South Africa.

O Taste and See

The Christian statement that only He who does the will of the Father will ever know the true doctrine is philosophically accurate. Imagination may help a little: but in the moral life, and (still more) in the devotional life we touch something concrete which will at once begin to correct the growing emptiness of our idea of God. One moment even of feeble contrition or blurred thankfulness will, at least in some degree, head us off from the abyss of abstraction. It is Reason herself which teaches us not to rely on Reason only in this matter. For Reason knows that she cannot work without materials. When it becomes clear that you cannot find out by reasoning whether the cat is in the linen-cupboard, it is Reason herself who whispers, 'Go and look. This is not my job: it is a matter for the senses'. So here. The materials for correcting our abstract conception of God cannot be supplied by Reason: she will be the first to tell you to go and try experience—'Oh, taste and see!' For of course she will have already pointed out that your present position is absurd. As long as we remain Erudite Limpets we are forgetting that if no one had ever seen more of God than we, we should have no reason even to believe Him immaterial, immutable, impassible and all the rest of it. Even that negative knowledge which seems to us so enlightened is only a relic left over from the positive knowledge of better men—only the pattern which that heavenly wave left on the sand when it retreated.

—from *Miracles*

Enemies of Goodness

It is no use either saying that if there is a God of that sort—an impersonal absolute goodness—then you do not like Him and are not going to bother about Him. For the trouble is that one part of you is on His side and really agrees with his disapproval of human greed and trickery and exploitation. You may want Him to make an exception in your own case, to let you off this one time; but you know at bottom that unless the power behind the world really and unalterably detests that sort of behaviour, then He cannot be good. On the other hand, we know that if there does exist an absolute goodness it must hate most of what we do. This is the terrible fix we are in. If the universe is not governed by an absolute goodness, then all our efforts are in the long run hopeless. But if it is, then we are making ourselves enemies to that goodness every day, and are not in the least likely to do any better tomorrow, and so our case is hopeless again. We cannot do without it, and we cannot do with it. God is the only comfort, He is also the supreme terror: the thing we most need and the thing we most want to hide from. He is our only possible ally, and we have made ourselves His enemies. Some people talk as if meeting the gaze of absolute goodness would be fun. They need to think again. They are still only playing with religion. Goodness is either the great safety or the great danger—according to the way you react to it. And we have reacted the wrong way.

—from *Mere Christianity*

A Pleasant Theology

One reason why many people find Creative Evolution so attractive is that it gives one much of the emotional comfort of believing in God and none of the less pleasant consequences. When you are feeling fit and the sun is shining and you do not want to believe that the whole universe is a mere mechanical dance of atoms, it is nice to be able to think of this great mysterious Force rolling on through the centuries and carrying you on its crest. If, on the other hand, you want to do something rather shabby, the Life-Force, being only a blind force, with no morals and no mind, will never interfere with you like that troublesome God we learned about when we were children. The Life-Force is a sort of tame God. You can switch it on when you want, but it will not bother you. All the thrills of religion and none of the cost. Is the Life-Force the greatest achievement of wishful thinking the world has yet seen?

—from *Mere Christianity*

1943 *The Abolition of Man* is published by Oxford University Press.

Damned Nonsense

If you do not take the distinction between good and bad very seriously, then it is easy to say that anything you find in this world is a part of God. But, of course, if you think some things really bad, and God really good, then you cannot talk like that. You must believe that God is separate from the world and that some of the things we see in it are contrary to His will. Confronted with a cancer or a slum the Pantheist can say, 'If you could only see it from the divine point of view, you would realise that this also is God.' The Christian replies, 'Don't talk damned nonsense.' For Christianity is a fighting religion. It thinks God made the world—that space and time, heat and cold, and all the colours and tastes, and all the animals and vegetables, are things that God 'made up out of His head' as a man makes up a story. But it also thinks that a great many things have gone wrong with the world that God made and that God insists, and insists very loudly, on our putting them right again.

—from *Mere Christianity*

1955 Lewis takes up residence in Magdalene College, Cambridge.

Something Beyond

I think all Christians would agree with me if I said that though Christianity seems at the first to be all about morality, all about duties and rules and guilt and virtue, yet it leads you on, out of all that, into something beyond. One has a glimpse of a country where they do not talk of those things, except perhaps as a joke. Every one there is filled full with what we should call goodness as a mirror is filled with light. But they do not call it goodness. They do not call it anything. They are not thinking of it. They are too busy looking at the source from which it comes. But this is near the stage where the road passes over the rim of our world. No one's eyes can see very far beyond that: lots of people's eyes can see further than mine.

—from *Mere Christianity*

Somebody Who?

We have two bits of evidence about the Somebody [behind the Moral Law]. One is the universe He has made. If we used that as our only clue, then I think we should have to conclude that He was a great artist (for the universe is a very beautiful place), but also that He is quite merciless and no friend to man (for the universe is a very dangerous and terrifying place). The other bit of evidence is that Moral Law which He has put into our minds. And this is a better bit of evidence than the other, because it is inside information. You find out more about God from the Moral Law than from the universe in general just as you find out more about a man by listening to his conversation than by looking at a house he has built.

—from *Mere Christianity*

A Good Time Was Had by All

By the goodness of God we mean nowadays almost exclusively His lovingness; and in this we may be right. And by Love, in this context, most of us mean kindness—the desire to see others than the self happy; not happy in this way or in that, but just happy. What would really satisfy us would be a God who said of anything we happened to like doing, 'What does it matter so long as they are contented?' We want, in fact, not so much a Father in Heaven as a grandfather in heaven—a senile benevolence who, as they say, 'liked to see young people enjoying themselves', and whose plan for the universe was simply that it might be truly said at the end of each day, 'a good time was had by all'. Not many people, I admit, would formulate a theology in precisely those terms: but a conception not very different lurks at the back of many minds. I do not claim to be an exception: I should very much like to live in a universe which was governed on such lines. But since it is abundantly clear that I don't, and since I have reason to believe, nevertheless, that God is Love, I conclude that my conception of love needs correction.

—from *The Problem of Pain*

1950 Lewis receives his first letter from American fan Joy Davidman Gresham.

More Than Mere Kindness

There is kindness in Love: but Love and kindness are not coterminous, and when kindness (in the sense given above) is separated from the other elements of Love, it involves a certain fundamental indifference to its object, and even something like contempt of it. Kindness consents very readily to the removal of its object—we have all met people whose kindness to animals is constantly leading them to kill animals lest they should suffer. Kindness, merely as such, cares not whether its object becomes good or bad, provided only that it escapes suffering. As Scripture points out, it is bastards who are spoiled: the legitimate sons, who are to carry on the family tradition, are punished [Hebrews 12:8]. It is for people whom we care nothing about that we demand happiness on any terms: with our friends, our lovers, our children, we are exacting and would rather see them suffer much than be happy in contemptible and estranging modes. If God is Love, He is, by definition, something more than mere kindness. And it appears, from all the records, that though He has often rebuked us and condemned us, He has never regarded us with contempt. He has paid us the intolerable compliment of loving us, in the deepest, most tragic, most inexorable sense.

—from *The Problem of Pain*

1942 Lewis begins his second series of BBC talks entitled "What Christians Believe." These talks were later published in *Broadcast Talks* (or, in the U.S., *The Case for Christianity*) and comprise Book 2 in *Mere Christianity*.

Amazing Love, How Can It Be?

When Christianity says that God loves man, it means that God *loves* man: not that He has some 'disinterested', because really indifferent, concern for our welfare, but that, in awful and surprising truth, we are the objects of His love. You asked for a loving God: you have one. The great spirit you so lightly invoked, the 'lord of terrible aspect', is present: not a senile benevolence that drowsily wishes you to be happy in your own way, not the cold philanthropy of a conscientious magistrate, nor the care of a host who feels responsible for the comfort of his guests, but the consuming fire Himself, the Love that made the worlds, persistent as the artist's love for his work and despotic as a man's love for a dog, provident and venerable as a father's love for a child, jealous, inexorable, exacting as love between the sexes. How this should be, I do not know: it passes reason to explain why any creatures, not to say creatures such as we, should have a value so prodigious in their Creator's eyes. It is certainly a burden of glory not only beyond our deserts but also, except in rare moments of grace, beyond our desiring; we are inclined, like the maidens in the old play, to deprecate the love of Zeus. But the fact seems unquestionable.

—from *The Problem of Pain*

1951 Janie King Moore (Mrs. Moore) dies at the age of seventy-eight in Oxford and is buried at Holy Trinity Church in Headington Quarry, Oxford. Mrs. Moore (the mother of Lewis's army buddy Paddy Moore) and her daughter Maureen come under Lewis's care after Paddy's death in World War I.

War in Heaven

The Screwtape Letters is a fictional correspondence between a senior tempter, Screwtape, and his protégé, Wormwood. In this letter Screwtape attempts to explain the great Quarrel between the Enemy (God) and the "father" of all tempters, Satan:

What does He stand to make out of them? That is the insoluble question. I do not see that it can do any harm to tell you that this very problem was a chief cause of Our Father's quarrel with the Enemy. When the creation of man was first mooted and when, even at that stage, the Enemy freely confessed that He foresaw a certain episode about a cross, Our Father very naturally sought an interview and asked for an explanation. The Enemy gave no reply except to produce the cock-and-bull story about disinterested love which He has been circulating ever since. This Our Father naturally could not accept. He implored the Enemy to lay His cards on the table, and gave Him every opportunity. He admitted that he felt a real anxiety to know the secret; the Enemy replied 'I wish with all my heart that you did.' It was, I imagine, at this stage in the interview that Our Father's disgust at such an unprovoked lack of confidence caused him to remove himself an infinite distance from the Presence with a suddenness which has given rise to the ridiculous Enemy story that he was forcibly thrown out of Heaven. Since then, we have begun to see why our Oppressor was so secretive. His throne depends on the secret. Members of His faction have frequently admitted that if ever we came to understand what He means by love, the war would be over and we should re-enter Heaven. And there lies the great task. We know that He cannot really love: nobody can: it doesn't make sense. If we could only find out what He is *really* up to!

—from *The Screwtape Letters*

1919 Lewis (age twenty) is demobilized from his military service in World War I and returns to Oxford.

Blurry Visions of God

When you come to knowing God, the initiative lies on His side. If He does not show Himself, nothing you can do will enable you to find Him. And, in fact, He shows much more of Himself to some people than to others—not because He has favourites, but because it is impossible for Him to show Himself to a man whose whole mind and character are in the wrong condition. Just as sunlight, though it has no favourites, cannot be reflected in a dusty mirror as clearly as in a clean one.

You can put this another way by saying that while in other sciences the instruments you use are things external to yourself (things like microscopes and telescopes), the instrument through which you see God is your whole self. And if a man's self is not kept clean and bright, his glimpse of God will be blurred—like the Moon seen through a dirty telescope. That is why horrible nations have horrible religions: they have been looking at God through a dirty lens.

—from *Mere Christianity*

1946 *The Great Divorce* is published by Geoffrey Bles/The Centenary Press, London.

Our Highest Activity

If the world exists not chiefly that we may love God but that God may love us, yet that very fact, on a deeper level, is so for our sakes. If He who in Himself can lack nothing chooses to need us, it is because we need to be needed. Before and behind all the relations of God to man, as we now learn them from Christianity, yawns the abyss of a Divine act of pure giving—the election of man, from nonentity, to be the beloved of God, and therefore (in some sense) the needed and desired of God, who but for that act needs and desires nothing, since He eternally has, and is, all goodness. And that act is for our sakes. It is good for us to know love; and best for us to know the love of the best object, God. But to know it as a love in which we were primarily the wooers and God the wooed, in which we sought and He was found, in which His conformity to our needs, not ours to His, came first, would be to know it in a form false to the very nature of things. For we are only creatures: our role must always be that of patient to agent, female to male, mirror to light, echo to voice. Our highest activity must be response, not initiative. To experience the love of God in a true, and not an illusory form, is therefore to experience it as our surrender to His demand, our conformity to His desire: to experience it in the opposite way is, as it were, a solecism against the grammar of being.

—from *The Problem of Pain*

Our Three Responses to God

It is not simply that God has arbitrarily made us such that He is our only good. Rather God is the only good of all creatures: and by necessity, each must find its good in that kind and degree of the fruition of God which is proper to its nature. The kind and degree may vary with the creature's nature: but that there ever could be any other good, is an atheistic dream. George Macdonald, in a passage I cannot now find, represents God as saying to men, 'You must be strong with my strength and blessed with my blessedness, *for I have no other to give you.*' That is the conclusion of the whole matter. God gives what He has, not what He has not: He gives the happiness that there is, not the happiness that is not. To be God—to be like God and to share His goodness in creaturely response—to be miserable—these are the only three alternatives. If we will not learn to eat the only food that the universe grows—the only food that any possible universe ever can grow—then we must starve eternally.

—from *The Problem of Pain*

Always Now

Everyone who believes in God at all believes that He knows what you and I are going to do tomorrow. But if He knows I am going to do so-and-so, how can I be free to do otherwise? Well, here once again, the difficulty comes from thinking that God is progressing along the Time-line like us: the only difference being that He can see ahead and we cannot. Well, if that were true, if God *foresaw* our acts, it would be very hard to understand how we could be free not to do them. But suppose God is outside and above the Time-line. In that case, what we call 'tomorrow' is visible to Him in just the same way as what we call 'today'. All the days are 'Now' for Him. He does not remember you doing things yesterday; He simply sees you doing them, because, though you have lost yesterday, He has not. He does not 'foresee' you doing things tomorrow; He simply sees you doing them: because, though tomorrow is not yet there for you, it is for Him. You never supposed that your actions at this moment were any less free because God knows what you are doing. Well, He knows your tomorrow's actions in just the same way—because He is already in tomorrow and can simply watch you. In a sense, He does not know your action till you have done it: but then the moment at which you have done it is already 'Now' for Him.

—from *Mere Christianity*

Just a Bit of Coloured Paper?

I remember once when I had been giving a talk to the R.A.F., an old, hard-bitten officer got up and said, 'I've no use for all that stuff. But, mind you, I'm a religious man too. I know there's a God. I've felt Him: out alone in the desert at night: the tremendous mystery. And that's just why I don't believe all your neat little dogmas and formulas about Him. To anyone who's met the real thing they all seem so petty and pedantic and unreal!'

Now in a sense I quite agreed with that man. I think he had probably had a real experience of God in the desert. And when he turned from that experience to the Christian creeds, I think he really was turning from something real to something less real. In the same way, if a man has once looked at the Atlantic from the beach, and then goes and looks at a map of the Atlantic, he also will be turning from something real to something less real: turning from real waves to a bit of coloured paper. But here comes the point. The map is admittedly only coloured paper, but there are two things you have to remember about it. In the first place, it is based on what hundreds and thousands of people have found out by sailing the real Atlantic. In that way it has behind it masses of experience just as real as the one you could have from the beach; only, while yours would be a single glimpse, the map fits all those different experiences together. In the second place, if you want to go anywhere, the map is absolutely necessary. As long as you are content with walks on the beach, your own glimpses are far more fun than looking at a map. But the map is going to be more use than walks on the beach if you want to get to America.

—from *Mere Christianity*

Traveling Without a Map

Now, Theology is like the map. Merely learning and thinking about the Christian doctrines, if you stop there, is less real and less exciting than the sort of thing my friend got in the desert. Doctrines are not God: they are only a kind of map. But that map is based on the experience of hundreds of people who really were in touch with God—experiences compared with which any thrills or pious feelings you and I are likely to get on our own are very elementary and very confused. And secondly, if you want to get any further, you must use the map. You see, what happened to that man in the desert may have been real, and was certainly exciting, but nothing comes of it. It leads nowhere. There is nothing to do about it. In fact, that is just why a vague religion—all about feeling God in nature, and so on—is so attractive. It is all thrills and no work: like watching the waves from the beach. But you will not get to Newfoundland by studying the Atlantic that way, and you will not get eternal life by simply feeling the presence of God in flowers or music. Neither will you get anywhere by looking at maps without going to sea. Nor will you be very safe if you go to sea without a map.

—from *Mere Christianity*

Gradually the Truth Condenses...

Theology, while saying that a special illumination has been vouchsafed to Christians and (earlier) to Jews, also says that there is some divine illumination vouchsafed to all men. The Divine light, we are told, "lighteneth every man." We should, therefore, expect to find in the imagination of great Pagan teachers and myth makers some glimpse of that theme which we believe to be the very plot of the whole cosmic story—the theme of incarnation, death, and rebirth. And the differences between the Pagan Christs (Balder, Osiris, etc.) and the Christ Himself is much what we should expect to find. The Pagan stories are all about someone dying and rising, either every year, or else nobody knows where and nobody knows when. The Christian story is about a historical personage, whose execution can be dated pretty accurately, under a named Roman magistrate, and with whom the society that He founded is in a continuous relation down to the present day. It is not the difference between falsehood and truth. It is the difference between a real event on the one hand and dim dreams or premonitions of that same event on the other. It is like watching something come gradually into focus; first it hangs in the clouds of myth and ritual, vast and vague, then it condenses, grows hard and in a sense small, as a historical event in first century Palestine.

—from "Is Theology Poetry?" *(The Weight of Glory)*

From Poetic Myth to Humble Fact

The essential meaning of all things came down from the "heaven" of myth to the "earth" of history. In so doing, it partly emptied itself of its glory, as Christ emptied Himself of His glory to be Man. That is the real explanation of the fact that Theology, far from defeating its rivals by a superior poetry, is, in a superficial but quite real sense, less poetical than they. That is why the New Testament is, in the same sense, less poetical than the Old. Have you not often felt in Church, if the first lesson is some great passage, that the second lesson is somehow small by comparison—almost, if one might say so, humdrum? So it is and so it must be. That is the humiliation of myth into fact, of God into Man; what is everywhere and always, imageless and ineffable, only to be glimpsed in dream and symbol and the acted poetry of ritual becomes small, solid—no bigger than a man who can lie asleep in a rowing boat on the Lake of Galilee. You may say that this, after all, is a still deeper poetry. I will not contradict you. The humiliation leads to a greater glory. But the humiliation of God and the shrinking or condensation of the myth as it becomes fact are also quite real.

—from "Is Theology Poetry?" (*The Weight of Glory*)

God's Remedies

And what did God do? First of all He left us conscience, the sense of right and wrong: and all through history there have been people trying (some of them very hard) to obey it. None of them ever quite succeeded. Secondly, He sent the human race what I call good dreams: I mean those queer stories scattered all through the heathen religions about a god who dies and comes to life again and, by his death, has somehow given new life to men. Thirdly, He selected one particular people and spent several centuries hammering into their heads the sort of God He was—that there was only one of Him and that He cared about right conduct. Those people were the Jews, and the Old Testament gives an account of the hammering process.

Then comes the real shock. Among these Jews there suddenly turns up a man who goes about talking as if He was God. He claims to forgive sins. He says He has always existed. He says He is coming to judge the world at the end of time. Now let us get this clear. Among Pantheists, like the Indians, anyone might say that he was a part of God, or one with God: there would be nothing very odd about it. But this man, since He was a Jew, could not mean that kind of God. God, in their language, meant the Being outside the world, who had made it and was infinitely different from anything else. And when you have grasped that, you will see that what this man said was, quite simply, the most shocking thing that has ever been uttered by human lips.

—from *Mere Christianity*

1959 Lewis attends the first meeting of the Commission to Revise the Psalms, at the invitation of Archbishop of Canterbury Geoffrey Fisher.

On Authority

There are three things that spread the Christ-life to us: baptism, belief, and that mysterious action which different Christians call by different names—Holy Communion, the Mass, the Lord's Supper. At least, those are the three ordinary methods. ....

I cannot myself see why these things should be the conductors of the new kind of life. .... But though I cannot see why it should be so, I can tell you why I believe it is so. I have explained why I have to believe that Jesus was (and is) God. And it seems plain as a matter of history that He taught His followers that the new life was communicated in this way. In other words, I believe it on His authority. Do not be scared by the word authority. Believing things on authority only means believing them because you have been told them by someone you think trustworthy. Ninety-nine per cent of the things you believe are believed on authority. I believe there is such a place as New York. I have not seen it myself. I could not prove by abstract reasoning that there must be such a place. I believe it because reliable people have told me so. The ordinary man believes in the Solar System, atoms, evolution, and the circulation of the blood on authority—because the scientists say so. Every historical statement in the world is believed on authority. None of us has seen the Norman Conquest or the defeat of the Armada. None of us could prove them by pure logic as you prove a thing in mathematics. We believe them simply because people who did see them have left writings that tell us about them: in fact, on authority. A man who jibbed at authority in other things as some people do in religion would have to be content to know nothing all his life.

—from *Mere Christianity*

1926 Lewis gives his first lecture as a don in the English School at Oxford, entitled "Some Eighteenth-Century Precursors of the Romantic Movement."

Finding Comfort

All I am doing is to ask people to face the facts—to understand the questions which Christianity claims to answer. And they are very terrifying facts. I wish it was possible to say something more agreeable. But I must say what I think true. Of course, I quite agree that the Christian religion is, in the long run, a thing of unspeakable comfort. But it does not begin in comfort; it begins in the dismay I have been describing, and it is no use at all trying to go on to that comfort without first going through that dismay. In religion, as in war and everything else, comfort is the one thing you cannot get by looking for it. If you look for truth, you may find comfort in the end: if you look for comfort you will not get either comfort or truth—only soft soap and wishful thinking to begin with and, in the end, despair.

—from *Mere Christianity*

We Couldn't Make It Up

Besides being complicated, reality, in my experience, is usually odd. It is not neat, not obvious, not what you expect. For instance, when you have grasped that the earth and the other planets all go round the sun, you would naturally expect that all the planets were made to match— all at equal distances from each other, say, or distances that regularly increased, or all the same size, or else getting bigger or smaller as you go further from the sun. In fact, you find no rhyme or reason (that we can see) about either the sizes or the distances; and some of them have one moon, one has four, one has two, some have none, and one has a ring.

Reality, in fact, is usually something you could not have guessed. That is one of the reasons I believe Christianity. It is a religion you could not have guessed. If it offered us just the kind of universe we had always expected, I should feel we were making it up. But, in fact, it is not the sort of thing anyone would have made up. It has just that queer twist about it that real things have.

—from *Mere Christianity*

January 1917 Lewis (age eighteen) returns to Great Bookham, Surrey, and William T. Kirkpatrick ("the Great Knock") to prepare for Responsions, the entrance examination for Oxford University.

Not Like a River but Like a Tree

We are not living in a world where all roads are radii of a circle and where all, if followed long enough, will therefore draw gradually nearer and finally meet at the centre: rather in a world where every road, after a few miles, forks into two, and each of those into two again, and at each fork you must make a decision. Even on the biological level life is not like a river but like a tree. It does not move towards unity but away from it and the creatures grow further apart as they increase in perfection. Good, as it ripens, becomes continually more different not only from evil but from other good.

—from *The Great Divorce*, Preface

1942 The Oxford University Socratic Club, Somerville College, Oxford, holds its first meeting. Lewis serves as its first president.

Being Good

Even the best Christian that ever lived is not acting on his own steam—he is only nourishing or protecting a life he could never have acquired by his own efforts. And that has practical consequences. As long as the natural life is in your body, it will do a lot towards repairing that body. Cut it, and up to a point it will heal, as a dead body would not. A live body is not one that never gets hurt, but one that can to some extent repair itself. In the same way a Christian is not a man who never goes wrong, but a man who is enabled to repent and pick himself up and begin over again after each stumble—because the Christ-life is inside him, repairing him all the time, enabling him to repeat (in some degree) the kind of voluntary death which Christ Himself carried out.

That is why the Christian is in a different position from other people who are trying to be good. They hope, by being good, to please God if there is one; or—if they think there is not—at least they hope to deserve approval from good men. But the Christian thinks any good he does comes from the Christ-life inside him. He does not think God will love us because we are good, but that God will make us good because He loves us; just as the roof of a greenhouse does not attract the sun because it is bright, but becomes bright because the sun shines on it.

—from *Mere Christianity*

1964 *Letters to Malcolm: Chiefly on Prayer* is published by Geoffrey Bles, London.

Finding a Balance

Screwtape offers ways to cleverly exploit the Patient's dry spell:

But there is an even better way of exploiting the trough; I mean through the patient's own thoughts about it. As always, the first step is to keep knowledge out of his mind. Do not let him suspect the law of undulation. Let him assume that the first ardours of his conversion might have been expected to last, and ought to have lasted, forever, and that his present dryness is an equally permanent condition. Having once got this misconception well fixed in his head, you may then proceed in various ways. It all depends on whether your man is of the desponding type who can be tempted to despair, or of the wishful-thinking type who can be assured that all is well. The former type is getting rare among the humans. If your patient should happen to belong to it, everything is easy. You have only got to keep him out of the way of experienced Christians (an easy task nowadays), to direct his attention to the appropriate passages in scripture, and then to set him to work on the desperate design of recovering his old feelings by sheer will-power, and the game is ours. If he is of the more hopeful type your job is to make him acquiesce in the present low temperature of his spirit and gradually become content with it, persuading himself that it is not so low after all. In a week or two you will be making him doubt whether the first days of his Christianity were not, perhaps, a little excessive. Talk to him about 'moderation in all things'. If you can once get him to the point of thinking that 'religion is all very well up to a point', you can feel quite happy about his soul. A moderated religion is as good for us as no religion at all—and more amusing.

—from *The Screwtape Letters*

A Slip of the Tongue

"O God, the protector of all that trust in thee, without whom nothing is strong, nothing is holy: Increase and multiply upon us thy mercy; that, through being our ruler and guide, we may so pass through things temporal, that we finally lose not the things eternal: Grant this, O heavenly Father, for the sake of Jesus Christ our Lord. Amen."

Not long ago when I was using the collect for the fourth Sunday after Trinity in my private prayers I found that I had made a slip of the tongue. I had meant to pray that I might so pass through things temporal that I finally lost not the things eternal; I found I had prayed so to pass through things eternal that I finally lost not the things temporal. Of course, I don't think that a slip of the tongue is a sin. I am not sure that I am even a strict enough Freudian to believe that all such slips, without exception, are deeply significant. But I think some of them are significant, and I thought this was one of that sort. I thought that what I had inadvertently said very nearly expressed something I had really wished.

Very nearly; not, of course, precisely. I had never been quite stupid enough to think that the eternal could, strictly, be "passed through." What I had wanted to pass through without prejudice to my things temporal was those hours or moments in which I attended to the eternal, in which I exposed myself to it.

—from "A Slip of the Tongue" *(The Weight of Glory)*

1899 Clive Staples ("Jack") Lewis baptized in St. Mark's, Belfast, by his grandfather, the Reverend Thomas Hamilton, Rector of St. Mark's.

1956 Lewis delivers his last sermon, "A Slip of the Tongue," in the chapel of Magdalene College (Cambridge) at Evensong.

Proceed with Great Caution

I mean this sort of thing. I say my prayers, I read a book of devotion, I prepare for, or receive, the Sacrament. But while I do these things, there is, so to speak, a voice inside me that urges caution. It tells me to be careful, to keep my head, not to go too far, not to burn my boats. I come into the presence of God with a great fear lest anything should happen to me within that presence which will prove too intolerably inconvenient when I have come out again into my "ordinary" life. I don't want to be carried away into any resolution which I shall afterwards regret. For I know I shall be feeling quite different after breakfast; I don't want anything to happen to me at the altar which will run up too big a bill to pay then. It would be very disagreeable, for instance, to take the duty of charity (while I am at the altar) so seriously that after breakfast I had to tear up the really stunning reply I had written to an impudent correspondent yesterday and meant to post today. It would be very tiresome to commit myself to a programme of temperance which would cut off my after-breakfast cigarette (or, at best, make it cruelly alternative to a cigarette later in the morning). Even repentance of past acts will have to be paid for. By repenting, one acknowledges them as sins—therefore not to be repeated. Better leave that issue undecided.

The root principle of all these precautions is the same: to guard the things temporal.

—from "A Slip of the Tongue" *(The Weight of Glory)*

My Lifeline to the Temporal

This is my endlessly recurrent temptation: to go down to that Sea (I think St. John of the Cross called God a sea) and there neither dive nor swim nor float, but only dabble and splash, careful not to get out of my depth and holding on to the lifeline which connects me with my things temporal.

It is different from the temptations that met us at the beginning of the Christian life. Then we fought (at least I fought) against admitting the claims of the eternal at all. And when we had fought, and been beaten, and surrendered, we supposed that all would be fairly plain sailing. This temptation comes later. It is addressed to those who have already admitted the claim in principle and are even making some sort of effort to meet it. Our temptation is to look eagerly for the minimum that will be accepted. We are in fact very like honest but reluctant taxpayers. We approve of an income tax in principle. We make our returns truthfully. But we dread a rise in the tax. We are very careful to pay no more than is necessary. And we hope—we very ardently hope—that after we have paid it there will still be enough left to live on.

—from "A Slip of the Tongue" (The Weight of Glory)

January 1919 Lewis joins and is elected secretary of the Martlet Society, a literary society at University College, Oxford.

FEBRUARY

Swimming Lessons Are Better

And notice that those cautions which the tempter whispers in our ears are all plausible. Indeed, I don't think he often tries to deceive us (after early youth) with a direct lie. The plausibility is this. It is really possible to be carried away by religious emotion—*enthusiasm* as our ancestors called it—into resolutions and attitudes which we shall, not sinfully but rationally, not when we are more worldly but when we are wiser, have cause to regret. We can become scrupulous or fanatical; we can, in what seems zeal but is really presumption, embrace tasks never intended for us. That is the truth in the temptation. The lie consists in the suggestion that our best protection is a prudent regard for the safety of our pocket, our habitual indulgences, and our ambitions. But that is quite false. Our real protection is to be sought elsewhere: in common Christian usage, in moral theology, in steady rational thinking, in the advice of good friends and good books, and (if need be) in a skilled spiritual director. Swimming lessons are better than a lifeline to the shore.

—from "A Slip of the Tongue" *(The Weight of Glory)*

1918 Lewis (age nineteen) is hospitalized with trench fever at
Le Treport, France, for one month.

Just a Bit of My Own, Please

For it is not so much of our time and so much of our attention that God demands; it is not even all our time and all our attention; it is ourselves. For each of us the Baptist's words are true: "He must increase and I decrease." He will be infinitely merciful to our repeated failures; I know no promise that He will accept a deliberate compromise. For He has, in the last resort, nothing to give us but Himself; and He can give that only insofar as our self-affirming will retires and makes room for Him in our souls. Let us make up our minds to it; there will be nothing "of our own" left over to live on, no "ordinary" life. I do not mean that each of us will necessarily be called to be a martyr or even an ascetic. That's as may be. For some (nobody knows which) the Christian life will include much leisure, many occupations we naturally like. But these will be received from God's hands. In a perfect Christian they would be as much part of his "religion," his "service," as his hardest duties, and his feasts would be as Christian as his fasts. What cannot be admitted—what must exist only as an undefeated but daily resisted enemy—is the idea of something that is "our own," some area in which we are to be "out of school," on which God has no claim.

For He claims all, because He is love and must bless. He cannot bless us unless He has us. When we try to keep within us an area that is our own, we try to keep an area of death. Therefore, in love, He claims all. There's no bargaining with Him.

—from "A Slip of the Tongue" *(The Weight of Glory)*

Count the Cost

Law, in his terrible, cool voice, said, ... "If you have not chosen the Kingdom of God, it will make in the end no difference what you have chosen instead." Those are hard words to take. Will it really make no difference whether it was women or patriotism, cocaine or art, whisky or a seat in the Cabinet, money or science? Well, surely no difference that matters. We shall have missed the end for which we are formed and rejected the only thing that satisfies. Does it matter to a man dying in a desert by which choice of route he missed the only well?

It is a remarkable fact that on this subject Heaven and Hell speak with one voice. The tempter tells me, "Take care. Think how much this good resolve, the acceptance of this Grace, is going to cost." But Our Lord equally tells us to count the cost. Even in human affairs great importance is attached to the agreement of those whose testimony hardly ever agrees. Here, more. Between them it would seem to be pretty clear that paddling [near the shore] is of little consequence. What matters, what Heaven desires and Hell fears, is precisely that further step, out of our depth, out of our own control.

—from "A Slip of the Tongue" *(The Weight of Glory)*

Begin Again Daily

I do not think any efforts of my own will can end once and for all this craving for limited liabilities, this fatal reservation. Only God can. I have good faith and hope He will. Of course, I don't mean I can therefore, as they say, "sit back." What God does for us, He does in us. The process of doing it will appear to me (and not falsely) to be the daily or hourly repeated exercises of my own will in renouncing this attitude, especially each morning, for it grows all over me like a new shell each night. Failures will be forgiven; it is acquiescence that is fatal, the permitted, regularised presence of an area in ourselves which we still claim for our own. We may never, this side of death, drive the invader out of our territory, but we must be in the Resistance, not in the Vichy government. And this, so far as I can yet see, must be begun again every day. Our morning prayer should be that in the *Imitation: Da hodie perfecte incipere*—grant me to make an unflawed beginning today, for I have done nothing yet.

—from "A Slip of the Tongue" *(The Weight of Glory)*

A Critical Distinction

All sorts of people are fond of repeating the Christian statement that 'God is love'. But they seem not to notice that the words 'God is love' have no real meaning unless God contains at least two Persons. Love is something that one person has for another person. If God was a single person, then before the world was made, He was not love. Of course, what these people mean when they say that God is love is often something quite different: they really mean 'Love is God'. They really mean that our feelings of love, however and wherever they arise, and whatever results they produce, are to be treated with great respect. Perhaps they are: but that is something quite different from what Christians mean by the statement 'God is love'. They believe that the living, dynamic activity of love has been going on in God forever and has created everything else.

And that, by the way, is perhaps the most important difference between Christianity and all other religions: that in Christianity God is not a static thing—not even a person—but a dynamic, pulsating activity, a life, almost a kind of drama. Almost, if you will not think me irreverent, a kind of dance.

—from *Mere Christianity*

Father and Son

We must think of the Son always, so to speak, streaming forth from the Father, like light from a lamp, or heat from a fire, or thoughts from a mind. He is the self-expression of the Father—what the Father has to say. And there never was a time when He was not saying it. But have you noticed what is happening? All these pictures of light or heat are making it sound as if the Father and Son were two things instead of two Persons. So that after all, the New Testament picture of a Father and a Son turns out to be much more accurate than anything we try to substitute for it. That is what always happens when you go away from the words of the Bible. It is quite right to go away from them for a moment in order to make some special point clear. But you must always go back. Naturally God knows how to describe Himself much better than we know how to describe Him. He knows that Father and Son is more like the relation between the First and Second Persons than anything else we can think of. Much the most important thing to know is that it is a relation of love. The Father delights in His Son; the Son looks up to His Father.

—from *Mere Christianity*

The Spirit of God

The union between the Father and the Son is such a live concrete thing that this union itself is also a Person. I know this is almost inconceivable, but look at it thus. You know that among human beings, when they get together in a family, or a club, or a trade union, people talk about the 'spirit' of that family, or club, or trade union. They talk about its 'spirit' because the individual members, when they are together, do really develop particular ways of talking and behaving which they would not have if they were apart. It is as if a sort of communal personality came into existence. Of course, it is not a real person: it is only rather like a person. But that is just one of the differences between God and us. What grows out of the joint life of the Father and Son is a real Person, is in fact the Third of the three Persons who are God.

This third Person is called, in technical language, the Holy Ghost or the 'spirit' of God. Do not be worried or surprised if you find it (or Him) rather vaguer or more shadowy in your mind than the other two. I think there is a reason why that must be so. In the Christian life you are not usually looking *at* Him. He is always acting through you. If you think of the Father as something 'out there', in front of you, and of the Son as someone standing at your side, helping you to pray, trying to turn you into another son, then you have to think of the third Person as something inside you, or behind you. Perhaps some people might find it easier to begin with the third Person and work backwards. God is love, and that love works through men—especially through the whole community of Christians. But this spirit of love is, from all eternity, a love going on between the Father and the Son.

—from *Mere Christianity*

43

Ever New Constructions

Screwtape considers the value of pursuing the "historical Jesus":

You will find that a good many Christian-political writers think that Christianity began going wrong, and departing from the doctrine of its Founder, at a very early stage. Now this idea must be used by us to encourage once again the conception of a 'historical Jesus' to be found by clearing away later 'accretions and perversions' and then to be contrasted with the whole Christian tradition. In the last generation we promoted the construction of such a 'historical Jesus' on liberal and humanitarian lines; we are now putting forward a new 'historical Jesus' on Marxian, catastrophic, and revolutionary lines. The advantages of these constructions, which we intend to change every thirty years or so, are manifold. In the first place they all tend to direct men's devotion to something which does not exist, for each 'historical Jesus' is unhistorical. The documents say what they say and cannot be added to; each new 'historical Jesus' therefore has to be got out of them by suppression at one point and exaggeration at another, and by that sort of guessing (*brilliant* is the adjective we teach humans to apply to it) on which no one would risk ten shillings in ordinary life, but which is enough to produce a crop of new Napoleons, new Shakespeares, and new Swifts, in every publisher's autumn list.

—from *The Screwtape Letters*

With a Bit of Coaxing

Screwtape, on manipulating the "historical Jesus":

The 'historical Jesus' then, however dangerous He may seem to be to us at some particular point, is always to be encouraged. About the general connection between Christianity and politics, our position is more delicate. Certainly we do not want men to allow their Christianity to flow over into their political life, for the establishment of anything like a really just society would be a major disaster. On the other hand we do want, and want very much, to make men treat Christianity as a means; preferably, of course, as a means to their own advancement, but, failing that, as a means to anything—even to social justice. The thing to do is to get a man at first to value social justice as a thing which the Enemy demands, and then work him on to the stage at which he values Christianity because it may produce social justice. For the Enemy will not be used as a convenience. Men or nations who think they can revive the Faith in order to make a good society might just as well think they can use the stairs of Heaven as a short cut to the nearest chemist's shop. Fortunately it is quite easy to coax humans round this little corner. Only today I have found a passage in a Christian writer where he recommends his own version of Christianity on the ground that 'only such a faith can outlast the death of old cultures and the birth of new civilisations'. You see the little rift? 'Believe this, not because it is true, but for some other reason.' That's the game.

—from *The Screwtape Letters*

1942 *The Screwtape Letters* is published by Geoffrey Bles, London.

Unequal Love

It is idle to say that men are of equal value. If value is taken in a worldly sense—if we mean that all men are equally useful or beautiful or good or entertaining—then it is nonsense. If it means that all are of equal value as immortal souls, then I think it conceals a dangerous error. The infinite value of each human soul is not a Christian doctrine. God did not die for man because of some value He perceived in him. The value of each human soul considered simply in itself, out of relation to God, is zero. As St. Paul writes, to have died for valuable men would have been not divine but merely heroic; but God died for sinners. He loved us not because we were lovable, but because He is Love. It may be that He loves all equally—He certainly loved all to the death—and I am not certain what the expression means. If there is equality, it is in His love, not in us.

Equality is a quantitative term and therefore love often knows nothing of it. Authority exercised with humility and obedience accepted with delight are the very lines along which our spirits live. Even in the life of the affections, much more in the Body of Christ, we step outside that world which says "I am as good as you." It is like turning from a march to a dance. It is like taking off our clothes. We become, as Chesterton said, taller when we bow; we become lowlier when we instruct. It delights me that there should be moments in the services of my own Church when the priest stands and I kneel. As democracy becomes more complete in the outer world and opportunities for reverence are successively removed, the refreshment, the cleansing, and invigorating returns to inequality, which the Church offers us, become more and more necessary.

—from "Membership" *(The Weight of Glory)*

1945 Lewis reads "Membership" to the Society of St. Alban and St. Sergius, Oxford.

A Good Infection

And now, what does it all matter? It matters more than anything else in the world. The whole dance, or drama, or pattern of this three-Personal life is to be played out in each one of us: or (putting it the other way round) each one of us has got to enter that pattern, take his place in that dance. There is no other way to the happiness for which we were made. Good things as well as bad, you know, are caught by a kind of infection. If you want to get warm you must stand near the fire: if you want to be wet you must get into the water. If you want joy, power, peace, eternal life, you must get close to, or even into, the thing that has them. They are not a sort of prize which God could, if He chose, just hand out to anyone. They are a great fountain of energy and beauty spurting up at the very centre of reality. If you are close to it, the spray will wet you: if you are not, you will remain dry. Once a man is united to God, how could he not live forever? Once a man is separated from God, what can he do but wither and die?

—from *Mere Christianity*

What Christianity Offers

Now the whole offer which Christianity makes is this: that we can, if we let God have His way, come to share in the life of Christ. If we do, we shall then be sharing a life which was begotten, not made, which always has existed and always will exist. Christ is the Son of God. If we share in this kind of life we also shall be sons of God. We shall love the Father as He does and the Holy Ghost will arise in us. He came to this world and became a man in order to spread to other men the kind of life He has—by what I call 'good infection'. Every Christian is to become a little Christ. The whole purpose of becoming a Christian is simply nothing else.

—from *Mere Christianity*

The Absurd Claim

We can all understand how a man forgives offences against himself. You tread on my toes and I forgive you, you steal my money and I forgive you. But what should we make of a man, himself unrobbed and untrodden on, who announced that he forgave you for treading on other men's toes and stealing other men's money? Asinine fatuity is the kindest description we should give of his conduct. Yet this is what Jesus did. He told people that their sins were forgiven, and never waited to consult all the other people whom their sins had undoubtedly injured. He unhesitatingly behaved as if He was the party chiefly concerned, the person chiefly offended in all offences. This makes sense only if He really was the God whose laws are broken and whose love is wounded in every sin. In the mouth of any speaker who is not God, these words would imply what I can only regard as a silliness and conceit unrivalled by any other character in history.

Yet (and this is the strange, significant thing) even His enemies, when they read the Gospels, do not usually get the impression of silliness and conceit. Still less do unprejudiced readers. Christ says that He is 'humble and meek' and we believe Him; not noticing that, if He were merely a man, humility and meekness are the very last characteristics we could attribute to some of His sayings.

—from *Mere Christianity*

Not a Matter of Opinion

I am trying here to prevent anyone saying the really foolish thing that people often say about Him: 'I'm ready to accept Jesus as a great moral teacher, but I don't accept His claim to be God.' That is the one thing we must not say. A man who was merely a man and said the sort of things Jesus said would not be a great moral teacher. He would either be a lunatic—on a level with the man who says he is a poached egg—or else he would be the Devil of Hell. You must make your choice. Either this man was, and is, the Son of God: or else a madman or something worse. You can shut Him up for a fool, you can spit at Him and kill Him as a demon; or you can fall at His feet and call Him Lord and God. But let us not come with any patronising nonsense about His being great human teacher. He has not left that open to us. He did not intend to.

—from *Mere Christianity*

No Shortage of Good Ideas

When you get down to it, is not the popular idea of Christianity simply this: that Jesus Christ was a great moral teacher and that if only we took His advice we might be able to establish a better social order and avoid another war? Now, mind you, that is quite true. But it tells you much less than the whole truth about Christianity and it has no practical importance at all.

It is quite true that if we took Christ's advice we should soon be living in a happier world. You need not even go as far as Christ. If we did all that Plato or Aristotle or Confucius told us, we should get on a great deal better than we do. And so what? We never have followed the advice of the great teachers. Why are we likely to begin now? Why are we more likely to follow Christ than any of the others? Because He is the best moral teacher? But that makes it even less likely that we shall follow Him. If we cannot take the elementary lessons, is it likely we are going to take the most advanced one? If Christianity only means one more bit of good advice, then Christianity is of no importance. There has been no lack of good advice for the last four thousand years. A bit more makes no difference.

—from *Mere Christianity*

1908 Lewis's mother, Flora Lewis, undergoes major cancer surgery.

Two Quick Clarifications

The first thing to get clear about Christian morality between man and man is that in this department Christ did not come to preach any brand new morality. The Golden Rule of the New Testament (Do as you would be done by) is a summing up of what every one, at bottom, had always known to be right. Really great moral teachers never do introduce new moralities: it is quacks and cranks who do that. As Dr Johnson said, 'People need to be reminded more often than they need to be instructed.' The real job of every moral teacher is to keep on bringing us back, time after time, to the old simple principles which we are all so anxious not to see; like bringing a horse back and back to the fence it has refused to jump or bringing a child back and back to the bit in its lesson that it wants to shirk.

The second thing to get clear is that Christianity has not, and does not profess to have, a detailed political programme for applying 'Do as you would be done by' to a particular society at a particular moment. It could not have. It is meant for all men at all times and the particular programme which suited one place or time would not suit another. And, anyhow, that is not how Christianity works. When it tells you to feed the hungry it does not give you lessons in cookery. When it tells you to read the Scriptures it does not give you lessons in Hebrew and Greek, or even in English grammar. It was never intended to replace or supersede the ordinary human arts and sciences: it is rather a director which will set them all to the right jobs, and a source of energy which will give them all new life, if only they will put themselves at its disposal.

—from *Mere Christianity*

Bad Gas

God made us: invented us as a man invents an engine. A car is made to run on petrol, and it would not run properly on anything else. Now God designed the human machine to run on Himself. He Himself is the fuel our spirits were designed to burn, or the food our spirits were designed to feed on. There is no other. That is why it is just no good asking God to make us happy in our own way without bothering about religion. God cannot give us a happiness and peace apart from Himself, because it is not there. There is no such thing.

That is the key to history. Terrific energy is expended—civilisations are built up—excellent institutions devised; but each time something goes wrong. Some fatal flaw always brings the selfish and cruel people to the top and it all slides back into misery and ruin. In fact, the machine conks. It seems to start up all right and runs a few yards, and then it breaks down. They are trying to run it on the wrong juice. That is what Satan has done to us humans.

—from *Mere Christianity*

Competition Rather Than Courtesy

If the fixed nature of matter prevents it from being always, and in all its dispositions, equally agreeable even to a single soul, much less is it possible for the matter of the universe at any moment to be distributed so that it is equally convenient and pleasurable to each member of a society. If a man travelling in one direction is having a journey down hill, a man going in the opposite direction must be going up hill. If even a pebble lies where I want it to lie, it cannot, except by a coincidence, be where you want it to lie. And this is very far from being an evil: on the contrary, it furnishes occasion for all those acts of courtesy, respect, and unselfishness by which love and good humour and modesty express themselves. But it certainly leaves the way open to a great evil, that of competition and hostility. And if souls are free, they cannot be prevented from dealing with the problem by competition instead of courtesy. And once they have advanced to actual hostility, they can then exploit the fixed nature of matter to hurt one another. The permanent nature of wood which enables us to use it as a beam also enables us to use it for hitting our neighbour on the head. The permanent nature of matter in general means that when human beings fight, the victory ordinarily goes to those who have superior weapons, skill, and numbers, even if their cause is unjust.

—from *The Problem of Pain*

Fixed Laws of Nature and Freedom of Will

We can, perhaps, conceive of a world in which God corrected the results of this abuse of free will by His creatures at every moment: so that a wooden beam became soft as grass when it was used as a weapon, and the air refused to obey me if I attempted to set up in it the sound-waves that carry lies or insults. But such a world would be one in which wrong actions were impossible, and in which, therefore, freedom of the will would be void; nay, if the principle were carried out to its logical conclusion, evil thoughts would be impossible, for the cerebral matter which we use in thinking would refuse its task when we attempted to frame them. All matter in the neighbourhood of a wicked man would be liable to undergo unpredictable alterations. That God can and does, on occasions, modify the behaviour of matter and produce what we call miracles, is part of Christian faith; but the very conception of a common, and therefore stable, world, demands that these occasions should be extremely rare. In a game of chess you can make certain arbitrary concessions to your opponent, which stand to the ordinary rules of the game as miracles stand to the laws of nature. You can deprive yourself of a castle, or allow the other man sometimes to take back a move made inadvertently. But if you conceded everything that at any moment happened to suit him—if all his moves were revocable and if all your pieces disappeared whenever their position on the board was not to his liking—then you could not have a game at all. So it is with the life of souls in a world: fixed laws, consequences unfolding by causal necessity, the whole natural order, are at once limits within which their common life is confined and also the sole condition under which any such life is possible. Try to exclude the possibility of suffering which the order of nature and the existence of free wills involve, and you find that you have excluded life itself.

—from *The Problem of Pain*

The Holy Eraser

It would, no doubt, have been possible for God to remove by miracle the results of the first sin ever committed by a human being; but this would not have been much good unless He was prepared to remove the results of the second sin, and of the third, and so on forever. If the miracles ceased, then sooner or later we might have reached our present lamentable situation: if they did not, then a world thus continually underpropped and corrected by Divine interference, would have been a world in which nothing important ever depended on human choice, and in which choice itself would soon cease from the certainty that one of the apparent alternatives before you would lead to no results and was therefore not really an alternative. As we saw, the chess player's freedom to play chess depends on the rigidity of the squares and the moves.

—from *The Problem of Pain*

Voluntarily United

God created things which had free will. That means creatures which can go either wrong or right. Some people think they can imagine a creature which was free but had no possibility of going wrong; I cannot. If a thing is free to be good it is also free to be bad. And free will is what has made evil possible. Why, then, did God give them free will? Because free will, though it makes evil possible, is also the only thing that makes possible any love or goodness or joy worth having. A world of automata—of creatures that worked like machines—would hardly be worth creating. The happiness which God designs for His higher creatures is the happiness of being freely, voluntarily united to Him and to each other in an ecstasy of love and delight compared with which the most rapturous love between a man and a woman on this earth is mere milk and water. And for that they must be free.

—from *Mere Christianity*

Second-Guessing God's Wisdom

Of course God knew what would happen if they [creatures with free will] used their freedom the wrong way: apparently He thought it worth the risk. Perhaps we feel inclined to disagree with Him. But there is a difficulty about disagreeing with God. He is the source from which all your reasoning power comes: you could not be right and He wrong any more than a stream can rise higher than its own source. When you are arguing against Him you are arguing against the very power that makes you able to argue at all: it is like cutting off the branch you are sitting on. If God thinks this state of war in the universe a price worth paying for free will—that is, for making a live world in which creatures can do real good or harm and something of real importance can happen, instead of a toy world which only moves when He pulls the strings—then we may take it it is worth paying.

—from *Mere Christianity*

1944 Lewis delivers the first of seven talks on "Beyond Personality" over the BBC. These talks later appear as Book 4 of *Mere Christianity*.

The Core Corruption

The moment you have a self at all, there is a possibility of putting yourself first—wanting to be the centre—wanting to be God, in fact. That was the sin of Satan: and that was the sin he taught the human race. Some people think the fall of man had something to do with sex, but that is a mistake. (The story in the Book of Genesis rather suggests that some corruption in our sexual nature followed the fall and was its result, not its cause.) What Satan put into the heads of our remote ancestors was the idea that they could 'be like gods'—could set up on their own as if they had created themselves—be their own masters—invent some sort of happiness for themselves outside God, apart from God. And out of that hopeless attempt has come nearly all that we call human history—money, poverty, ambition, war, prostitution, classes, empires, slavery—the long terrible story of man trying to find something other than God which will make him happy.

—from *Mere Christianity*

Human Will, the Weak Point of Creation

We have no idea in what particular act, or series of acts, the self-contradictory, impossible wish found expression. For all I can see, it might have concerned the literal eating of a fruit, but the question is of no consequence.

This act of self-will on the part of the creature, which constitutes an utter falseness to its true creaturely position, is the only sin that can be conceived as the Fall. For the difficulty about the first sin is that it must be very heinous, or its consequences would not be so terrible, and yet it must be something which a being free from the temptations of fallen man could conceivably have committed. The turning from God to self fulfils both conditions. It is a sin possible even to Paradisal man, because the mere existence of a self—the mere fact that we call it 'me'—includes, from the first, the danger of self-idolatry. Since I am I, I must make an act of self-surrender, however small or however easy, in living to God rather than to myself. This is, if you like, the 'weak spot' in the very nature of creation, the risk which God apparently thinks worth taking.

—from *The Problem of Pain*

1943 Lewis delivers the first of three Riddell Memorial Lectures, later published as *The Abolition of Man*.

Becoming Yourself

Screwtape clarifies the Enemy's intent:

Of course I know that the Enemy also wants to detach men from themselves, but in a different way. Remember always, that He really likes the little vermin, and sets an absurd value on the distinctness of every one of them. When He talks of their losing their selves, He only means abandoning the clamour of self-will; once they have done that, He really gives them back all their personality, and boasts (I am afraid, sincerely) that when they are wholly His they will be more themselves than ever. Hence, while He is delighted to see them sacrificing even their innocent wills to His, He hates to see them drifting away from their own nature for any other reason. And we should always encourage them to do so.

—from *The Screwtape Letters*

A Real Right and Wrong

Whenever you find a man who says he does not believe in a real Right and Wrong, you will find the same man going back on this a moment later. He may break his promise to you, but if you try breaking one to him he will be complaining 'It's not fair' before you can say Jack Robinson. A nation may say treaties don't matter; but then, next minute, they spoil their case by saying that the particular treaty they want to break was an unfair one. But if treaties do not matter, and if there is no such thing as Right and Wrong—in other words, if there is no Law of Nature—what is the difference between a fair treaty and an unfair one? Have they not let the cat out of the bag and shown that, whatever they say, they really know the Law of Nature just like anyone else?

It seems, then, we are forced to believe in a real Right and Wrong. People may be sometimes mistaken about them, just as people sometimes get their sums wrong; but they are not a matter of mere taste and opinion any more than the multiplication table.

—from *Mere Christianity*

The Rules

I hope you will not misunderstand what I am going to say. I am not preaching, and Heaven knows I do not pretend to be better than anyone else. I am only trying to call attention to a fact; the fact that this year, or this month, or, more likely, this very day, we have failed to practise ourselves the kind of behaviour we expect from other people. There may be all sorts of excuses for us. That time you were so unfair to the children was when you were very tired. That slightly shady business about the money—the one you have almost forgotten—came when you were very hard-up. And what you promised to do for old So-and-so and have never done—well, you never would have promised if you had known how frightfully busy you were going to be. And as for your behaviour to your wife (or husband) or sister (or brother) if I knew how irritating they could be, I would not wonder at it—and who the dickens am I, anyway? I am just the same. That is to say, I do not succeed in keeping the Law of Nature very well, and the moment anyone tells me I am not keeping it, there starts up in my mind a string of excuses as long as your arm. The question at the moment is not whether they are good excuses. The point is that they are one more proof of how deeply, whether we like it or not, we believe in the Law of Nature. If we do not believe in decent behaviour, why should we be so anxious to make excuses for not having behaved decently? The truth is, we believe in decency so much—we feel the Rule of Law pressing on us so—that we cannot bear to face the fact that we are breaking it, and consequently we try to shift the responsibility. For you notice that it is only for our bad behaviour that we find all these explanations. It is only our bad temper that we put down to being tired or worried or hungry; we put our good temper down to ourselves.

—from *Mere Christianity*

Impulse Control

It is a mistake to think that some of our impulses—say mother love or patriotism—are good, and others, like sex or the fighting instinct, are bad. All we mean is that the occasions on which the fighting instinct or the sexual desire need to be restrained are rather more frequent than those for restraining mother love or patriotism. But there are situations in which it is the duty of a married man to encourage his sexual impulse and of a soldier to encourage the fighting instinct. There are also occasions on which a mother's love for her own children or a man's love for his own country have to be suppressed or they will lead to unfairness towards other people's children or countries. Strictly speaking, there are no such things as good and bad impulses. Think once again of a piano. It has not got two kinds of notes on it, the 'right' notes and the 'wrong' ones. Every single note is right at one time and wrong at another. . . . .

By the way, the point is of great practical consequence. The most dangerous thing you can do is to take any one impulse of your own nature and set it up as the thing you ought to follow at all costs. There is not one of them which will not make us into devils if we set it up as an absolute guide. You might think love of humanity in general was safe, but it is not. If you leave out justice you will find yourself breaking agreements and faking evidence in trials 'for the sake of humanity', and become in the end a cruel and treacherous man.

—from *Mere Christianity*

Not Moral Perfection

The Holiness of God is something more and other than moral perfection: His claim upon us is something more and other than the claim of moral duty. I do not deny it: but this conception, like that of corporate guilt, is very easily used as an evasion of the real issue. God may be more than moral goodness: He is not less. The road to the promised land runs past Sinai. The moral law may exist to be transcended: but there is no transcending it for those who have not first admitted its claims upon them, and then tried with all their strength to meet that claim, and fairly and squarely faced the fact of their failure.

—from *The Problem of Pain*

MARCH

Morality: A Quick Lesson

There are two ways in which the human machine goes wrong. One is when human individuals drift apart from one another, or else collide with one another and do one another damage, by cheating or bullying. The other is when things go wrong inside the individual—when the different parts of him (his different faculties and desires and so on) either drift apart or interfere with one another. You can get the idea plain if you think of us as a fleet of ships sailing in formation. The voyage will be a success only, in the first place, if the ships do not collide and get in one another's way; and, secondly, if each ship is seaworthy and has her engines in good order. As a matter of fact, you cannot have either of these two things without the other. If the ships keep on having collisions they will not remain seaworthy very long. On the other hand, if their steering gears are out of order they will not be able to avoid collisions. Or, if you like, think of humanity as a band playing a tune. To get a good result, you need two things. Each player's individual instrument must be in tune and also each must come in at the right moment so as to combine with all the others.

But there is one thing we have not yet taken into account. We have not asked where the fleet is trying to get to, or what piece of music the band is trying to play. The instruments might be all in tune and might all come in at the right moment, but even so the performance would not be a success if they had been engaged to provide dance music and actually played nothing but Dead Marches. And however well the fleet sailed, its voyage would be a failure if it were meant to reach New York and actually arrived at Calcutta.

—from *Mere Christianity*

The Moral Dilemma

Morality, then, seems to be concerned with three things. Firstly, with fair play and harmony between individuals. Secondly, with what might be called tidying up or harmonising the things inside each individual. Thirdly, with the general purpose of human life as a whole: what man was made for: what course the whole fleet ought to be on: what tune the conductor of the band wants it to play. . . . .

Almost all people at all times have agreed (in theory) that human beings ought to be honest and kind and helpful to one another. But though it is natural to begin with all that, if our thinking about morality stops there, we might just as well not have thought at all. Unless we go on to the second thing—the tidying up inside each human being—we are only deceiving ourselves.

What is the good of telling the ships how to steer so as to avoid collisions if, in fact, they are such crazy old tubs that they cannot be steered at all? What is the good of drawing up, on paper, rules for social behaviour, if we know that, in fact, our greed, cowardice, ill temper, and self-conceit are going to prevent us from keeping them? I do not mean for a moment that we ought not to think, and think hard, about improvements in our social and economic system. What I do mean is that all that thinking will be mere moonshine unless we realise that nothing but the courage and unselfishness of individuals is ever going to make any system work properly. It is easy enough to remove the particular kinds of graft or bullying that go on under the present system: but as long as men are twisters or bullies they will find some new way of carrying on the old game under the new system. You cannot make men good by law: and without good men you cannot have a good society.

—from *Mere Christianity*

Just Deserts

A bad man, happy, is a man without the least inkling that his actions do not 'answer', that they are not in accord with the laws of the universe.

A perception of this truth lies at the back of the universal human feeling that bad men ought to suffer. It is no use turning up our noses at this feeling, as if it were wholly base. On its mildest level it appeals to everyone's sense of justice. Once when my brother and I, as very small boys, were drawing pictures at the same table, I jerked his elbow and caused him to make an irrelevant line across the middle of his work; the matter was amicably settled by my allowing him to draw a line of equal length across mine. That is, I was 'put in his place', made to see my negligence from the other end. On a sterner level the same idea appears as 'retributive punishment', or 'giving a man what he deserves'. Some enlightened people would like to banish all conceptions of retribution or desert from their theory of punishment and place its value wholly in the deterrence of others or the reform of the criminal himself. They do not see that by so doing they render all punishment unjust. What can be more immoral than to inflict suffering on me for the sake of deterring others if I do not *deserve* it? And if I do deserve it, you are admitting the claims of 'retribution'. And what can be more outrageous than to catch me and submit me to a disagreeable process of moral improvement without my consent, unless (once more) I *deserve* it?

—from *The Problem of Pain*

The Impulse for Vengeance

Revenge loses sight of the end in the means, but its end is not wholly bad—it wants the evil of the bad man to be to him what it is to everyone else. This is proved by the fact that the avenger wants the guilty party not merely to suffer, but to suffer at his hands, and to know it, and to know why. Hence the impulse to taunt the guilty man with his crime at the moment of taking vengeance: hence, too, such natural expressions as 'I wonder how he'd like it if the same thing were done to him' or 'I'll teach him'. For the same reason when we are going to abuse a man in words we say we are going to 'let him know what we think of him'.

—from *The Problem of Pain*

Face the Bad

Now at the moment when a man feels real guilt—moments too rare in our lives—all these blasphemies vanish away. Much, we may feel, can be excused to human infirmities: but not *this*—this incredibly mean and ugly action which none of our friends would have done, which even such a thorough-going little rotter as X would have been ashamed of, which we would not for the world allow to be published. At such a moment we really do know that our character, as revealed in this action, is, and ought to be, hateful to all good men, and, if there are powers above man, to them. A God who did not regard this with unappeasable distaste would not be a good being. We cannot even wish for such a God—it is like wishing that every nose in the universe were abolished, that smell of hay or roses or the sea should never again delight any creature, because our own breath happens to stink.

When we merely *say* that we are bad, the 'wrath' of God seems a barbarous doctrine; as soon as we *perceive* our badness, it appears inevitable, a mere corollary from God's goodness. To keep ever before us the insight derived from such a moment as I have been describing, to learn to detect the same real inexcusable corruption under more and more of its complex disguises, is therefore indispensable to a real understanding of the Christian faith. This is not, of course, a new doctrine. I am attempting nothing very splendid in this chapter. I am merely trying to get my reader (and, still more, myself) over a *pons asinorum*—to take the first step out of fools' paradise and utter illusion.

—from *The Problem of Pain*

The Truth About Ourselves

Every man, not very holy or very arrogant, has to 'live up to' the outward appearance of other men: he knows there is that within him which falls far below even his most careless public behaviour, even his loosest talk. In an instant of time—while your friend hesitates for a word—what things pass through your mind? We have never told the whole truth. We may confess ugly *facts*—the meanest cowardice or the shabbiest and most prosaic impurity—but the *tone* is false. The very act of confessing—an infinitesimally hypocritical glance—a dash of humour—all this contrives to dissociate the facts from your very self. No one could guess how familiar and, in a sense, congenial to your soul these things were, how much of a piece with all the rest: down there, in the dreaming inner warmth, they struck no such discordant note, were not nearly so odd and detachable from the rest of you, as they seem when they are turned into words. We imply, and often believe, that habitual vices are exceptional single acts, and make the opposite mistake about our virtues—like the bad tennis player who calls his normal form his 'bad days' and mistakes his rare successes for his normal. I do not think it is our fault that we cannot tell the real truth about ourselves; the persistent, life-long, inner murmur of spite, jealousy, prurience, greed and self-complacence, simply will not go into words. But the important thing is that we should not mistake our inevitably limited utterances for a full account of the worst that is inside.

—from *The Problem of Pain*

Time Does Not Cancel Sin

We have a strange illusion that mere time cancels sin. I have heard others, and I have heard myself, recounting cruelties and falsehoods committed in boyhood as if they were no concern of the present speaker's, and even with laughter. But mere time does nothing either to the fact or to the guilt of a sin. The guilt is washed out not by time but by repentance and the blood of Christ: if we have repented these early sins we should remember the price of our forgiveness and be humble. As for the fact of a sin, is it probable that anything cancels it? All times are eternally present to God. Is it not at least possible that along some one line of His multi-dimensional eternity He sees you forever in the nursery pulling the wings off a fly, forever toadying, lying, and lusting as a schoolboy, forever in that moment of cowardice or insolence as a subaltern? It may be that salvation consists not in the cancelling of these eternal moments but in the perfected humanity that bears the shame forever, rejoicing in the occasion which it furnished to God's compassion and glad that it should be common knowledge to the universe. Perhaps in that eternal moment St Peter—he will forgive me if I am wrong—forever denies his Master. If so, it would indeed be true that the joys of Heaven are for most of us, in our present condition, 'an acquired taste'—and certain ways of life may render the taste impossible of acquisition. Perhaps the lost are those who dare not go to such a *public* place. Of course I do not know that this is true; but I think the possibility is worth keeping in mind.

—from *The Problem of Pain*

Bad Company

We must guard against the feeling that there is 'safety in numbers'. It is natural to feel that if *all* men are as bad as the Christians say, then badness must be very excusable. If all the boys plough in the examination, surely the papers must have been too hard? And so the masters at that school feel till they learn that there are other schools where ninety per cent of the boys passed on the same papers. Then they begin to suspect that the fault did not lie with the examiners. Again, many of us have had the experience of living in some local pocket of human society—some particular school, college, regiment or profession where the tone was bad. And inside that pocket certain actions were regarded as merely normal ('Everyone does it') and certain others as impracticably virtuous and Quixotic. But when we emerged from that bad society we made the horrible discovery that in the outer world our 'normal' was the kind of thing that no decent person ever dreamed of doing, and our 'Quixotic' was taken for granted as the minimum standard of decency. What had seemed to us morbid and fantastic scruples so long as we were in the 'pocket' now turned out to be the only moments of sanity we there enjoyed. It is wise to face the possibility that the whole human race (being a small thing in the universe) is, in fact, just such a local pocket of evil—an isolated bad school or regiment inside which minimum decency passes for heroic virtue and utter corruption for pardonable imperfection.

—from *The Problem of Pain*

Virtues in Different Ages

If, then, you are ever tempted to think that we modern Western Europeans cannot really be so very bad because we are, comparatively speaking, humane—if, in other words, you think God might be content with us on that ground—ask yourself whether you think God ought to have been content with the cruelty of cruel ages because they excelled in courage or chastity. You will see at once that this is an impossibility. From considering how the cruelty of our ancestors looks to us, you may get some inkling how our softness, worldliness, and timidity would have looked to them, and hence how both must look to God.

—from *The Problem of Pain*

Enemy-Occupied Territory

One of the things that surprised me when I first read the New Testament seriously was that it talked so much about a Dark Power in the universe—a mighty evil spirit who was held to be the Power behind death and disease, and sin. The difference is that Christianity thinks this Dark Power was created by God, and was good when he was created, and went wrong. Christianity agrees with Dualism that this universe is at war. But it does not think this is a war between independent powers. It thinks it is a civil war, a rebellion, and that we are living in a part of the universe occupied by the rebel.

Enemy-occupied territory—that is what this world is. Christianity is the story of how the rightful king has landed, you might say landed in disguise, and is calling us all to take part in a great campaign of sabotage. When you go to church you are really listening-in to the secret wireless from our friends: that is why the enemy is so anxious to prevent us from going. He does it by playing on our conceit and laziness and intellectual snobbery. I know someone will ask me, 'Do you really mean, at this time of day, to re-introduce our old friend the devil—hoofs and horns and all?' Well, what the time of day has to do with it I do not know. And I am not particular about the hoofs and horns. But in other respects my answer is 'Yes, I do.' I do not claim to know anything about his personal appearance. If anybody really wants to know him better I would say to that person, 'Don't worry. If you really want to, you will. Whether you'll like it when you do is another question.'

—from *Mere Christianity*

A Simple (Albeit Comical) Argument for Christian Theology

Almost the whole of Christian theology could perhaps be deduced from the two facts (a) That men make coarse jokes, and (b) That they feel the dead to be uncanny. The coarse joke proclaims that we have here an animal which finds its own animality either objectionable or funny. Unless there had been a quarrel between the spirit and the organism I do not see how this could be: it is the very mark of the two not being 'at home' together. But it is very difficult to imagine such a state of affairs as original—to suppose a creature which from the very first was half shocked and half tickled to death at the mere fact of being the creature it is. I do not perceive that dogs see anything funny about being dogs: I suspect that angels see nothing funny about being angels. Our feeling about the dead is equally odd. It is idle to say that we dislike corpses because we are afraid of ghosts. You might say with equal truth that we fear ghosts because we dislike corpses—for the ghost owes much of its horror to the associated ideas of pallor, decay, coffins, shrouds, and worms. In reality we hate the division which makes possible the conception of either corpse or ghost. Because the thing ought not to be divided, each of the halves into which it falls by division is detestable. The explanations which Naturalism gives both of bodily shame and of our feeling about the dead are not satisfactory. It refers us to primitive taboos and superstitions—as if these themselves were not obviously results of the thing to be explained. But once accept the Christian doctrine that man was originally a unity and that the present division is unnatural, and all the phenomena fall into place.

—from *Miracles*

So What About God's Authority?

Christians, then, believe that an evil power has made himself for the present the Prince of this World. And, of course, that raises problems. Is this state of affairs in accordance with God's will, or not? If it is, He is a strange God, you will say: and if it is not, how can anything happen contrary to the will of a being with absolute power?

But anyone who has been in authority knows how a thing can be in accordance with your will in one way and not in another. It may be quite sensible for a mother to say to the children, 'I'm not going to go and make you tidy the schoolroom every night. You've got to learn to keep it tidy on your own.' Then she goes up one night and finds the Teddy bear and the ink and the French Grammar all lying in the grate. That is against her will. She would prefer the children to be tidy. But on the other hand, it is her will which has left the children free to be untidy. The same thing arises in any regiment, or trade union, or school. You make a thing voluntary and then half the people do not do it. That is not what you willed, but your will has made it possible.

—from *Mere Christianity*

Our Imperfect World: Creation in Process

We ask how the Nature created by a good God comes to be in this [depraved] condition? By which question we may mean either how she comes to be imperfect—to leave 'room for improvement' as the schoolmasters say in their reports—or else, how she comes to be positively depraved. If we ask the question in the first sense, the Christian answer (I think) is that God, from the first, created her such as to reach her perfection by a process in time. He made an Earth at first 'without form and void' and brought it by degrees to its perfection. In this, as elsewhere, we see the familiar pattern—descent from God to the formless Earth and reascent from the formless to the finished. In that sense a certain degree of 'evolutionism' or 'developmentalism' is inherent in Christianity.

—from *Miracles*

Our Imperfect World: Creation Corrupted

So much for Nature's imperfection; her positive depravity calls for a very different explanation. According to the Christians this is all due to sin: the sin both of men and of powerful, non-human beings, supernatural but created. .... To be sure, the morbid inquisitiveness about such beings which led our ancestors to a pseudo-science of Demonology, is to be sternly discouraged: our attitude should be that of the sensible citizen in wartime who believes that there are enemy spies in our midst but disbelieves nearly every particular spy story. We must limit ourselves to the general statement that beings in a different, and higher 'Nature' which is *partially* interlocked with ours have, like men, fallen and have tampered with things inside our frontier. The doctrine, besides proving itself fruitful of good in each man's spiritual life, helps to protect us from shallowly optimistic or pessimistic views of Nature. To call her either 'good' or 'evil' is boys' philosophy. We find ourselves in a world of transporting pleasures, ravishing beauties, and tantalising possibilities, but all constantly being destroyed, all coming to nothing. Nature has all the air of a good thing spoiled.

The sin, both of men and of angels, was rendered possible by the fact that God gave them free will: thus surrendering a portion of His omnipotence (it is again a deathlike or descending movement) because He saw that from a world of free creatures, even though they fell, He could work out (and this is the reascent) a deeper happiness and a fuller splendour than any world of automata would admit.

—from *Miracles*

Once Begun...

This doctrine of a universal redemption spreading outwards from the redemption of Man, mythological as it will seem to modern minds, is in reality far more philosophical than any theory which holds that God, having once entered Nature, should leave her, and leave her substantially unchanged, or that the glorification of one creature could be realised without the glorification of the whole system. God never undoes anything but evil, never does good to undo it again. The union between God and Nature in the Person of Christ admits no divorce. He will not go *out* of Nature again and she must be glorified in all ways which this miraculous union demands. When spring comes it 'leaves no corner of the land untouched'; even a pebble dropped in a pond sends circles to the margin.

—from *Miracles*

Correcting Our Arithmetic

Would you think I was joking if I said that you can put a clock back, and that if the clock is wrong it is often a very sensible thing to do? . . . . We all want progress. But progress means getting nearer to the place where you want to be. And if you have taken a wrong turning, then to go forward does not get you any nearer. If you are on the wrong road, progress means doing an about-turn and walking back to the right road; and in that case the man who turns back soonest is the most progressive man. We have all seen this when doing arithmetic. When I have started a sum the wrong way, the sooner I admit this and go back and start again, the faster I shall get on. There is nothing progressive about being pig headed and refusing to admit a mistake. And I think if you look at the present state of the world, it is pretty plain that humanity has been making some big mistake. We are on the wrong road. And if that is so, we must go back. Going back is the quickest way on.

—from *Mere Christianity*

With Every Choice

People often think of Christian morality as a kind of bargain in which God says, 'If you keep a lot of rules I'll reward you, and if you don't I'll do the other thing.' I do not think that is the best way of looking at it. I would much rather say that every time you make a choice you are turning the central part of you, the part of you that chooses, into something a little different from what it was before. And taking your life as a whole, with all your innumerable choices, all your life long you are slowly turning this central thing either into a heavenly creature or into a hellish creature: either into a creature that is in harmony with God, and with other creatures, and with itself, or else into one that is in a state of war and hatred with God, and with its fellow-creatures, and with itself. To be the one kind of creature is heaven: that is, it is joy and peace and knowledge and power. To be the other means madness, horror, idiocy, rage, impotence, and eternal loneliness. Each of us at each moment is progressing to the one state or the other.

—from *Mere Christianity*

Understanding Evil

Remember that, as I said, the right direction leads not only to peace but to knowledge. When a man is getting better he understands more and more clearly the evil that is still left in him. When a man is getting worse he understands his own badness less and less. A moderately bad man knows he is not very good: a thoroughly bad man thinks he is all right. This is common sense, really. You understand sleep when you are awake, not while you are sleeping. You can see mistakes in arithmetic when your mind is working properly: while you are making them you cannot see them. You can understand the nature of drunkenness when you are sober, not when you are drunk. Good people know about both good and evil: bad people do not know about either.

—from *Mere Christianity*

The Essential Vice

There is one vice of which no man in the world is free; which every one in the world loathes when he sees it in someone else; and of which hardly any people, except Christians, ever imagine that they are guilty themselves. I have heard people admit that they are bad-tempered, or that they cannot keep their heads about girls or drink, or even that they are cowards. I do not think I have ever heard anyone who was not a Christian accuse himself of this vice. And at the same time I have very seldom met anyone, who was not a Christian, who showed the slightest mercy to it in others. There is no fault which makes a man more unpopular, and no fault which we are more unconscious of in ourselves. And the more we have it ourselves, the more we dislike it in others.

The vice I am talking of is Pride or Self-Conceit: and the virtue opposite to it, in Christian morals, is called Humility. You may remember, when I was talking about sexual morality, I warned you that the centre of Christian morals did not lie there. Well, now, we have come to the centre. According to Christian teachers, the essential vice, the utmost evil, is Pride. Unchastity, anger, greed, drunkenness, and all that, are mere fleabites in comparison: it was through Pride that the devil became the devil: Pride leads to every other vice: it is the complete anti-God state of mind.

—from *Mere Christianity*

1956 *The Last Battle* (the final volume of *The Chronicles of Narnia*) is published by The Bodley Head, London.

The Proud Competitor

If you want to find out how proud you are the easiest way is to ask yourself, 'How much do I dislike it when other people snub me, or refuse to take any notice of me, or shove their oar in, or patronise me, or show off?' The point is that each person's pride is in competition with every one else's pride. It is because I wanted to be the big noise at the party that I am so annoyed at someone else being the big noise. Two of a trade never agree. Now what you want to get clear is that Pride is *essentially* competitive—is competitive by its very nature—while the other vices are competitive only, so to speak, by accident. Pride gets no pleasure out of having something, only out of having more of it than the next man. We say that people are proud of being rich, or clever, or good-looking, but they are not. They are proud of being richer, or cleverer, or better-looking than others. If everyone else became equally rich, or clever, or good-looking there would be nothing to be proud about. It is the comparison that makes you proud: the pleasure of being above the rest. Once the element of competition has gone, pride has gone. That is why I say that Pride is essentially competitive in a way the other vices are not. .... Greed may drive men into competition if there is not enough to go round; but the proud man, even when he has got more than he can possibly want, will try to get still more just to assert his power. Nearly all those evils in the world which people put down to greed or selfishness are really far more the result of Pride.

—from *Mere Christianity*

1919 Lewis's first book, *Spirits in Bondage: A Cycle of Lyrics*, is published by William Heinemann, London, under the pseudonym of Clive Hamilton.

How Marriage Reconciles

Lewis, grieving the death of his wife, Joy:

'It was too perfect to last,' so I am tempted to say of our marriage. But it can be meant in two ways. It may be grimly pessimistic—as if God no sooner saw two of His creatures happy than He stopped it ('None of that here!'). As if He were like the Hostess at the sherry-party who separates two guests the moment they show signs of having got into a real conversation. But it could also mean 'This had reached its proper perfection. This had become what it had in it to be. Therefore of course it would not be prolonged.' As if God said, 'Good; you have mastered that exercise. I am very pleased with it. And now you are ready to go on to the next.' When you have learned to do quadratics and enjoy doing them you will not be set them much longer. The teacher moves you on.

For we did learn and achieve something. There is, hidden or flaunted, a sword between the sexes till an entire marriage reconciles them. It is arrogance in us to call frankness, fairness, and chivalry 'masculine' when we see them in a woman; it is arrogance in them to describe a man's sensitiveness or tact or tenderness as 'feminine.' But also what poor, warped fragments of humanity most mere men and mere women must be to make the implications of that arrogance plausible. Marriage heals this. Jointly the two become fully human. 'In the image of God created He *them*.' Thus, by a paradox, this carnival of sexuality leads us out beyond our sexes.

—from *A Grief Observed*

1957 Jack Lewis and Joy Davidman Gresham, united in a civil marriage the previous year, are married in an ecclesiastical ceremony in Wingfield-Morris Hospital by the Rev. Peter Bide. Bide also performs a healing service for Joy, who is believed to be dying of cancer.

Too Proud to Know God

The Christians are right: it is Pride which has been the chief cause of misery in every nation and every family since the world began. Other vices may sometimes bring people together: you may find good fellowship and jokes and friendliness among drunken people or unchaste people. But pride always means enmity—it *is* enmity. And not only enmity between man and man, but enmity to God.

In God you come up against something which is in every respect immeasurably superior to yourself. Unless you know God as that—and, therefore, know yourself as nothing in comparison—you do not know God at all. As long as you are proud you cannot know God. A proud man is always looking down on things and people: and, of course, as long as you are looking down, you cannot see something that is above you.

—from *Mere Christianity*

1921 William T. Kirkpatrick, Lewis's beloved tutor (1914–1917), dies at age seventy-one.

Forget Yourself

How is it that people who are quite obviously eaten up with Pride can say they believe in God and appear to themselves very religious? I am afraid it means they are worshipping an imaginary God. They theoretically admit themselves to be nothing in the presence of this phantom God, but are really all the time imagining how He approves of them and thinks them far better than ordinary people. that is, they pay a pennyworth of imaginary humility to Him and get out of it a pound's worth of Pride towards their fellow-men. I suppose it was of those people Christ was thinking when He said that some would preach about Him and cast out devils in His name, only to be told at the end of the world that He had never known them. And any of us may at any moment be in this death-trap. Luckily, we have a test. Whenever we find that our religious life is making us feel that we are good—above all, that we are better than someone else—I think we may be sure that we are being acted on, not by God, but by the devil. The real test of being in the presence of God is, that you either forget about yourself altogether or see yourself as a small, dirty object. It is better to forget about yourself altogether.

—from *Mere Christianity*

Dictatorship of Pride

It is a terrible thing that the worst of all the vices [Pride] can smuggle itself into the very centre of our religious life. But you can see why. The other, and less bad, vices come from the devil working on us through our animal nature. But this does not come through our animal nature at all. It comes direct from Hell. It is purely spiritual: consequently it is far more subtle and deadly. For the same reason, Pride can often be used to beat down the simpler vices. Teachers, in fact, often appeal to a boy's Pride, or, as they call it, his self-respect, to make him behave decently: many a man has overcome cowardice, or lust, or ill-temper, by learning to think that they are beneath his dignity—that is, by Pride. The devil laughs. He is perfectly content to see you becoming chaste and brave and self-controlled provided, all the time, he is setting up in you the Dictatorship of Pride—just as he would be quite content to see your chilblains cured if he was allowed, in return, to give you cancer. For Pride is spiritual cancer: it eats up the very possibility of love, or contentment, or even common sense.

—from *Mere Christianity*

1918 Edward "Paddy" Moore, Lewis's army roommate and friend, is reported missing in action. It is later learned that Paddy had been killed in action on March 21, 1918, resisting the German attack at Pargny, France.

A Humble Fault

Pleasure in being praised is not Pride. The child who is patted on the back for doing a lesson well, the woman whose beauty is praised by her lover, the saved soul to whom Christ says 'Well done,' are pleased and ought to be. For here the pleasure lies not in what you are but in the fact that you have pleased someone you wanted (and rightly wanted) to please. The trouble begins when you pass from thinking, 'I have pleased him; all is well,' to thinking, 'What a fine person I must be to have done it.' The more you delight in yourself and the less you delight in the praise, the worse you are becoming. When you delight wholly in yourself and do not care about the praise at all, you have reached the bottom. That is why vanity, though it is the sort of Pride which shows most on the surface, is really the least bad and most pardonable sort. The vain person wants praise, applause, admiration, too much and is always angling for it. It is a fault, but a child-like and even (in an odd way) a humble fault. It shows that you are not yet completely contented with your own admiration. You value other people enough to want them to look at you. You are, in fact, still human.

—from *Mere Christianity*

Diabolical Pride

The real black, diabolical Pride, comes when you look down on others so much that you do not care what they think of you. Of course, it is very right, and often our duty, not to care what people think of us, if we do so for the right reason; namely, because we care so incomparably more what God thinks. But the Proud man has a different reason for not caring. He says 'Why should I care for the applause of that rabble as if their opinion were worth anything? And even if their opinions were of value, am I the sort of man to blush with pleasure at a compliment like some chit of a girl at her first dance? No, I am an integrated, adult personality. All I have done has been done to satisfy my own ideals—or my artistic conscience—or the traditions of my family—or, in a word, because I'm That Kind of Chap. If the mob like it, let them. They're nothing to me.' In this way real thorough-going pride may act as a check on vanity; for, as I said a moment ago, the devil loves 'curing' a small fault by giving you a great one. We must try not to be vain, but we must never call in our Pride to cure our vanity.

—from *Mere Christianity*

1959 Lewis is elected Honorary Fellow of University College, Oxford.

School Pride

We say in English that a man is 'proud' of his son, or his father, or his school, or regiment, and it may be asked whether 'pride' in this sense is a sin. I think it depends on what, exactly, we mean by 'proud of'. Very often, in such sentences, the phrase 'is proud of' means 'has a warm-hearted admiration for'. Such an admiration is, of course, very far from being a sin. But it might, perhaps, mean that the person in question gives himself airs on the ground of his distinguished father, or because he belongs to a famous regiment. This would, clearly, be a fault; but even then, it would be better than being proud simply of himself. To love and admire anything outside yourself is to take one step away from utter spiritual ruin; though we shall not be well so long as we love and admire anything more than we love and admire God.

—from *Mere Christianity*

Point of Contact

We must not think Pride is something God forbids because He is offended at it, or that Humility is something He demands as due to His own dignity—as if God Himself was proud. He is not in the least worried about His dignity. The point is, He wants you to know Him: wants to give you Himself. And He and you are two things of such a kind that if you really get into any kind of touch with Him you will, in fact, be humble—delightedly humble, feeling the infinite relief of having for once got rid of all the silly nonsense about your own dignity which has made you restless and unhappy all your life. He is trying to make you humble in order to make this moment possible: trying to take off a lot of silly, ugly, fancy-dress in which we have all got ourselves up and are strutting about like the little idiots we are. I wish I had got a bit further with humility myself: if I had, I could probably tell you more about the relief, the comfort, of taking the fancy-dress off—getting rid of the false self, with all its 'Look at me' and 'Aren't I a good boy?' and all its posing and posturing. To get even near it, even for a moment, is like a drink of cold water to a man in a desert.

—from *Mere Christianity*

1960 *The Four Loves* is published by Geoffrey Bles, London.

The First Step

Do not imagine that if you meet a really humble man he will be what most people call 'humble' nowadays: he will not be a sort of greasy, smarmy person, who is always telling you that, of course, he is nobody. Probably all you will think about him is that he seemed a cheerful, intelligent chap who took a real interest in what *you* said to *him*. If you do dislike him it will be because you feel a little envious of anyone who seems to enjoy life so easily. He will not be thinking about humility: he will not be thinking about himself at all.

If anyone would like to acquire humility, I can, I think, tell him the first step. The first step is to realise that one is proud. And a biggish step, too. At least, nothing whatever can be done before it. If you think you are not conceited, it means you are very conceited indeed.

—from *Mere Christianity*

Humility 101

Screwtape examines the virtue of Humility:

Your patient has become humble; have you drawn his attention to the fact? All virtues are less formidable to us once the man is aware that he has them, but this is specially true of humility. Catch him at the moment when he is really poor in spirit and smuggle into his mind the gratifying reflection, 'By jove! I'm being humble', and almost immediately pride—pride at his own humility—will appear. If he awakes to the danger and tries to smother this new form of pride, make him proud of his attempt—and so on, through as many stages as you please. But don't try this too long, for fear you awake his sense of humour and proportion, in which case he will merely laugh at you and go to bed.

But there are other profitable ways of fixing his attention on the virtue of Humility. By this virtue, as by all the others, our Enemy wants to turn the man's attention away from self to Him, and to the man's neighbours. All the abjection and self-hatred are designed, in the long run, solely for this end; unless they attain this end they do us little harm; and they may even do us good if they keep the man concerned with himself, and, above all, if self-contempt can be made the starting-point for contempt of other selves, and thus for gloom, cynicism, and cruelty.

—from *The Screwtape Letters*

Humility, the Wrong End

Screwtape continues his examination of the virtue of Humility:

You must therefore conceal from the patient the true end of Humility. Let him think of it not as self-forgetfulness but as a certain kind of opinion (namely, a low opinion) of his own talents and character. Some talents, I gather, he really has. Fix in his mind the idea that humility consists in trying to believe those talents to be less valuable than he believes them to be. No doubt they *are* in fact less valuable than he believes, but that is not the point. The great thing is to make him value an opinion for some quality other than truth, thus introducing an element of dishonesty and make-believe into the heart of what otherwise threatens to become a virtue. By this method thousands of humans have been brought to think that humility means pretty women trying to believe they are ugly and clever men trying to believe they are fools. And since what they are trying to believe may, in some cases, be manifest nonsense, they cannot succeed in believing it and we have the chance of keeping their minds endlessly revolving on themselves in an effort to achieve the impossible.

—from *The Screwtape Letters*

1920 Lewis takes First in Classical Honour Moderations ("Mods")–
Greek and Latin texts–and begins reading *Literae Humaniores.*

APRIL

Humility, the Right End

Screwtape continues his examination of the virtue of Humility:

To anticipate the Enemy's strategy, we must consider His aims. The Enemy wants to bring the man to a state of mind in which he could design the best cathedral in the world, and know it to be the best, and rejoice in the fact, without being any more (or less) or otherwise glad at having done it than he would be if it had been done by another. The Enemy wants him, in the end, to be so free from any bias in his own favour that he can rejoice in his own talents as frankly and gratefully as in his neighbour's talents—or in a sunrise, an elephant, or a waterfall. He wants each man, in the long run, to be able to recognise all creatures (even himself) as glorious and excellent things. He wants to kill their animal self-love as soon as possible; but it is His long-term policy, I fear, to restore to them a new kind of self-love—a charity and gratitude for all selves, including their own; when they have really learned to love their neighbours as themselves, they will be allowed to love themselves as their neighbours. For we must never forget what is the most repellent and inexplicable trait in our Enemy; He *really* loves the hairless bipeds He has created and always gives back to them with His right hand what He has taken away with His left.

—from *The Screwtape Letters*

April 1957 Joy Gresham Lewis leaves the hospital with little hope of recovery, and is moved to The Kilns as Lewis's wife, joining her sons, David and Douglas.

The Primary Sin

Traditional doctrine points to a sin against God, an act of disobedience, not a sin against the neighbour. And certainly, if we are to hold the doctrine of the Fall in any real sense, we must look for the great sin on a deeper and more timeless level than that of social morality.

This sin has been described by Saint Augustine as the result of Pride, of the movement whereby a creature (that is, an essentially dependent being whose principle of existence lies not in itself but in another) tries to set up on its own, to exist for itself. Such a sin requires no complex social conditions, no extended experience, no great intellectual development. From the moment a creature becomes aware of God as God and of itself as self, the terrible alternative of choosing God or self for the centre is opened to it. This sin is committed daily by young children and ignorant peasants as well as by sophisticated persons, by solitaries no less than by those who live in society: it is the fall in every individual life, and in each day of each individual life, the basic sin behind all particular sins: at this very moment you and I are either committing it, or about to commit it, or repenting it.

—from *The Problem of Pain*

3 APRIL

The Gentle Slope to Nothing

Screwtape reveals Nothing:

The Christians describe the Enemy as one 'without whom Nothing is strong'. And Nothing is very strong: strong enough to steal away a man's best years not in sweet sins but in a dreary flickering of the mind over it knows not what and knows not why, in the gratification of curiosities so feeble that the man is only half aware of them, in drumming of fingers and kicking of heels, in whistling tunes that he does not like, or in the long, dim labyrinth of reveries that have not even lust or ambition to give them a relish, but which, once chance association has started them, the creature is too weak and fuddled to shake off.

You will say that these are very small sins; and doubtless, like all young tempters, you are anxious to be able to report spectacular wickedness. But do remember, the only thing that matters is the extent to which you separate the man from the Enemy. It does not matter how small the sins are provided that their cumulative effect is to edge the man away from the Light and out into the Nothing. Murder is no better than cards if cards can do the trick. Indeed the safest road to Hell is the gradual one—the gentle slope, soft underfoot, without sudden turnings, without milestones, without signposts.

—from *The Screwtape Letters*

1960 After learning of the return of Joy's cancer, Jack and Joy
vacation in Greece with Roger Lancelyn Green and his wife, Joy.

Closer to God—or Closer to Hell?

Screwtape expands on fundamental sins:

You complain that my last letter does not make it clear whether I regard *being in love* as a desirable state for a human or not. But really, Wormwood, that is the sort of question one expects *them* to ask! Leave them to discuss whether 'Love', or patriotism, or celibacy, or candles on altars, or teetotalism, or education, are 'good' or 'bad'. Can't you see there's no answer? Nothing matters at all except the tendency of a given state of mind, in given circumstances, to move a particular patient at a particular moment nearer to the Enemy or nearer to us. Thus it would be quite a good thing to make the patient decide that 'Love' is 'good' or 'bad'. If he is an arrogant man with a contempt for the body really based on delicacy but mistaken by him for purity— and one who takes pleasure in flouting what most of his fellows approve—by all means let him decide against love. Instil into him an overweening asceticism and then, when you have separated his sexuality from all that might humanise it, weigh in on him with it in some much more brutal and cynical form. If, on the other hand, he is an emotional, gullible man, feed him on minor poets and fifth-rate novelists of the old school until you have made him believe that 'Love' is both irresistible and somehow intrinsically meritorious. This belief is not much help, I grant you, in producing casual unchastity; but it is an incomparable recipe for prolonged, 'noble', romantic, tragic adulteries, ending, if all goes well, in murders and suicides.

—from *The Screwtape Letters*

A Matter of Meanings

Screwtape examines the matter of Unselfishness:

The grand problem is that of 'Unselfishness'. Note, once again, the admirable work of our Philological Arm in substituting the negative unselfishness for the Enemy's positive Charity. Thanks to this you can, from the very outset, teach a man to surrender benefits not that others may be happy in having them but that he may be unselfish in forgoing them. That is a great point gained. Another great help, where the parties concerned are male and female, is the divergence of view about Unselfishness which we have built up between the sexes. A woman means by Unselfishness chiefly taking trouble for others; a man means not giving trouble to others. As a result, a woman who is quite far gone in the Enemy's service will make a nuisance of herself on a larger scale than any man except those whom Our Father has dominated completely; and, conversely, a man will live long in the Enemy's camp before he undertakes as much spontaneous work to please others as a quite ordinary woman may do every day. Thus while the woman thinks of doing good offices and the man of respecting other people's rights, each sex, without any obvious unreason, can and does regard the other as radically selfish.

—from *The Screwtape Letters*

The Unselfishness Game

Screwtape's gleeful tale of the unselfish family:

This game is best played with more than two players, in a family with grown-up children for example. Something quite trivial, like having tea in the garden, is proposed. One member takes care to make it quite clear (though not in so many words) that he would rather not but is, of course, prepared to do so out of 'Unselfishness'. The others instantly withdraw their proposal, ostensibly through their 'Unselfishness', but really because they don't want to be used as a sort of lay figure on which the first speaker practises petty altruisms. But he is not going to be done out of his debauch of Unselfishness either. He insists on doing 'what the others want'. They insist on doing what he wants. Passions are roused. Soon someone is saying 'Very well then, I won't have any tea at all!', and a real quarrel ensues with bitter resentment on both sides. You see how it is done? If each side had been frankly contending for its own real wish, they would all have kept within the bounds of reason and courtesy; but just because the contention is reversed and each side is fighting the other side's battle, all the bitterness which really flows from thwarted self-righteousness and obstinacy and the accumulated grudges of the last ten years is concealed from them by the nominal or official 'Unselfishness' of what they are doing or, at least, held to be excused by it. .... A sensible human once said, 'If people knew how much ill-feeling Unselfishness occasions, it would not be so often recommended from the pulpit'; and again, 'She's the sort of woman who lives for others—you can always tell the others by their hunted expression.'

—from *The Screwtape Letters*

Half-Hearted Desires

If you asked twenty good men today what they thought the highest of the virtues, nineteen of them would reply, Unselfishness. But if you had asked almost any of the great Christians of old, he would have replied, Love. You see what has happened? A negative term has been substituted for a positive, and this is of more than philological importance. The negative idea of Unselfishness carries with it the suggestion not primarily of securing good things for others, but of going without them ourselves, as if our abstinence and not their happiness was the important point. I do not think this is the Christian virtue of Love. The New Testament has lots to say about self-denial, but not about self-denial as an end in itself. We are told to deny ourselves and to take up our crosses in order that we may follow Christ; and nearly every description of what we shall ultimately find if we do so contains an appeal to desire. If there lurks in most modern minds the notion that to desire our own good and earnestly to hope for the enjoyment of it is a bad thing, I submit that this notion has crept in from Kant and the Stoics and is no part of the Christian faith. Indeed, if we consider the unblushing promises of reward and the staggering nature of the rewards promised in the Gospels, it would seem that Our Lord finds our desires not too strong, but too weak. We are half-hearted creatures, fooling about with drink and sex and ambition when infinite joy is offered us, like an ignorant child who wants to go on making mud pies in a slum because he cannot imagine what is meant by the offer of a holiday at the sea. We are far too easily pleased.

—from "The Weight of Glory" (The Weight of Glory)

A Gradual Turning

Screwtape reiterates his premise:

Whichever he adopts, your main task will be the same. Let him begin by treating the Patriotism or the Pacifism as a part of his religion. Then let him, under the influence of partisan spirit, come to regard it as the most important part. Then quietly and gradually nurse him on to the stage at which the religion becomes merely part of the 'cause', in which Christianity is valued chiefly because of the excellent arguments it can produce in favour of the British war-effort or of Pacifism. The attitude which you want to guard against is that in which temporal affairs are treated primarily as material for obedience. Once you have made the World an end, and faith a means, you have almost won your man, and it makes very little difference what kind of worldly end he is pursuing. Provided that meetings, pamphlets, policies, movements, causes, and crusades, matter more to him than prayers and sacraments and charity, he is ours—and the more 'religious' (on those terms) the more securely ours. I could show you a pretty cageful down here.

—from *The Screwtape Letters*

The Horror of the Same Old Thing

Screwtape reveals a powerful tool for distraction:

What we want, if men become Christians at all, is to keep them in the state of mind I call 'Christianity And'. You know—Christianity and the Crisis, Christianity and the New Psychology, Christianity and the New Order, Christianity and Faith Healing, Christianity and Psychical Research, Christianity and Vegetarianism, Christianity and Spelling Reform. If they must be Christians let them at least be Christians with a difference. Substitute for the faith itself some Fashion with a Christian colouring. Work on their horror of the Same Old Thing.

The horror of the Same Old Thing is one of the most valuable passions we have produced in the human heart—an endless source of heresies in religion, folly in counsel, infidelity in marriage, and inconstancy in friendship. The humans live in time, and experience reality successively. To experience much of it, therefore, they must experience many different things; in other words, they must experience change. And since they need change, the Enemy (being a hedonist at heart) has made change pleasurable to them, just as He has made eating pleasurable. But since He does not wish them to make change, any more than eating, an end in itself, He has balanced the love of change in them by a love of permanence. He has contrived to gratify both tastes together in the very world He has made, by that union of change and permanence which we call Rhythm. He gives them the seasons, each season different yet every year the same, so that spring is always felt as a novelty yet always as the recurrence of an immemorial theme. He gives them in His Church a spiritual year; they change from a fast to a feast, but it is the same feast as before.

—from *The Screwtape Letters*

1973 Warren Hamilton Lewis, C. S. Lewis's older brother, dies at age seventy-eight at The Kilns, Oxford.

The Demand for Novelty

Screwtape shows how the pleasure of change is corrupted into a demand for novelty:

Now just as we pick out and exaggerate the pleasure of eating to produce gluttony, so we pick out this natural pleasantness of change and twist it into a demand for absolute novelty. This demand is entirely our workmanship. If we neglect our duty, men will be not only contented but transported by the mixed novelty and familiarity of snowdrops *this* January, sunrise *this* morning, plum pudding *this* Christmas. Children, until we have taught them better, will be perfectly happy with a seasonal round of games in which conkers succeed hopscotch as regularly as autumn follows summer. Only by our incessant efforts is the demand for infinite, or unrhythmical, change kept up.

This demand is valuable in various ways. In the first place it diminishes pleasure while increasing desire. The pleasure of novelty is by its very nature more subject than any other to the law of diminishing returns. And continued novelty costs money, so that the desire for it spells avarice or unhappiness or both. And again, the more rapacious this desire, the sooner it must eat up all the innocent sources of pleasure and pass on to those the Enemy forbids. Thus by inflaming the horror of the Same Old Thing we have recently made the Arts, for example, less dangerous to us than, perhaps, they have ever been, 'low-brow' and 'high-brow' artists alike being now daily drawn into fresh, and still fresh, excesses of lasciviousness, unreason, cruelty, and pride.

—from *The Screwtape Letters*

The Thrill Is Gone

What is more (and I can hardly find words to tell you how important I think this), it is just the people who are ready to submit to the loss of the thrill and settle down to the sober interest, who are then most likely to meet new thrills in some quite different direction. The man who has learned to fly and become a good pilot will suddenly discover music; the man who has settled down to live in the beauty spot will discover gardening.

This is, I think, one little part of what Christ meant by saying that a thing will not really live unless it first dies. It is simply no good trying to keep any thrill: that is the very worst thing you can do. Let the thrill go—let it die away—go on through that period of death into the quieter interest and happiness that follow—and you will find you are living in a world of new thrills all the time. But if you decide to make thrills your regular diet and try to prolong them artificially, they will all get weaker and weaker, and fewer and fewer, and you will be a bored, disillusioned old man for the rest of your life. It is because so few people understand this that you find many middle-aged men and women maundering about their lost youth, at the very age when new horizons ought to be appearing and new doors opening all round them. It is much better fun to learn to swim than to go on endlessly (and hopelessly) trying to get back the feeling you had when you first went paddling as a small boy.

—from *Mere Christianity*

My Time Is My Own

Screwtape outlines a fundamental deception:

Men are not angered by mere misfortune but by misfortune conceived as injury. And the sense of injury depends on the feeling that a legitimate claim has been denied. The more claims on life, therefore, that your patient can be induced to make, the more often he will feel injured and, as a result, ill-tempered. Now you will have noticed that nothing throws him into a passion so easily as to find a tract of time which he reckoned on having at his own disposal unexpectedly taken from him. It is the unexpected visitor (when he looked forward to a quiet evening), or the friend's talkative wife (turning up when he looked forward to a *tête-à-tête* with the friend), that throw him out of gear. Now he is not yet so uncharitable or slothful that these small demands on his courtesy are *in themselves* too much for it. They anger him because he regards his time as his own and feels that it is being stolen. You must therefore zealously guard in his mind the curious assumption 'My time is my own'. Let him have the feeling that he starts each day as the lawful possessor of twenty-four hours. Let him feel as a grievous tax that portion of this property which he has to make over to his employers, and as a generous donation that further portion which he allows to religious duties. But what he must never be permitted to doubt is that the total from which these deductions have been made was, in some mysterious sense, his own personal birthright.

—from *The Screwtape Letters*

Uninspected Assumptions

Screwtape instructs Wormwood on muddled thinking:

The assumption which you want him to go on making is so absurd that, if once it is questioned, even we cannot find a shred of argument in its defence. The man can neither make, nor retain, one moment of time; it all comes to him by pure gift; he might as well regard the sun and moon as his chattels. He is also, in theory, committed to a total service of the Enemy; and if the Enemy appeared to him in bodily form and demanded that total service for even one day, he would not refuse. He would be greatly relieved if that one day involved nothing harder than listening to the conversation of a foolish woman; and he would be relieved almost to the pitch of disappointment if for one half-hour in that day the Enemy said 'Now you may go and amuse yourself'. Now if he thinks about his assumption for a moment, even he is bound to realise that he is actually in this situation every day. When I speak of preserving this assumption in his mind, therefore, the last thing I mean you to do is to furnish him with arguments in its defence. There aren't any. Your task is purely negative. Don't let his thoughts come anywhere near it. Wrap a darkness about it, and in the centre of that darkness let his sense of ownership-in-Time lie silent, uninspected, and operative.

—from *The Screwtape Letters*

Nuances of Ownership

Screwtape encourages confusion and pride:

The sense of ownership in general is always to be encouraged. The humans are always putting up claims to ownership which sound equally funny in Heaven and in Hell and we must keep them doing so. Much of the modem resistance to chastity comes from men's belief that they 'own' their bodies—those vast and perilous estates, pulsating with the energy that made the worlds, in which they find themselves without their consent and from which they are ejected at the pleasure of Another! It is as if a royal child whom his father has placed, for love's sake, in titular command of some great province, under the real rule of wise counsellors, should come to fancy he really owns the cities, the forests, and the corn, in the same way as he owns the bricks on the nursery floor.

We produce this sense of ownership not only by pride but by confusion. We teach them not to notice the different senses of the possessive pronoun—the finely graded differences that run from 'my boots' through 'my dog', 'my servant', 'my wife', 'my father', 'my master' and 'my country', to 'my God'. They can be taught to reduce all these senses to that of 'my boots', the 'my' of ownership.

—from *The Screwtape Letters*

Mine, Mine, Mine

Screwtape acknowledges the truth about ownership:

Even in the nursery a child can be taught to mean by 'my teddy bear' *not* the old imagined recipient of affection to whom it stands in a special relation (for that is what the Enemy will teach them to mean if we are not careful) but 'the bear I can pull to pieces if I like'. And at the other end of the scale, we have taught men to say 'my God' in a sense not really very different from 'my boots', meaning 'the God on whom I have a claim for my distinguished services and whom I exploit from the pulpit—the God I have done a corner in'.

And all the time the joke is that the word 'Mine' in its fully possessive sense cannot be uttered by a human being about anything. In the long run either Our Father or the Enemy will say 'Mine' of each thing that exists, and specially of each man. They will find out in the end, never fear, to whom their time, their souls, and their bodies really belong—certainly not to *them*, whatever happens. At present the Enemy says 'Mine' of everything on the pedantic, legalistic ground that He made it: Our Father hopes in the end to say 'Mine' of all things on the more realistic and dynamic ground of conquest.

—from *The Screwtape Letters*

1918 Lewis is wounded by a British shell on Mount Berenchon during the Battle of Arras.

A Mother's Love

A Ghost argues with the Bright Spirit who was her brother Reginald:

'It's a lie. A wicked, cruel lie. How could anyone love their son more than I did? Haven't I lived only for his memory all these years?'

'That was rather a mistake, Pam. In your heart of hearts you know it was.'

'What was a mistake?'

'All that ten years' ritual of grief. Keeping his room exactly as he'd left it; keeping anniversaries; refusing to leave that house though Dick and Muriel were both wretched there.'

'Of course they didn't care. I know that. I soon learned to expect no real sympathy from them.'

'You're wrong. No man ever felt his son's death more than Dick. Not many girls loved their brothers better than Muriel. It wasn't against Michael they revolted: it was against you—against having their whole life dominated by the tyranny of the past: and not really even Michael's past, but your past.'

'You are heartless. Everyone is heartless. The past was all I had.'

'It was all you chose to have. It was the wrong way to deal with a sorrow. It was Egyptian—like embalming a dead body.'

'Oh, of course. I'm wrong. Everything I say or do is wrong, according to you.'

'But of course!' said the Spirit, shining with love and mirth so that my eyes were dazzled. 'That's what we all find when we reach this country. We've all been wrong! That's the great joke. There's no need to go on pretending one was right! After that we begin living.'

—from *The Great Divorce*

Domestic Tyranny

Lewis, grieving the death of his wife, Joy:

Keeping promises to the dead, or to anyone else, is very well. But I begin to see that 'respect for the wishes of the dead' is a trap. Yesterday I stopped myself only in time from saying about some trifle 'H. wouldn't have liked that.' This is unfair to the others. I should soon be using 'what H. would have liked' as an instrument of domestic tyranny, with her supposed likings becoming a thinner and thinner disguise for my own.

—from *A Grief Observed*

God at Her Elbow

Lewis, grieving the death of his wife, Joy:

On the other hand, 'Knock and it shall be opened.' But does knocking mean hammering and kicking the door like a maniac? And there's also 'To him that hath shall be given.' After all, you must have a capacity to receive, or even omnipotence can't give. Perhaps your own passion temporarily destroys the capacity.

For all sorts of mistakes are possible when you are dealing with Him. Long ago, before we were married, H. was haunted all one morning as she went about her work with the obscure sense of God (so to speak) 'at her elbow,' demanding her attention. And of course, not being a perfected saint, she had the feeling that it would be a question, as it usually is, of some unrepented sin or tedious duty. At last she gave in—I know how one puts it off—and faced Him. But the message was, 'I want to *give* you something' and instantly she entered into joy.

—from *A Grief Observed*

1915 Helen Joy Davidman is born in New York City.

Signs of Attrition

Screwtape advises Wormwood on using time to wear down a soul:
The Enemy has guarded him from you through the first great wave of temptations. But, if only he can be kept alive, you have time itself for your ally. The long, dull, monotonous years of middle-aged prosperity or middle-aged adversity are excellent campaigning weather. You see, it is so hard for these creatures to *persevere*. The routine of adversity, the gradual decay of youthful loves and youthful hopes, the quiet despair (hardly felt as pain) of ever overcoming the chronic temptations with which we have again and again defeated them, the drabness which we create in their lives and the inarticulate resentment with which we teach them to respond to it—all this provides admirable opportunities of wearing out a soul by attrition. If, on the other hand, the middle years prove prosperous, our position is even stronger. Prosperity knits a man to the World. He feels that he is 'finding his place in it', while really it is finding its place in him. His increasing reputation, his widening circle of acquaintances, his sense of importance, the growing pressure of absorbing and agreeable work, build up in him a sense of being really at home in earth, which is just what we want. You will notice that the young are generally less unwilling to die than the middle-aged and the old.

—from *The Screwtape Letters*

1943 *Christian Behaviour: A Further Series of Broadcast Talks* is published by Geoffrey Bles/The Centenary Press, London.

Unravelling Souls

Screwtape's observations on how long life on earth can enhance Hell's work:

The truth is that the Enemy, having oddly destined these mere animals to life in His own eternal world, has guarded them pretty effectively from the danger of feeling at home anywhere else. That is why we must often wish long life to our patients; seventy years is not a day too much for the difficult task of unravelling their souls from Heaven and building up a firm attachment to the earth. While they are young we find them always shooting off at a tangent. Even if we contrive to keep them ignorant of explicit religion, the incalculable winds of fantasy and music and poetry—the mere face of a girl, the song of a bird, or the sight of a horizon—are always blowing our whole structure away. They *will* not apply themselves steadily to worldly advancement, prudent connections, and the policy of safety first. So inveterate is their appetite for Heaven that our best method, at this stage, of attaching them to earth is to make them believe that earth can be turned into Heaven at some future date by politics or eugenics or 'science' or psychology, or what not. Real worldliness is a work of time—assisted, of course, by pride, for we teach them to describe the creeping death as good sense or Maturity or Experience. *Experience,* in the peculiar sense we teach them to give it, is, by the by, a most useful word. A great human philosopher nearly let our secret out when he said that where Virtue is concerned 'Experience is the mother of illusion'; but thanks to a change in Fashion, and also, of course, to the Historical Point of View, we have largely rendered his book innocuous.

—from *The Screwtape Letters*

1943 *Perelandra* (the second volume of Lewis's *Space Trilogy*) is published by The Bodley Head, London.

The Secret Thread

There have been times when I think we do not desire heaven; but more often I find myself wondering whether, in our heart of hearts, we have ever desired anything else. You may have noticed that the books you really love are bound together by a secret thread. You know very well what is the common quality that makes you love them, though you cannot put it into words: but most of your friends do not see it at all, and often wonder why, liking this, you should also like that. Again, you have stood before some landscape, which seems to embody what you have been looking for all your life; and then turned to the friend at your side who appears to be seeing what you saw—but at the first words a gulf yawns between you, and you realise that this landscape means something totally different to him, that he is pursuing an alien vision and cares nothing for the ineffable suggestion by which you are transported. Even in your hobbies, has there not always been some secret attraction which the others are curiously ignorant of—something, not to be identified with, but always on the verge of breaking through, the smell of cut wood in the workshop or the clap-clap of water against the boat's side?

—from *The Problem of Pain*

1905 The Lewis family—Albert, Flora, Warnie, and Jack—moves from Dundela Villas to Little Lea, on the outskirts of Belfast.

The Hint of More

Are not all lifelong friendships born at the moment when at last you meet another human being who has some inkling (but faint and uncertain even in the best) of that something which you were born desiring, and which, beneath the flux of other desires and in all the momentary silences between the louder passions, night and day, year by year, from childhood to old age, you are looking for, watching for, listening for? You have never *had* it. All the things that have ever deeply possessed your soul have been but hints of it—tantalising glimpses, promises never quite fulfilled, echoes that died away just as they caught your ear. But if it should really become manifest—if there ever came an echo that did not die away but swelled into the sound itself—you would know it. Beyond all possibility of doubt you would say 'Here at last is the thing I was made for.' We cannot tell each other about it. It is the secret signature of each soul, the incommunicable and unappeasable want, the thing we desired before we met our wives or made our friends or chose our work, and which we shall still desire on our deathbeds, when the mind no longer knows wife or friend or work. While we are, this is. If we lose this, we lose all.

—from *The Problem of Pain*

A Most Complete Wife

Lewis, grieving the death of his wife, Joy:

For a good wife contains so many persons in herself. What was H. not to me? She was my daughter and my mother, my pupil and my teacher, my subject and my sovereign; and always, holding all these in solution, my trusty comrade, friend, shipmate, fellow-soldier. My mistress; but at the same time all that any man friend (and I have good ones) has ever been to me. Perhaps more. If we had never fallen in love we should have none the less been always together, and created a scandal. That's what I meant when I once praised her for her 'masculine virtues.' But she soon put a stop to that by asking how I'd like to be praised for my feminine ones. It was a good *riposte*, dear. Yet there was something of the Amazon, something of Penthesileia and Camilla. And you, as well as I, were glad it should be there. You were glad I should recognize it.

Solomon calls his bride Sister. Could a woman be a complete wife unless, for a moment, in one particular mood, a man felt almost inclined to call her Brother?

—from *A Grief Observed*

1956 Jack Lewis and Joy Davidman Gresham are married in a civil ceremony at the registry office on St. Giles Street, Oxford.

A World Starving

No Christian and, indeed, no historian could accept the epigram which defines religion as "what a man does with his solitude." It was one of the Wesleys, I think, who said that the New Testament knows nothing of solitary religion. We are forbidden to neglect the assembling of ourselves together. Christianity is already institutional in the earliest of its documents. The Church is the Bride of Christ. We are members of one another.

In our own age the idea that religion belongs to our private life—that it is, in fact, an occupation for the individual's hour of leisure—is at once paradoxical, dangerous, and natural. It is paradoxical because this exaltation of the individual in the religious field springs up in an age when collectivism is ruthlessly defeating the individual in every other field. .... There is a crowd of busybodies, self-appointed masters of ceremonies, whose life is devoted to destroying solitude wherever solitude still exists. They call it "taking the young people out of themselves," or "waking them up," or "overcoming their apathy." If an Augustine, a Vaughan, a Traherne, or a Wordsworth should be born in the modern world, the leaders of a youth organization would soon cure him. If a really good home, such as the home of Alcinous and Arete in the *Odyssey* or the Rostovs in *War and Peace* or any of Charlotte M. Yonge's families, existed today, it would be denounced as *bourgeois* and every engine of destruction would be levelled against it. And even where the planners fail and someone is left physically by himself, the wireless has seen to it that he will be—in a sense not intended by Scipio—never less alone than when alone. We live, in fact, in a world starved for solitude, silence, and privacy, and therefore starved for meditation and true friendship.

—from "Membership" *(The Weight of Glory)*

Welcome to the Family

The very word *membership* is of Christian origin, but it has been taken over by the world and emptied of all meaning. In any book on logic you may see the expression "members of a class." It must be most emphatically stated that the items or particulars included in a homogeneous class are almost the reverse of what St. Paul meant by *members*. By *members* . . . . he meant what we should call *organs*, things essentially different from, and complementary to, one another, things differing not only in structure and function but also in dignity. . . . . How true membership in a body differs from inclusion in a collective may be seen in the structure of a family. The grandfather, the parents, the grown-up son, the child, the dog, and the cat are true members (in the organic sense), precisely because they are not members or units of a homogeneous class. They are not interchangeable. Each person is almost a species in himself. The mother is not simply a different person from the daughter; she is a different kind of person. The grown-up brother is not simply one unit in the class children; he is a separate estate of the realm. The father and grandfather are almost as different as the cat and the dog. If you subtract any one member, you have not simply reduced the family in number; you have inflicted an injury on its structure. Its unity is a unity of unlikes, almost of incommensurables.

A dim perception of the richness inherent in this kind of unity is one reason why we enjoy a book like *The Wind in the Willows;* a trio such as Rat, Mole, and Badger symbolises the extreme differentiation of persons in harmonious union, which we know intuitively to be our true refuge both from solitude and from the collective.

—from "Membership" *(The Weight of Glory)*

Part of the Mystical Body

The Church will outlive the universe; in it the individual person will outlive the universe. Everything that is joined to the immortal head will share His immortality. We hear little of this from the Christian pulpit today. .... If we do not believe it, let us be honest and relegate the Christian faith to museums. If we do, let us give up the pretence that it makes no difference. For this is the real answer to every excessive claim made by the collective. It is mortal; we shall live forever. There will come a time when every culture, every institution, every nation, the human race, all biological life is extinct and every one of us is still alive. Immortality is promised to us, not to these generalities. It was not for societies or states that Christ died, but for men. In that sense Christianity must seem to secular collectivists to involve an almost frantic assertion of individuality. But then it is not the individual as such who will share Christ's victory over death. We shall share the victory by being in the Victor. A rejection, or in Scripture's strong language, a crucifixion of the natural self is the passport to everlasting life. Nothing that has not died will be resurrected. .... There lies the maddening ambiguity of our faith as it must appear to outsiders. It sets its face relentlessly against our natural individualism; on the other hand, it gives back to those who abandon individualism an eternal possession of their own personal being, even of their bodies. As mere biological entities, each with its separate will to live and to expand, we are apparently of no account; we are cross-fodder. But as organs in the Body of Christ, as stones and pillars in the temple, we are assured of our eternal self-identity and shall live to remember the galaxies as an old tale.
—from "Membership" *(The Weight of Glory)*

1917 Lewis (age eighteen) arrives at Oxford University to begin his studies.

To Become Really Doggy

True personality lies ahead—how far ahead, for most of us, I dare not say. And the key to it does not lie in ourselves. It will not be attained by development from within outwards. It will come to us when we occupy those places in the structure of the eternal cosmos for which we were designed or invented. As a colour first reveals its true quality when placed by an excellent artist in its pre-elected spot between certain others, as a spice reveals its true flavour when inserted just where and when a good cook wishes among the other ingredients, as the dog becomes really doggy only when he has taken his place in the household of man, so we shall then first be true persons when we have suffered ourselves to be fitted into our places. We are marble waiting to be shaped, metal waiting to be run into a mould. No doubt there are already, even in the unregenerate self, faint hints of what mould each is designed for, or what sort of pillar he will be. But it is, I think, a gross exaggeration to picture the saving of a soul as being, normally, at all like the development from seed to flower. The very words *repentance, regeneration, the New Man,* suggest something very different. Some tendencies in each natural man may have to be simply rejected.
—from "Membership" *(The Weight of Glory)*

1939 *The Personal Heresy* is published by Oxford University Press.

The Right Job

We have in our day started by getting the whole picture upside down. Starting with the doctrine that every individuality is "of infinite value," we then picture God as a kind of employment committee whose business it is to find suitable careers for souls, square holes for square pegs. In fact, however, the value of the individual does not lie in him. He is capable of receiving value. He receives it by union with Christ. There is no question of finding for him a place in the living temple which will do justice to his inherent value and give scope to his natural idiosyncrasy. The place was there first. The man was created for it. He will not be himself till he is there. We shall be true and everlasting and really divine persons only in Heaven, just as we are, even now, coloured bodies only in the light.

To say this is to repeat what everyone here admits already—that we are saved by grace, that in our flesh dwells no good thing, that we are, through and through, creatures not creators, derived beings, living not of ourselves but from Christ.

—from "Membership" *(The Weight of Glory)*

Two Final Points

If I seem to have complicated a simple matter, you will, I hope, forgive me. I have been anxious to bring out two points. I have wanted to try to expel that quite un-Christian worship of the human individual simply as such which is so rampant in modern thought side by side with our collectivism, for one error begets the opposite error and, far from neutralising, they aggravate each other. I mean the pestilent notion (one sees it in literary criticism) that each of us starts with a treasure called "personality" locked up inside him, and that to expand and express this, to guard it from interference, to be "original," is the main end of life. This is Pelagian, or worse, and it defeats even itself. No man who values originality will ever be original. But try to tell the truth as you see it, try to do any bit of work as well as it can be done for the work's sake, and what men call originality will come unsought. Even on that level, the submission of the individual to the function is already beginning to bring true personality to birth. And secondly, I have wanted to show that Christianity is not, in the long run, concerned either with individuals or communities. Neither the individual nor the community as popular thought understands them can inherit eternal life, neither the natural self, nor the collective mass, but a new creature.

—from "Membership" *(The Weight of Glory)*

Troughs and Peaks

Screwtape explains the law of undulation:

Humans are amphibians—half spirit and half animal. (The Enemy's determination to produce such a revolting hybrid was one of the things that determined Our Father to withdraw his support from Him.) As spirits they belong to the eternal world, but as animals they inhabit time. This means that while their spirit can be directed to an eternal object, their bodies, passions, and imaginations are in continual change, for to be in time means to change. Their nearest approach to constancy, therefore, is undulation—the repeated return to a level from which they repeatedly fall back, a series of troughs and peaks. If you had watched your patient carefully you would have seen this undulation in every department of his life—his interest in his work, his affection for his friends, his physical appetites, all go up and down. As long as he lives on earth periods of emotional and bodily richness and liveliness will alternate with periods of numbness and poverty. The dryness and dullness through which your patient is now going are not, as you fondly suppose, your workmanship; they are merely a natural phenomenon which will do us no good unless you make a good use of it.

—from *The Screwtape Letters*

MAY

Servants Who Become Sons

Screwtape reveals the Enemy's intentions:

Now it may surprise you to learn that in His [the Enemy's] efforts to get permanent possession of a soul, He relies on the troughs even more than on the peaks; some of His special favourites have gone through longer and deeper troughs than anyone else. The reason is this. To us a human is primarily food; our aim is the absorption of its will into ours, the increase of our own area of selfhood at its expense. But the obedience which the Enemy demands of men is quite a different thing. One must face the fact that all the talk about His love for men, and His service being perfect freedom, is not (as one would gladly believe) mere propaganda, but an appalling truth. He really *does* want to fill the universe with a lot of loathsome little replicas of Himself—creatures whose life, on its miniature scale, will be qualitatively like His own, not because He has absorbed them but because their wills freely conform to His. We want cattle who can finally become food; He wants servants who can finally become sons. We want to suck in, He wants to give out. We are empty and would be filled; He is full and flows over. Our war aim is a world in which Our Father Below has drawn all other beings into himself: the Enemy wants a world full of beings united to Him but still distinct.

—from *The Screwtape Letters*

May 1924 Lewis accepts a one-year temporary post at University College as a philosophy tutor.

...And Still Obeys

Screwtape elaborates on the Enemy's intentions:

Merely to override a human will (as His felt presence in any but the faintest and most mitigated degree would certainly do) would be for Him useless. He cannot ravish. He can only woo. For His ignoble idea is to eat the cake and have it; the creatures are to be one with Him, but yet themselves; merely to cancel them, or assimilate them, will not serve. He is prepared to do a little overriding at the beginning. He will set them off with communications of His presence which, though faint, seem great to them, with emotional sweetness, and easy conquest over temptation. But He never allows this state of affairs to last long. Sooner or later He withdraws, if not in fact, at least from their conscious experience, all those supports and incentives. He leaves the creature to stand up on its own legs—to carry out from the will alone duties which have lost all relish. It is during such trough periods, much more than during the peak periods, that it is growing into the sort of creature He wants it to be. Hence the prayers offered in the state of dryness are those which please Him best. .... He cannot 'tempt' to virtue as we do to vice. He wants them to learn to walk and must therefore take away His hand; and if only the will to walk is really there He is pleased even with their stumbles. Do not be deceived, Wormwood. Our cause is never more in danger than when a human, no longer desiring, but still intending, to do our Enemy's will, looks round upon a universe from which every trace of Him seems to have vanished, and asks why he has been forsaken, and still obeys.

—from *The Screwtape Letters*

1955 *The Magician's Nephew* (the sixth book written in *The Chronicles of Narnia*) is published by The Bodley Head, London.

At Just That Point in History

We believe that the death of Christ is just that point in history at which something absolutely unimaginable from outside shows through into our own world. And if we cannot picture even the atoms of which our own world is built, of course we are not going to be able to picture this. Indeed, if we found that we could fully understand it, that very fact would show it was not what it professes to be—the inconceivable, the uncreated, the thing from beyond nature, striking down into nature like lightning. You may ask what good it will be to us if we do not understand it. But that is easily answered. A man can eat his dinner without understanding exactly how food nourishes him. A man can accept what Christ has done without knowing how it works: indeed, he certainly would not know how it works until he has accepted it.

We are told that Christ was killed for us, that His death has washed out our sins, and that by dying He disabled death itself. That is the formula. That is Christianity. That is what has to be believed.

—from *Mere Christianity*

May 1941 *The Guardian* begins to publish *The Screwtape Letters* in weekly installments.

The Great Weapon

On the one hand Death is the triumph of Satan, the punishment of the Fall, and the last enemy. Christ shed tears at the grave of Lazarus and sweated blood in Gethsemane: the Life of Lives that was in Him detested this penal obscenity not less than we do, but more. On the other hand, only he who loses his life will save it. We are baptised into the *death* of Christ, and it is the remedy for the Fall. Death is, in fact, what some modern people call 'ambivalent'. It is Satan's great weapon and also God's great weapon: it is holy and unholy; our supreme disgrace and our only hope; the thing Christ came to conquer and the means by which He conquered.

—from *Miracles*

The Very Pattern of Reality

Humanity must embrace death freely, submit to it with total humility, drink it to the dregs, and so convert it into that mystical death which is the secret of life. But only a Man who did not need to have been a Man at all unless He had chosen, only one who served in our sad regiment as a volunteer, yet also only one who was perfectly a Man, could perform this perfect dying; and thus (which way you put it is unimportant) either defeat death or redeem it. He tasted death on behalf of all others. He is the representative 'Die-er' of the universe: and for that very reason the Resurrection and the Life. Or conversely, because He truly lives, He truly dies, for that is the very pattern of reality. Because the higher can descend into the lower He who from all eternity has been incessantly plunging Himself in the blessed death of self-surrender to the Father can also most fully descend into the horrible and (for us) involuntary death of the body. Because Vicariousness is the very idiom of the reality He has created, His death can become ours. The whole Miracle, far from denying what we already know of reality, writes the comment which makes that crabbed text plain: or rather, proves itself to be the text on which Nature was only the commentary. In science we have been reading only the notes to a poem; in Christianity we find the poem itself.

—from *Miracles*

New Life

In the long run God is no one but Himself and what He does is like nothing else. You could hardly expect it to be.

What, then, is the difference which He has made to the whole human mass? It is just this; that the business of becoming a son of God, of being turned from a created thing into a begotten thing, of passing over from the temporary biological life into timeless 'spiritual' life, has been done for us. Humanity is already 'saved' in principle. We individuals have to appropriate that salvation. But the really tough work—the bit we could not have done for ourselves—has been done for us. We have not got to try to climb up into spiritual life by our own efforts; it has already come down into the human race. If we will only lay ourselves open to the one Man in whom it was fully present, and who, in spite of being God, is also a real man, He will do it in us and for us. Remember what I said about 'good infection'. One of our own race has this new life: if we get close to Him we shall catch it from Him.

Of course, you can express this in all sorts of different ways. You can say that Christ died for our sins. You may say that the Father has forgiven us because Christ has done for us what we ought to have done. You may say that we are washed in the blood of the Lamb. You may say that Christ has defeated death. They are all true.

—from *Mere Christianity*

Vicarious Needs

But, you will ask, does this much mend matters? Is not this still injustice, though now the other way round? Where, at the first glance, we accused God of undue favour to His 'chosen', we are now tempted to accuse Him of undue disfavour. (The attempt to keep up both charges at the same time had better be dropped.) And certainly we have here come to a principle very deep-rooted in Christianity: what may be called the principle of *Vicariousness*. The Sinless Man suffers for the sinful, and, in their degree, all good men for all bad men. And this Vicariousness—no less than Death and Rebirth or Selectiveness—is also a characteristic of Nature. Self-sufficiency, living on one's own resources, is a thing impossible in her realm. Everything is indebted to everything else, sacrificed to everything else, dependent on everything else. And here too we must recognise that the principle is in itself neither good nor bad. The cat lives on the mouse in a way I think bad: the bees and the flowers live on one another in a more pleasing manner. The parasite lives on its 'host': but so also the unborn child on its mother. In social life without Vicariousness there would be no exploitation or oppression; but also no kindness or gratitude. It is a fountain both of love and hatred, both of misery and happiness. When we have understood this we shall no longer think that the depraved examples of Vicariousness in Nature forbid us to suppose that the principle itself is of divine origin.
—from *Miracles*

1945 World War II ends in Europe.

1964 *The Discarded Image* is published by Cambridge University Press, Cambridge.

It's Not Fair

I have heard some people complain that if Jesus was God as well as man, then His sufferings and death lose all value in their eyes, 'because it must have been so easy for Him'. Others may (very rightly) rebuke the ingratitude and ungraciousness of this objection; what staggers me is the misunderstanding it betrays. In one sense, of course, those who make it are right. They have even understated their own case. The perfect submission, the perfect suffering, the perfect death were not only easier to Jesus because He was God, but were possible only because He was God. But surely that is a very odd reason for not accepting them? The teacher is able to form the letters for the child because the teacher is grown-up and knows how to write. That, of course, makes it easier for the teacher; and only because it is easier for him can he help the child. If it rejected him because 'it's easy for grown-ups' and waited to learn writing from another child who could not write itself (and so had no 'unfair' advantage), it would not get on very quickly. If I am drowning in a rapid river, a man who still has one foot on the bank may give me a hand which saves my life. Ought I to shout back (between my gasps) 'No, it's not fair! You have an advantage! You're keeping one foot on the bank'? That advantage—call it 'unfair' if you like—is the only reason why he can be of any use to me. To what will you look for help if you will not look to that which is stronger than yourself?

—from *Mere Christianity*

Full Surrender

If God was prepared to let us off, why on earth did He not do so? And what possible point could there be in punishing an innocent person instead? None at all that I can see, if you are thinking of punishment in the police-court sense. On the other hand, if you think of a debt, there is plenty of point in a person who has some assets paying it on behalf of someone who has not. Or if you take 'paying the penalty', not in the sense of being punished, but in the more general sense of 'standing the racket' or 'footing the bill', then, of course, it is a matter of common experience that, when one person has got himself into a hole, the trouble of getting him out usually falls on a kind friend.

Now what was the sort of 'hole' man had got himself into? He had tried to set up on his own, to behave as if he belonged to himself. In other words, fallen man is not simply an imperfect creature who needs improvement: he is a rebel who must lay down his arms. Laying down your arms, surrendering, saying you are sorry, realising that you have been on the wrong track and getting ready to start life over again from the ground floor—that is the only way out of our 'hole'. This process of surrender—this movement full speed astern—is what Christians call repentance. Now repentance is no fun at all. It is something much harder than merely eating humble pie. It means unlearning all the self-conceit and self-will that we have been training ourselves into for thousands of years. It means killing part of yourself, undergoing a kind of death. In fact, it needs a good man to repent. And here comes the catch. Only a bad person needs to repent: only a good person can repent perfectly. The worse you are the more you need it and the less you can do it. The only person who could do it perfectly would be a perfect person—and he would not need it.

—from *Mere Christianity*

With God's Help

Remember, this repentance, this willing submission to humiliation and a kind of death, is not something God demands of you before He will take you back and which He could let you off if He chose: it is simply a description of what going back to Him is like. If you ask God to take you back without it, you are really asking Him to let you go back without going back. It cannot happen. Very well, then, we must go through with it. But the same badness which makes us need it, makes us unable to do it. Can we do it if God helps us? Yes, but what do we mean when we talk of God helping us? We mean God putting into us a bit of Himself, so to speak. He lends us a little of His reasoning powers and that is how we think: He puts a little of His love into us and that is how we love one another. When you teach a child writing, you hold its hand while it forms the letters: that is, it forms the letters because you are forming them. We love and reason because God loves and reasons and holds our hand while we do it.

—from *Mere Christianity*

Nice Is Not Enough

'Niceness'—wholesome, integrated personality—is an excellent thing. We must try by every medical, educational, economic, and political means in our power to produce a world where as many people as possible grow up 'nice'; just as we must try to produce a world where all have plenty to eat. But we must not suppose that even if we succeeded in making everyone nice we should have saved their souls. A world of nice people, content in their own niceness, looking no further, turned away from God, would be just as desperately in need of salvation as a miserable world—and might even be more difficult to save.

For mere improvement is not redemption, though redemption always improves people even here and now and will, in the end, improve them to a degree we cannot yet imagine. God became man to turn creatures into sons: not simply to produce better men of the old kind but to produce a new kind of man. It is not like teaching a horse to jump better and better but like turning a horse into a winged creature. Of course, once it has got its wings, it will soar over fences which could never have been jumped and thus beat the natural horse at its own game. But there may be a period, while the wings are just beginning to grow, when it cannot do so: and at that stage the lumps on the shoulders—no one could tell by looking at them that they are going to be wings—may even give it an awkward appearance.

—from *Mere Christianity*

1926 Lewis meets J. R. R. Tolkien.

That Some Day We May Ride Bare-Back

To shrink back from all that can be called Nature into negative spiritu-
ality is as if we ran away from horses instead of learning to ride. There
is in our present pilgrim condition plenty of room (more room than
most of us like) for abstinence and renunciation and mortifying our
natural desires. But behind all asceticism the thought should be, 'Who
will trust us with the true wealth if we cannot be trusted even with the
wealth that perishes?' Who will trust me with a spiritual body if I cannot control even an earthly body? These small and perishable bodies
we now have were given to us as ponies are given to schoolboys. We
must learn to manage: not that we may some day be free of horses
altogether but that some day we may ride bare-back, confident and
rejoicing, those greater mounts, those winged, shining and world-
shaking horses which perhaps even now expect us with impatience,
pawing and snorting in the King's stables. Not that the gallop would
be of any value unless it were a gallop with the King; but how else—
since He has retained His own charger—should we accompany Him?
—from *Miracles*

1947 *Miracles* is published by Geoffrey Bles/The Centenary Press,
London.

Recognizing Christ's New Men

The new step has been taken and is being taken. Already the new men are dotted here and there all over the earth. Some, as I have admitted, are still hardly recognisable: but others can be recognised. Every now and then one meets them. Their very voices and faces are different from ours: stronger, quieter, happier, more radiant. They begin where most of us leave off. They are, I say, recognisable; but you must know what to look for. They will not be very like the idea of 'religious people' which you have formed from your general reading. They do not draw attention to themselves. You tend to think that you are being kind to them when they are really being kind to you. They love you more than other men do, but they need you less. (We must get over wanting to be needed: in some goodish people, specially women, that is the hardest of all temptations to resist.) They will usually seem to have a lot of time: you will wonder where it comes from. When you have recognised one of them, you will recognise the next one much more easily. And I strongly suspect (but how should I know?) that they recognise one another immediately and infallibly, across every barrier of colour, sex, class, age, and even of creeds. In that way, to become holy is rather like joining a secret society. To put it at the very lowest, it must be great *fun*.

—from *Mere Christianity*

1959 Lewis is made Doctor of Letters by Manchester University.

Imagine Being Who You Really Are

To become new men means losing what we now call 'ourselves'. Out of our selves, into Christ, we must go. His will is to become ours and we are to think His thoughts, to 'have the mind of Christ' as the Bible says. And if Christ is one, and if He is thus to be 'in' us all, shall we not be exactly the same? It certainly sounds like it; but in fact it is not so.

It is difficult here to get a good illustration; because, of course, no other two things are related to each other just as the Creator is related to one of His creatures. But I will try two very imperfect illustrations which may give a hint of the truth. Imagine a lot of people who have always lived in the dark. You come and try to describe to them what light is like. You might tell them that if they come into the light that same light would fall on them all and they would all reflect it and thus become what we call visible. Is it not quite possible that they would imagine that, since they were all receiving the same light, and all reacting to it in the same way (i.e. all reflecting it), they would all look alike? Whereas you and I know that the light will in fact bring out, or show up, how different they are. Or again, suppose a person who knew nothing about salt. You give him a pinch to taste and he experiences a particular strong, sharp taste. You then tell him that in your country people use salt in all their cookery. Might he not reply 'In that case I suppose all your dishes taste exactly the same: because the taste of that stuff you have just given me is so strong that it will kill the taste of everything else.' But you and I know that the real effect of salt is exactly the opposite. So far from killing the taste of the egg and the tripe and the cabbage, it actually brings it out. They do not show their real taste till you have added the salt.

—from *Mere Christianity*

My Own Personality

The more we get what we now call 'ourselves' out of the way and let Him take us over, the more truly ourselves we become. There is so much of Him that millions and millions of 'little Christs', all different, will still be too few to express Him fully. He made them all. He invented—as an author invents characters in a novel—all the different men that you and I were intended to be. In that sense our real selves are all waiting for us in Him. It is no good trying to 'be myself' without Him. The more I resist Him and try to live on my own, the more I become dominated by my own heredity and upbringing and surroundings and natural desires. In fact what I so proudly call 'Myself' becomes merely the meeting place for trains of events which I never started and which I cannot stop. What I call 'My wishes' become merely the desires thrown up by my physical organism or pumped into me by other men's thoughts or even suggested to me by devils. Eggs and alcohol and a good night's sleep will be the real origins of what I flatter myself by regarding as my own highly personal and discriminating decision to make love to the girl opposite to me in the railway carriage. Propaganda will be the real origin of what I regard as my own personal political ideas. I am not, in my natural state, nearly so much of a person as I like to believe: most of what I call 'me' can be very easily explained. It is when I turn to Christ, when I give myself up to His Personality, that I first begin to have a real personality of my own.

—from *Mere Christianity*

1945 Charles Williams, Lewis's friend and fellow Inkling, dies at age fifty-eight.

All Good Masters Are Servants

The question we want to ask about Man's 'central' position in this drama is really on a level with the disciples' question, 'Which of them was the greatest?' It is the sort of question which God does not answer. If from Man's point of view the re-creation of non-human and even inanimate Nature appears a mere by-product of his own redemption, then equally from some remote, non-human point of view Man's redemption may seem merely the preliminary to this more widely diffused springtime, and the very permission of Man's fall may be supposed to have had that larger end in view. Both attitudes will be right if they will consent to drop the words *mere* and *merely*. Where a God who is totally purposive and totally foreseeing acts upon a Nature which is totally interlocked, there can be no accidents or loose ends, nothing whatever of which we can safely use the word *merely*. Nothing is 'merely a by-product' of anything else. All results are intended from the first. What is subservient from one point of view is the main purpose from another. No thing or event is first or highest in a sense which forbids it to be also last and lowest. The partner who bows to Man in one movement of the dance receives Man's reverences in another. To be high or central means to abdicate continually: to be low means to be raised: all good masters are servants: God washes the feet of men.

—from *Miracles*

God's Arrangements

In Christ a new kind of man appeared: and the new kind of life which began in Him is to be put into us.

How is this to be done? Now, please remember how we acquired the old, ordinary kind of life. We derived it from others, from our father and mother and all our ancestors, without our consent—and by a very curious process, involving pleasure, pain, and danger. A process you would never have guessed. Most of us spend a good many years in childhood trying to guess it: and some children, when they are first told, do not believe it—and I am not sure that I blame them, for it is very odd. Now the God who arranged that process is the same God who arranges how the new kind of life—the Christ-life—is to be spread. We must be prepared for it being odd too. He did not consult us when He invented sex: He has not consulted us either when He invented this.

There are three things that spread the Christ-life to us: baptism, belief, and that mysterious action which different Christians call by different names—Holy Communion, the Mass, the Lord's Supper. At least, those are the three ordinary methods. . . . .

I cannot myself see why these things should be the conductors of the new kind of life. But then, if one did not happen to know, I should never have seen any connection between a particular physical pleasure and the appearance of a new human being in the world. We have to take reality as it comes to us: there is no good jabbering about what it ought to be like or what we should have expected it to be like.

—from *Mere Christianity*

Blessed Matter

And let me make it quite clear that when Christians say the Christ-life is in them, they do not mean simply something mental or moral. When they speak of being 'in Christ' or of Christ being 'in them', this is not simply a way of saying that they are thinking about Christ or copying Him. They mean that Christ is actually operating through them; that the whole mass of Christians are the physical organism through which Christ acts—that we are His fingers and muscles, the cells of His body. And perhaps that explains one or two things. It explains why this new life is spread not only by purely mental acts like belief, but by bodily acts like baptism and Holy Communion. It is not merely the spreading of an idea; it is more like evolution—a biological or superbiological fact. There is no good trying to be more spiritual than God. God never meant man to be a purely spiritual creature. That is why He uses material things like bread and wine to put the new life into us. We may think this rather crude and unspiritual. God does not: He invented eating. He likes matter. He invented it.

—from *Mere Christianity*

1862 Florence Augusta ("Flora") Hamilton, mother of C. S. ("Jack") Lewis, is born in Queenstown, County Cork, Ireland.

Carriers of Christ

Some of you may feel that this is very unlike your own experience. You may say 'I've never had the sense of being helped by an invisible Christ, but I often have been helped by other human beings.' That is rather like the woman in the first war who said that if there were a bread shortage it would not bother her house because they always ate toast. If there is no bread there will be no toast. If there were no help from Christ, there would be no help from other human beings. He works on us in all sorts of ways: not only through what we think our 'religious life'. He works through Nature, through our own bodies, through books, sometimes through experiences which seem (at the time) *anti*-Christian. When a young man who has been going to church in a routine way honestly realises that he does not believe in Christianity and stops going—provided he does it for honesty's sake and not just to annoy his parents—the spirit of Christ is probably nearer to him then than it ever was before. But above all, He works on us through each other.

Men are mirrors, or 'carriers' of Christ to other men. Sometimes unconscious carriers. This 'good infection' can be carried by those who have not got it themselves. People who were not Christians themselves helped me to Christianity. But usually it is those who know Him that bring Him to others. That is why the Church, the whole body of Christians showing Him to one another, is so important. You might say that when two Christians are following Christ together there is not twice as much Christianity as when they are apart, but sixteen times as much.

—from *Mere Christianity*

A Body—Muscular, Vital, and Diverse

The society into which the Christian is called at baptism is not a collective but a Body. It is in fact that Body of which the family is an image on the natural level. .... We are summoned from the outset to combine as creatures with our Creator, as mortals with immortal, as redeemed sinners with sinless Redeemer. His presence, the interaction between Him and us, must always be the overwhelmingly dominant factor in the life we are to lead within the Body, and any conception of Christian fellowship which does not mean primarily fellowship with Him is out of court. After that it seems almost trivial to trace further down the diversity of operations to the unity of the Spirit. But it is very plainly there. There are priests divided from the laity, catechumens divided from those who are in full fellowship. There is authority of husbands over wives and parents over children. There is, in forms too subtle for official embodiment, a continual interchange of complementary ministrations. We are all constantly teaching and learning, forgiving and being forgiven, representing Christ to man when we intercede, and man to Christ when others intercede for us. The sacrifice of selfish privacy which is daily demanded of us is daily repaid a hundredfold in the true growth of personality which the life of the Body encourages. Those who are members of one another become as diverse as the hand and the ear. That is why the worldlings are so monotonously alike compared with the almost fantastic variety of the saints. Obedience is the road to freedom, humility the road to pleasure, unity the road to personality.

—from "Membership" *(The Weight of Glory)*

1925 Lewis is elected Fellow of Magdalen College, Oxford.

1960 Joy undergoes her last surgery.

Should the Church Take the Lead?

People say, 'The Church ought to give us a lead.' That is true if they mean it in the right way, but false if they mean it in the wrong way. By the Church they ought to mean the whole body of practising Christians. And when they say that the Church should give us a lead, they ought to mean that some Christians—those who happen to have the right talents—should be economists and statesmen, and that all economists and statesmen should be Christians, and that their whole efforts in politics and economics should be directed to putting 'Do as you would be done by' into action. If that happened, and if we others were really ready to take it, then we should find the Christian solution for our own social problems pretty quickly. But, of course, when they ask for a lead from the Church most people mean they want the clergy to put out a political programme. That is silly. The clergy are those particular people within the whole Church who have been specially trained and set aside to look after what concerns us as creatures who are going to live for ever: and we are asking them to do a quite different job for which they have not been trained. The job is really on us, on the laymen. The application of Christian principles, say, to trade unionism or education, must come from Christian trade unionists and Christian schoolmasters: just as Christian literature comes from Christian novelists and dramatists—not from the bench of bishops getting together and trying to write plays and novels in their spare time.

—from *Mere Christianity*

1936 *Allegory of Love* is published by Clarendon Press, Oxford.

A Christian Society

The New Testament, without going into details, gives us a pretty clear hint of what a fully Christian society would be like. Perhaps it gives us more than we can take. It tells us that there are to be no passengers or parasites: if man does not work, he ought not to eat. Every one is to work with his own hands, and what is more, every one's work is to produce something good: there will be no manufacture of silly luxuries and then of sillier advertisements to persuade us to buy them. And there is to be no 'swank' or 'side', no putting on airs. To that extent a Christian society would be what we now call Leftist. On the other hand, it is always insisting on obedience—obedience (and outward marks of respect) from all of us to properly appointed magistrates, from children to parents, and (I am afraid this is going to be very unpopular) from wives to husbands. Thirdly, it is to be a cheerful society: full of singing and rejoicing, and regarding worry or anxiety as wrong. Courtesy is one of the Christian virtues; and the New Testament hates what it calls 'busybodies'.

If there were such a society in existence and you or I visited it, I think we should come away with a curious impression. We should feel that its economic life was very socialistic and, in that sense, 'advanced', but that its family life and its code of manners were rather old fashioned—perhaps even ceremonious and aristocratic. Each of us would like some bits of it, but I am afraid very few of us would like the whole thing. That is just what one would expect if Christianity is the total plan for the human machine. We have all departed from that total plan in different ways, and each of us wants to make out that his own modification of the original plan is the plan itself. You will find this again and again about anything that is really Christian: every one is attracted by bits of it and wants to pick out those bits and leave the rest.

—from *Mere Christianity*

The Longest Way Round

I am going to venture on a guess as to how this section has affected any who have read it. My guess is that there are some Leftist people among them who are very angry that it has not gone further in that direction, and some people of an opposite sort who are angry because they think it has gone much too far. If so, that brings us right up against the real snag in all this drawing up of blueprints for a Christian society. Most of us are not really approaching the subject in order to find out what Christianity says: we are approaching it in the hope of finding support from Christianity for the views of our own party. We are looking for an ally where we are offered either a Master or—a Judge. I am just the same. There are bits in this section that I wanted to leave out. And that is why nothing whatever is going to come of such talks unless we go a much longer way round. A Christian society is not going to arrive until most of us really want it: and we are not going to want it until we become fully Christian. I may repeat 'Do as you would be done by' till I am black in the face, but I cannot really carry it out till I love my neighbour as myself: and I cannot learn to love my neighbour as myself till I learn to love God: and I cannot learn to love God except by learning to obey Him. And so, as I warned you, we are driven on to something more inward—driven on from social matters to religious matters. For the longest way round is the shortest way home.

—from *Mere Christianity*

For No Other Purpose

This is the whole of Christianity. There is nothing else. It is so easy to get muddled about that. It is easy to think that the Church has a lot of different objects—education, building, missions, holding services. Just as it is easy to think the State has a lot of different objects—military, political, economic, and what not. But in a way things are much simpler than that. The State exists simply to promote and to protect the ordinary happiness of human beings in this life. A husband and wife chatting over a fire, a couple of friends having a game of darts in a pub, a man reading a book in his own room or digging in his own garden—that is what the State is there for. And unless they are helping to increase and prolong and protect such moments, all the laws, parliaments, armies, courts, police, economics, etc., are simply a waste of time. In the same way the Church exists for nothing else but to draw men into Christ, to make them little Christs. If they are not doing that, all the cathedrals, clergy, missions, sermons, even the Bible itself, are simply a waste of time. God became Man for no other purpose. It is even doubtful, you know, whether the whole universe was created for any other purpose.

—from *Mere Christianity*

May 1918 Lewis is transferred to Endsleigh Palace Hospital, London, to continue recovering from his battle wounds.

A Gentle Welcome

I hope no reader will suppose that 'mere' Christianity is here put forward as an alternative to the creeds of the existing communions. .... It is more like a hall out of which doors open into several rooms. If I can bring anyone into that hall I shall have done what I attempted. But it is in the rooms, not in the hall, that there are fires and chairs and meals. The hall is a place to wait in, a place from which to try the various doors, not a place to live in. For that purpose the worst of the rooms (whichever that may be) is, I think, preferable. It is true that some people may find they have to wait in the hall for a considerable time, while others feel certain almost at once which door they must knock at. I do not know why there is this difference, but I am sure God keeps no one waiting unless He sees that it is good for him to wait. When you do get into your room you will find that the long wait has done you some kind of good which you would not have had otherwise. But you must regard it as waiting, not as camping. You must keep on praying for light: and, of course, even in the hall, you must begin trying to obey the rules which are common to the whole house. And above all you must be asking which door is the true one; not which pleases you best by its paint and panelling. In plain language, the question should never be: 'Do I like that kind of service?' but 'Are these doctrines true: Is holiness here? Does my conscience move me towards this? Is my reluctance to knock at this door due to my pride, or my mere taste, or my personal dislike of this particular door-keeper?'

When you have reached your own room, be kind to those who have chosen different doors and to those who are still in the hall. If they are wrong they need your prayers all the more; and if they are your enemies, then you are under orders to pray for them. That is one of the rules common to the whole house.

—from *Mere Christianity*, Preface

Creating Hatred in Church

Screwtape offers insights on using church for evil ends:

I think I warned you before that if your patient can't be kept out of the Church, he ought at least to be violently attached to some party within it. I don't mean on really doctrinal issues; about those, the more lukewarm he is the better. And it isn't the doctrines on which we chiefly depend for producing malice. The real fun is working up hatred between those who *say* 'mass' and those who *say* 'holy communion' when neither party could possibly state the difference between, say, Hooker's doctrine and Thomas Aquinas', in any form which would hold water for five minutes. And all the purely indifferent things—candles and clothes and what not—are an admirable ground for our activities. We have quite removed from men's minds what that pestilent fellow Paul used to teach about food and other unessentials—namely, that the human without scruples should always give in to the human with scruples. You would think they could not fail to see the application. You would expect to find the 'low' churchman genuflecting and crossing himself lest the weak conscience of his 'high' brother should be moved to irreverence, and the 'high' one refraining from these exercises lest he should betray his 'low' brother into idolatry. And so it would have been but for our ceaseless labour. Without that the variety of usage within the Church of England might have become a positive hotbed of charity and humility.

—from *The Screwtape Letters*

May 1933 *The Pilgrim's Regress* is published by J. M. Dent, London.

A Suitable Church

Screwtape expands on developing church participation for evil ends:

Surely you know that if a man can't be cured of churchgoing, the next best thing is to send him all over the neighbourhood looking for the church that 'suits' him until he becomes a taster or connoisseur of churches.

The reasons are obvious. In the first place the parochial organisation should always be attacked, because, being a unity of place and not of likings, it brings people of different classes and psychology together in the kind of unity the Enemy desires. The congregational principle, on the other hand, makes each church into a kind of club, and finally, if all goes well, into a coterie or faction. In the second place, the search for a 'suitable' church makes the man a critic where the Enemy wants him to be a pupil. What He wants of the layman in church is an attitude which may, indeed, be critical in the sense of rejecting what is false or unhelpful, but which is wholly uncritical in the sense that it does not appraise—does not waste time in thinking about what it rejects, but lays itself open in uncommenting, humble receptivity to any nourishment that is going. (You see how grovelling, how unspiritual, how irredeemably vulgar He is!) This attitude, especially during sermons, creates the condition (most hostile to our whole policy) in which platitudes can become really audible to a human soul. There is hardly any sermon, or any book, which may not be dangerous to us if it is received in this temper.

—from *The Screwtape Letters*

Hints of Our Future

"We know not what we shall be"; but we may be sure we shall be more, not less, than we were on earth. Our natural experiences (sensory, emotional, imaginative) are only like the drawing, like pencilled lines on flat paper. If they vanish in the risen life, they will vanish only as pencil lines vanish from the real landscape, not as a candle flame that is put out but as a candle flame which becomes invisible because someone has pulled up the blind, thrown open the shutters, and let in the blaze of the risen sun.

—from "Transposition" *(The Weight of Glory)*

1944 "Transposition" is preached in the chapel of Mansfield College, Oxford, on the Feast of Pentecost.

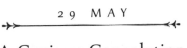

A Curious Consolation

It is at her centre, where her truest children dwell, that each communion is really closest to every other in spirit, if not in doctrine. And this suggests that at the centre of each there is a something, or a Someone, who against all divergencies of belief, all differences of temperament, all memories of mutual persecution, speaks with the same voice.

—from *Mere Christianity,* Preface

1874 G. K. Chesterton (d. 1936), one of Lewis's primary spiritual influences, is born.

Work Offered to God

I reject at once an idea which lingers in the mind of some modern people that cultural activities are in their own right spiritual and meritorious—as though scholars and poets were intrinsically more pleasing to God than scavengers and bootblacks. I think it was Matthew Arnold who first used the English word *spiritual* in the sense of the German *geistlich*, and so inaugurated this most dangerous and most anti-Christian error. Let us clear it forever from our minds. The work of a Beethoven and the work of a charwoman become spiritual on precisely the same condition, that of being offered to God, of being done humbly "as to the Lord." This does not, of course, mean that it is for anyone a mere toss-up whether he should sweep rooms or compose symphonies. A mole must dig to the glory of God and a cock must crow. We are members of one body, but differentiated members, each with his own vocation.

—from "Learning in War-Time" (The Weight of Glory)

Avoid Clarity

Upon learning that Wormwood's Patient has become a Christian, Screwtape illustrates techniques for confusion:

One of our great allies at present is the Church itself. Do not misunderstand me. I do not mean the Church as we see her spread out through all time and space and rooted in eternity, terrible as an army with banners. That, I confess, is a spectacle which makes our boldest tempters uneasy. But fortunately it is quite invisible to these humans. All your patient sees is the half-finished, sham Gothic erection on the new building estate. When he goes inside, he sees the local grocer with rather an oily expression on his face bustling up to offer him one shiny little book containing a liturgy which neither of them understands, and one shabby little book containing corrupt texts of a number of religious lyrics, mostly bad, and in very small print. When he gets to his pew and looks round him he sees just that selection of his neighbours whom he has hitherto avoided. You want to lean pretty heavily on those neighbours. .... Provided that any of those neighbours sing out of tune, or have boots that squeak, or double chins, or odd clothes, the patient will quite easily believe that their religion must therefore be somehow ridiculous. At his present stage, you see, he has an idea of 'Christians' in his mind which he supposes to be spiritual but which, in fact, is largely pictorial. His mind is full of togas and sandals and armour and bare legs and the mere fact that the other people in church wear modern clothes is a real—though of course an unconscious—difficulty to him. Never let it come to the surface; never let him ask what he expected them to look like. Keep everything hazy in his mind now, and you will have all eternity wherein to amuse yourself by producing in him the peculiar kind of clarity which Hell affords.

—from *The Screwtape Letters*

JUNE

Untold Millions

Here is another thing that used to puzzle me. Is it not frightfully unfair that this new life should be confined to people who have heard of Christ and been able to believe in Him? But the truth is God has not told us what His arrangements about the other people are. We do know that no man can be saved except through Christ; we do not know that only those who know Him can be saved through Him. But in the meantime, if you are worried about the people outside, the most unreasonable thing you can do is to remain outside yourself. Christians are Christ's body, the organism through which He works. Every addition to that body enables Him to do more. If you want to help those outside you must add your own little cell to the body of Christ who alone can help them. Cutting off a man's fingers would be an odd way of getting him to do more work.

—from *Mere Christianity*

The Apostolic Witness

In the earliest days of Christianity an 'apostle' was first and foremost a man who claimed to be an eyewitness of the Resurrection. Only a few days after the Crucifixion when two candidates were nominated for the vacancy created by the treachery of Judas, their qualification was that they had known Jesus personally both before and after His death and could offer first-hand evidence of the Resurrection in addressing the outer world (Acts 1:22). A few days later St Peter, preaching the first Christian sermon, makes the same claim—'God raised Jesus, of which we all (we Christians) are witnesses' (Acts 2:32). In the first Letter to the Corinthians, St Paul bases his claim to apostleship on the same ground—'Am I not an apostle? Have I not seen the Lord Jesus?' (1:9).

As this qualification suggests, to preach Christianity meant primarily to preach the Resurrection. .... The Resurrection is the central theme in every Christian sermon reported in the Acts. The Resurrection, and its consequences, were the 'gospel' or good news which the Christians brought: what we call the 'gospels', the narratives of Our Lord's life and death, were composed later for the benefit of those who had already accepted the *gospel*. They were in no sense the basis of Christianity: they were written for those already converted. The miracle of the Resurrection, and the theology of that miracle, comes first: the biography comes later as a comment on it. .... The first fact in the history of Christendom is a number of people who say they have seen the Resurrection. If they had died without making anyone else believe this 'gospel' no gospels would ever have been written.

—from *Miracles*

What the Apostles Meant

When modern writers talk of the Resurrection they usually mean one particular moment—the discovery of the Empty Tomb and the appearance of Jesus a few yards away from it. The story of that moment is what Christian apologists now chiefly try to support and sceptics chiefly try to impugn. But this almost exclusive concentration on the first five minutes or so of the Resurrection would have astonished the earliest Christian teachers. In claiming to have seen the Resurrection they were not necessarily claiming to have seen *that*. Some of them had, some of them had not. It had no more importance than any of the other appearances of the risen Jesus—apart from the poetic and dramatic importance which the beginnings of things must always have. What they were claiming was that they had all, at one time or another, met Jesus during the six or seven weeks that followed His death. Sometimes they seem to have been alone when they did so, but on one occasion twelve of them saw Him together, and on another occasion about five hundred of them. St Paul says that the majority of the five hundred were still alive when he wrote the First Letter to the Corinthians, i.e. in about 55 AD.

The 'Resurrection' to which they bore witness was, in fact, not the action of rising from the dead but the state of having risen; a state, as they held, attested by intermittent meetings during a limited period (except for the special, and in some ways different, meeting vouchsafed to St Paul). This termination of the period is important, for .... there is no possibility of isolating the doctrine of the Resurrection from that of the Ascension.

—from *Miracles*

The Beginning of the New Creation

The Resurrection was not regarded simply or chiefly as evidence for the immortality of the soul. It is, of course, often so regarded today: I have heard a man maintain that 'the importance of the Resurrection is that it proves *survival*'. Such a view cannot at any point be reconciled with the language of the New Testament. On such a view Christ would simply have done what all men do when they die: the only novelty would have been that in His case we were allowed to see it happening. But there is not in Scripture the faintest suggestion that the Resurrection was new evidence for something that had *in fact* been always happening. The New Testament writers speak as if Christ's achievement in rising from the dead was the first event of its kind in the whole history of the universe. He is the 'first fruits', the 'pioneer of life'. He has forced open a door that has been locked since the death of the first man. He has met, fought, and beaten the King of Death. Everything is different because He has done so. This is the beginning of the New Creation: a new chapter in cosmic history has opened.

—from *Miracles*

1954 Lewis accepts the Chair of Medieval and Renaissance English at Cambridge University.

Like a Ghost, Yet Not

There are, I allow, certain respects in which the risen Christ resembles the 'ghost' of popular tradition. Like a ghost He 'appears' and 'disappears': locked doors are no obstacle to Him. On the other hand He Himself vigorously asserts that He is corporeal (Luke 24:39–40) and eats broiled fish. It is at this point that the modern reader becomes uncomfortable. He becomes more uncomfortable still at the word, 'Don't touch me; I have not yet gone up to the Father' (John 20:17). For voices and apparitions we are, in some measure, prepared. But what is this that must not be touched? What is all this about going 'up' to the Father? Is He not already 'with the Father' in the only sense that matters? What can 'going up' be except a metaphor for *that?* And if so, why has He 'not yet' gone? These discomforts arise because the story the 'apostles' actually had to tell begins at this point to conflict with the story we expect and are determined beforehand to read into their narrative.

We expect them to tell of a risen life which is purely 'spiritual' in the negative sense of that word: that is, we use the word 'spiritual' to mean not what it is but what it is not. We mean a life without space, without history, without environment, with no sensuous elements in it. We also, in our heart of hearts, tend to slur over the risen *manhood* of Jesus, to conceive Him, after death, simply returning into Deity, so that the Resurrection would be no more than the reversal or undoing of the Incarnation. That being so, all references to the risen *body* make us uneasy: they raise awkward questions.

—from *Miracles*

A Much Stranger Story Than Expected

It is at this point that awe and trembling fall upon us as we read the records. If the story is false, it is at least a much stranger story than we expected, something for which philosophical 'religion', psychical research, and popular superstition have all alike failed to prepare us. If the story is true, then a wholly new mode of being has arisen in the universe.

The body which lives in that new mode is like, and yet unlike, the body His friends knew before the execution. It is differently related to space and probably to time, but by no means cut off from all relation to them. It can perform the animal act of eating. It is so related to matter, as we know it, that it can be touched, though at first it had better not be touched. It has also a history before it which is in view from the first moment of the Resurrection; it is presently going to become different or go somewhere else. That is why the story of the Ascension cannot be separated from that of the Resurrection. All the accounts suggest that the appearances of the Risen Body came to an end; some describe an abrupt end about six weeks after the death. And they describe this abrupt end in a way which presents greater difficulties to the modern mind than any other part of Scripture. For here, surely, we get the implication of all those primitive crudities to which I have said that Christians are not committed: the vertical ascent like a balloon, the local Heaven, the decorated chair to the right of the Father's throne. 'He was caught up into the sky (*ouranos*)', says St Mark's Gospel 'and sat down at the right hand of God'. 'He was lifted up', says the author of Acts 'and a cloud cut Him off from their sight'.

—from *Miracles*

A Whole New Nature

The records represent Christ as passing after death (as no man had passed before) neither into a purely, that is, negatively, 'spiritual' mode of existence nor into a 'natural' life such as we know, but into a life which has its own, new Nature. It represents Him as withdrawing six weeks later, into some different mode of existence. It says—He says—that He goes 'to prepare a place for us'. This presumably means that He is about to create that whole new Nature which will provide the environment or conditions for His glorified humanity and, in Him, for ours. The picture is not what we expected—though whether it is less or more probable and philosophical on that account is another question. It is not the picture of an escape from any and every kind of Nature into some unconditioned and utterly transcendent life. It is the picture of a new human nature, and a new Nature in general, being brought into existence. We must, indeed, believe the risen body to be extremely different from the mortal body: but the existence, in that new state, of anything that could in any sense be described as 'body' at all, involves some sort of spatial relations and in the long run a whole new universe. That is the picture—not of unmaking but of remaking. The old field of space, time, matter, and the senses is to be weeded, dug, and sown for a new crop. We may be tired of that old field: God is not.

—from *Miracles*

No Ordinary People

There are no *ordinary* people. You have never talked to a mere mortal. Nations, cultures, arts, civilisations—these are mortal, and their life is to ours as the life of a gnat. But it is immortals whom we joke with, work with, marry, snub, and exploit—immortal horrors or everlasting splendours. This does not mean that we are to be perpetually solemn: We must play. But our merriment must be of that kind (and it is, in fact, the merriest kind) which exists between people who have, from the outset, taken each other seriously—no flippancy, no superiority, no presumption. And our charity must be a real and costly love, with deep feeling for the sins in spite of which we love the sinner—no mere tolerance, or indulgence which parodies love as flippancy parodies merriment. Next to the Blessed Sacrament itself, your neighbour is the holiest object presented to your senses. If he is your Christian neighbour, he is holy in almost the same way, for in him also Christ *vere latitat*—the glorifier and the glorified, Glory Himself, is truly hidden.
 —from "The Weight of Glory" *(The Weight of Glory)*

1941 Lewis preaches "The Weight of Glory" in Oxford University Church of St. Mary the Virgin.

What Did They See and What Did They Think They Saw?

To say that Christ's passage to a new 'Nature' could involve no such [upwards] movement, or no movement at all, within the 'Nature' he was leaving, is very arbitrary. Where there is passage, there is departure; and departure is an event in the region from which the traveller is departing. All this, even on the assumption that the Ascending Christ is in a three-dimensional space. If it is not that kind of body, and space is not that kind of space, then we are even less qualified to say what the spectators of this entirely new event might or might not see or feel as if they had seen. There is, of course, no question of a human body as we know it existing in interstellar space as we know it. The Ascension belongs to a New Nature. We are discussing only what the 'joint' between the Old Nature and the new, the precise moment of transition, would look like.

But what really worries us is the conviction that, whatever we say, the New Testament writers meant something quite different. We feel sure that they thought they had seen their Master setting off on a journey for a local 'Heaven' where God sat in a throne and where there was another throne waiting for Him. And I believe that in a sense that is just what they did think. And I believe that, for this reason, whatever they had actually seen (sense perception, almost by hypothesis, would be confused at such a moment) they would almost certainly have remembered it as a vertical movement. What we must not say is that they 'mistook' local 'Heavens' and celestial throne-rooms and the like for the 'spiritual' Heaven of union with God and supreme power and beatitude.

—from *Miracles*

Witness Reports

Heaven can mean (1) The unconditioned Divine Life beyond all worlds. (2) Blessed participation in that Life by a created spirit. (3) The whole Nature or system of conditions in which redeemed human spirits, still remaining human, can enjoy such participation fully and for ever. This is the Heaven Christ goes to 'prepare' for us. (4) The physical Heaven, the sky, the space in which Earth moves. What enables us to distinguish these senses and hold them clearly apart is not any special spiritual purity but the fact that we are the heirs to centuries of logical analysis: not that we are sons to Abraham but that we are sons to Aristotle. We are not to suppose that the writers of the New Testament mistook Heaven in sense four or three for Heaven in sense two or one. You cannot mistake a half sovereign for a sixpence until you know the English system of coinage—that is, until you know the difference between them. In their idea of Heaven all these meanings were latent, ready to be brought out by later analysis. They never thought merely of the blue sky or merely of a 'spiritual' heaven. When they looked up at the blue sky they never doubted that there, whence light and heat and the precious rain descended, was the home of God: but on the other hand, when they thought of one ascending to that Heaven they never doubted He was 'ascending' in what we should call a 'spiritual' sense.

—from *Miracles*

Reliable Eyewitnesses?

The fact that Galilean shepherds could not distinguish what they saw at the Ascension from that kind of ascent which, by its very nature, could never be seen at all, does not prove on the one hand that they were unspiritual, nor on the other that they saw nothing. A man who really believes that 'Heaven' is in the sky may well, in his heart, have a far truer and more spiritual conception of it than many a modern logician who could expose that fallacy with a few strokes of his pen. For he who does the will of the Father shall know the doctrine. Irrelevant material splendours in such a man's idea of the vision of God will do no harm, for they are not there for their own sakes. Purity from such images in a merely theoretical Christian's idea will do no good if they have been banished only by logical criticism.

—from *Miracles*

An Idea Why Heaven Is Always "Up"

It is not an accident that simple-minded people, however spiritual, should blend the ideas of God and Heaven and the blue sky. It is a fact, not a fiction, that light and life-giving heat do come down from the sky to Earth. The analogy of the sky's role to begetting and of the Earth's role to bearing is sound as far as it goes. The huge dome of the sky is of all things sensuously perceived the most like infinity. And when God made space and worlds that move in space, and clothed our world with air, and gave us such eyes and such imaginations as those we have, He knew what the sky would mean to us. And since nothing in His work is accidental, if He knew, He intended. We cannot be certain that this was not indeed one of the chief purposes for which Nature was created; still less that it was not one of the chief reasons why the withdrawal was allowed to affect human senses as a movement upwards. (A disappearance into the Earth would beget a wholly different religion.) The ancients in letting the spiritual symbolism of the sky flow straight into their minds without stopping to discover by analysis that it was a symbol, were not entirely mistaken. In one way they were perhaps less mistaken than we.

—from *Miracles*

Close Up and Small

Another way of expressing the real character of the miracles would be to say that though isolated from other actions, they are not isolated in either of the two ways we are apt to suppose. They are not, on the one hand, isolated from other Divine acts: they do close and small and, as it were, in focus what God at other times does so large that men do not attend to it. Neither are they isolated exactly as we suppose from other human acts: they anticipate powers which all men will have when they also are 'sons' of God and enter into that 'glorious liberty'. Christ's isolation is not that of a prodigy but of a pioneer. He is the first of His kind; He will not be the last.

—from *Miracles*

Fitting into the Pattern

It is therefore inaccurate to define a miracle as something that breaks the laws of Nature. It doesn't. If I knock out my pipe I alter the position of a great many atoms: in the long run, and to an infinitesimal degree, of all the atoms there are. Nature digests or assimilates this event with perfect ease and harmonises it in a twinkling with all other events. It is one more bit of raw material for the laws to apply to, and they apply. I have simply thrown one event into the general cataract of events and it finds itself at home there and conforms to all other events. If God annihilates or creates or deflects a unit of matter He has created a new situation at that point. Immediately all Nature domiciles this new situation, makes it at home in her realm, adapts all other events to it. It finds itself conforming to all the laws. If God creates a miraculous spermatozoon in the body of a virgin, it does not proceed to break any laws. The laws at once take it over. Nature is ready. Pregnancy follows, according to all the normal laws, and nine months later a child is born. We see every day that physical nature is not in the least incommoded by the daily inrush of events from biological nature or from psychological nature. If events ever come from beyond Nature altogether, she will be no more incommoded by them. Be sure she will rush to the point where she is invaded, as the defensive forces rush to a cut in our finger, and there hasten to accommodate the newcomer. The moment it enters her realm it obeys all her laws. Miraculous wine will intoxicate, miraculous conception will lead to pregnancy, inspired books will suffer all the ordinary processes of textual corruption, miraculous bread will be digested. The divine art of miracle is not an art of suspending the pattern to which events conform but of feeding new events into that pattern.

—from *Miracles*

How to Think About the Miracles of Jesus

I contend that in all these miracles [of Jesus] alike the incarnate God does suddenly and locally something that God has done or will do in general. Each miracle writes for us in small letters something that God has already written, or will write, in letters almost too large to be noticed, across the whole canvas of Nature. They focus at a particular point either God's actual, or His future, operations on the universe. When they reproduce operations we have already seen on the large scale they are miracles of the Old Creation: when they focus those which are still to come they are miracles of the New. Not one of them is isolated or anomalous: each carries the signature of the God whom we know through conscience and from Nature. Their authenticity is attested by the *style*.

Before going any further I should say that I do not propose to raise the question, which has before now been asked, whether Christ was able to do these things only because He was God or also because He was perfect man; for it is a possible view that if Man had never fallen all men would have been able to do the like. It is one of the glories of Christianity that we can say of this question, 'It doesn't matter.' Whatever may have been the powers of unfallen man, it appears that those of redeemed Man will be almost unlimited. Christ, reascending from His great dive, is bringing up Human Nature with Him. Where He goes, it goes too. It will be made 'like Him'. If in His miracles He is not acting as the Old Man might have done before his Fall, then He is acting as the New Man, every new man, will do after his redemption. When humanity, borne on His shoulders, passes with Him up from the cold dark water into the green warm water and out at last into the sunlight and the air, it also will be bright and coloured.

—from *Miracles*

Be Careful What You Think You Want

You are probably quite right in thinking that you will never see a miracle done: you are probably equally right in thinking that there was a natural explanation of anything in your past life which seemed, at the first glance, to be 'rum' or 'odd'. God does not shake miracles into Nature at random as if from a pepper-caster. They come on great occasions: they are found at the great ganglions of history—not of political or social history, but of that spiritual history which cannot be fully known by men. If your own life does not happen to be near one of those great ganglions, how should you expect to see one? If we were heroic missionaries, apostles, or martyrs, it would be a different matter. But why you or I? Unless you live near a railway, you will not see trains go past your windows. How likely is it that you or I will be present when a peace-treaty is signed, when a great scientific discovery is made, when a dictator commits suicide? That we should see a miracle is even less likely. Nor, if we understand, shall we be anxious to do so. 'Nothing almost sees miracles but misery'. Miracles and martyrdoms tend to bunch about the same areas of history—areas we have naturally no wish to frequent. Do not, I earnestly advise you, demand an ocular proof unless you are already perfectly certain that it is not forthcoming.

—from *Miracles*

1895 Warren Hamilton Lewis, C. S. Lewis's older brother, is born in Dundella Villa, on the outskirts of Belfast.

Threshold of Belief

And yet... and yet... It is that *and yet* which I fear more than any positive argument against miracles: that soft, tidal return of your habitual outlook as you close the book and the familiar four walls about you and the familiar noises from the street reassert themselves. Perhaps (if I dare suppose so much) you have been led on at times while you were reading, have felt ancient hopes and fears astir in your heart, have perhaps come almost to the threshold of belief—but now? No. It just won't do. Here is the ordinary, here is the 'real' world, round you again. The dream is ending; as all other similar dreams have always ended. For of course this is not the first time such a thing has happened. More than once in your life before this you have heard a strange story, read some odd book, seen something queer or imagined you have seen it, entertained some wild hope or terror: but always it ended in the same way. And always you wondered how you could, even for a moment, have expected it not to. For that 'real world' when you came back to it is so unanswerable. *Of course* the strange story was false, of course the voice was really subjective, of course the apparent portent was a coincidence. You are ashamed of yourself for having ever thought otherwise: ashamed, relieved, amused, disappointed, and angry all at once. You ought to have known that, as Arnold says, 'Miracles don't happen'.

—from *Miracles*

What the World Is Really Like

Screwtape on using a false concept of "real":

Probably the scenes he is now witnessing [in the London Blitz] will not provide material for an *intellectual* attack on his faith—your previous failures have put that out of your power. But there is a sort of attack on the emotions which can still be tried. It turns on making him *feel,* when first he sees human remains plastered on a wall, that this is 'what the world is *really* like' and that all his religion has been a fantasy. You will notice that we have got them completely fogged about the meaning of the word 'real'. They tell each other, of some great spiritual experience, 'All that *really* happened was that you heard some music in a lighted building'; here 'real' means the bare physical facts, separated from the other elements in the experience they actually had. On the other hand, they will also say 'It's all very well discussing that high dive as you sit here in an armchair, but wait till you get up there and see what it's *really* like': here 'real' is being used in the opposite sense to mean, not the physical facts (which they know already while discussing the matter in armchairs) but the emotional effect those facts will have on a human consciousness. Either application of the word could be defended; but our business is to keep the two going at once so that the emotional value of the word 'real' can be placed now on one side of the account, now on the other, as it happens to suit us.

—from *The Screwtape Letters*

Discerning What's Real

Screwtape twists Reality:

The general rule which we have now pretty well established among them is that in all experiences which can make them happier or better only the physical facts are 'real' while the spiritual elements are 'subjective'; in all experiences which can discourage or corrupt them the spiritual elements are the main reality and to ignore them is to be an escapist. Thus in birth the blood and pain are 'real', the rejoicing a mere subjective point of view; in death, the terror and ugliness reveal what death 'really means'. The hatefulness of a hated person is 'real'—in hatred you see men as they are, you are disillusioned; but the loveliness of a loved person is merely a subjective haze concealing a 'real' core of sexual appetite or economic association. Wars and poverty are 'really' horrible; peace and plenty are mere physical facts about which men happen to have certain sentiments. The creatures are always accusing one another of wanting 'to eat the cake and have it'; but thanks to our labours they are more often in the predicament of paying for the cake and not eating it. Your patient, properly handled, will have no difficulty in regarding his emotion at the sight of human entrails as a revelation of Reality and his emotion at the sight of happy children or fair weather as mere sentiment.

—from *The Screwtape Letters*

Everythingism

I mean by this [Everythingism] the belief that 'everything', or 'the whole show', must be self-existent, must be more important than every particular thing, and must contain all particular things in such a way that they cannot be really very different from one another—that they must be not merely 'at one', but one. Thus the Everythingist, if he starts from God, becomes a Pantheist; there must be nothing that is not God. If he starts from Nature he becomes a Naturalist; there must be nothing that is not Nature. He thinks that everything is in the long run 'merely' a precursor or a development or a relic or an instance or a disguise, of everything else. This philosophy I believe to be profoundly untrue. One of the moderns has said that reality is 'incorrigibly plural'. I think he is right. All things come from One. All things are related— related in different and complicated ways. But all things are not one. The word 'everything' should mean simply the total (a total to be reached, if we knew enough, by enumeration) of all the things that exist at a given moment. It must not be given a mental capital letter; must not (under the influence of picture thinking) be turned into a sort of pool in which particular things sink or even a cake in which they are the currants. Real things are sharp and knobbly and complicated and different. Everythingism is congenial to our minds because it is the natural philosophy of a totalitarian, mass-producing, conscripted age. That is why we must be perpetually on our guard against it.

—from *Miracles*

Wild Rumours

What man, in his natural condition, has not got, is Spiritual life—the higher and different sort of life that exists in God. We use the same word *life* for both: but if you thought that both must therefore be the same sort of thing, that would be like thinking that the 'greatness' of space and the 'greatness' of God were the same sort of greatness. In reality, the difference between Biological life and Spiritual life is so important that I am going to give them two distinct names. The Biological sort which comes to us through Nature, and which (like everything else in Nature) is always tending to run down and decay so that it can only be kept up by incessant subsidies from Nature in the form of air, water, food, etc., is *Bios*. The Spiritual life which is in God from all eternity, and which made the whole natural universe, is *Zoe*. *Bios* has, to be sure, a certain shadowy or symbolic resemblance to *Zoe*: but only the sort of resemblance there is between a photo and a place, or a statue and a man. A man who changed from having *Bios* to having *Zoe* would have gone through as big a change as a statue which changed from being a carved stone to being a real man.

And that is precisely what Christianity is about. This world is a great sculptor's shop. We are the statues and there is a rumour going round the shop that some of us are some day going to come to life.

—from *Mere Christianity*

God in Our Prayers

An ordinary simple Christian kneels down to say his prayers. He is trying to get into touch with God. But if he is a Christian he knows that what is prompting him to pray is also God: God, so to speak, inside him. But he also knows that all his real knowledge of God comes through Christ, the Man who was God—that Christ is standing beside him, helping him to pray, praying for him. You see what is happening. God is the thing to which he is praying—the goal he is trying to reach. God is also the thing inside him which is pushing him on—the motive power. God is also the road or bridge along which he is being pushed to that goal. So that the whole threefold life of the three-personal Being is actually going on in that ordinary little bedroom where an ordinary man is saying his prayers. The man is being caught up into the higher kinds of life—what I called *Zoe* or spiritual life: he is being pulled into God, by God, while still remaining himself.

—from *Mere Christianity*

Very Hard, Yet Very Easy

We were considering the Christian idea of 'putting on Christ', or first 'dressing up' as a son of God in order that you may finally become a real son. What I want to make clear is that this is not one among many jobs a Christian has to do; and it is not a sort of special exercise for the top class. It is the whole of Christianity. Christianity offers nothing else at all. . . . .

The Christian way is different: harder, and easier. Christ says 'Give me All. I don't want so much of your time and so much of your money and so much of your work: I want You. I have not come to torment your natural self, but to kill it. No half-measures are any good. I don't want to cut off a branch here and a branch there, I want to have the whole tree down. I don't want to drill the tooth, or crown it, or stop it, but to have it out. Hand over the whole natural self, all the desires which you think innocent as well as the ones you think wicked—the whole out-fit. I will give you a new self instead. In fact, I will give you Myself: my own will shall become yours.'

Both harder and easier than what we are all trying to do. You have noticed, I expect, that Christ Himself sometimes describes the Christian way as very hard, sometimes as very easy. He says, 'Take up your Cross'—in other words, it is like going to be beaten to death in a concentration camp. Next minute he says, 'My yoke is easy and my burden light.' He means both.

—from *Mere Christianity*

The Most Difficult Is the Easiest

Teachers will tell you that the laziest boy in the class is the one who works hardest in the end. They mean this. If you give two boys, say, a proposition in geometry to do, the one who is prepared to take trouble will try to understand it. The lazy boy will try to learn it by heart because, for the moment, that needs less effort. But six months later, when they are preparing for an exam, that lazy boy is doing hours and hours of miserable drudgery over things the other boy understands, and positively enjoys, in a few minutes. Laziness means more work in the long run. Or look at it this way. In a battle, or in mountain climbing, there is often one thing which it takes a lot of pluck to do; but it is also, in the long run, the safest thing to do. If you funk it, you will find yourself, hours later, in far worse danger. The cowardly thing is also the most dangerous thing.

It is like that here. The terrible thing, the almost impossible thing, is to hand over your whole self—all your wishes and precautions—to Christ. But it is far easier than what we are all trying to do instead. For what we are trying to do is to remain what we call 'ourselves', to keep personal happiness as our great aim in life, and yet at the same time be 'good'. We are all trying to let our mind and heart go their own way—centred on money or pleasure or ambition—and hoping, in spite of this, to behave honestly and chastely and humbly. And that is exactly what Christ warned us you could not do. As He said, a thistle cannot produce figs. If I am a field that contains nothing but grass-seed, I cannot produce wheat. Cutting the grass may keep it short: but I shall still produce grass and no wheat. If I want to produce wheat, the change must go deeper than the surface. I must be ploughed up and re-sown.

—from *Mere Christianity*

1961 Lewis is diagnosed as having an enlarged prostate gland; doctors ultimately determine that surgery would be too dangerous.

Let's Pretend

What do we do next? What difference does all this theology make? It can start making a difference tonight. If you are interested enough to have read thus far you are probably interested enough to make a shot at saying your prayers: and, whatever else you say, you will probably say the Lord's Prayer.

Its very first words are *Our Father*. Do you now see what those words mean? They mean quite frankly, that you are putting yourself in the place of a son of God. To put it bluntly, you are *dressing up as Christ*. If you like, you are pretending. Because, of course, the moment you realise what the words mean, you realise that you are not a son of God. You are not a being like The Son of God, whose will and interests are at one with those of the Father: you are a bundle of self-centred fears, hopes, greeds, jealousies, and self-conceit, all doomed to death. So that, in a way, this dressing up as Christ is a piece of outrageous cheek. But the odd thing is that He has ordered us to do it.

Why? What is the good of pretending to be what you are not? Well, even on the human level, you know, there are two kinds of pretending. There is a bad kind, where the pretence is there instead of the real thing; as when a man pretends he is going to help you instead of really helping you. But there is also a good kind, where the pretence leads up to the real thing. When you are not feeling particularly friendly but know you ought to be, the best thing you can do, very often, is to put on a friendly manner and behave as if you were a nicer person than you actually are. And in a few minutes, as we have all noticed, you will be really feeling friendlier than you were.

—from *Mere Christianity*

1918 Lewis is moved to a convalescent home in Ashton Court near Clifton, Bristol, to complete his recovery from battle injuries.

Pretending a Little Less

Very often the only way to get a quality in reality is to start behaving as if you had it already. That is why children's games are so important. They are always pretending to be grown-ups—playing soldiers, playing shop. But all the time, they are hardening their muscles and sharpening their wits so that the pretence of being grown-up helps them to grow up in earnest.

Now, the moment you realise 'Here I am, dressing up as Christ,' it is extremely likely that you will see at once some way in which at that very moment the pretence could be made less of a pretence and more of a reality. You will find several things going on in your mind which would not be going on there if you were really a son of God. Well, stop them. Or you may realise that, instead of saying your prayers, you ought to be downstairs writing a letter, or helping your wife to wash-up. Well, go and do it.

—from *Mere Christianity*

Pretence Becomes Reality

You see what is happening. The Christ Himself, the Son of God who is man (just like you) and God (just like His Father) is actually at your side and is already at that moment beginning to turn your pretence into a reality. This is not merely a fancy way of saying that your conscience is telling you what to do. If you simply ask your conscience, you get one result; if you remember that you are dressing up as Christ, you get a different one. There are lots of things which your conscience might not call definitely wrong (specially things in your mind) but which you will see at once you cannot go on doing if you are seriously trying to be like Christ. For you are no longer thinking simply about right and wrong; you are trying to catch the good infection from a Person. It is more like painting a portrait than like obeying a set of rules. And the odd thing is that while in one way it is much harder than keeping rules, in another way it is far easier.

The real Son of God is at your side. He is beginning to turn you into the same kind of thing as Himself. He is beginning, so to speak, to 'inject' His kind of life and thought, His *Zoe*, into you; beginning to turn the tin soldier into a live man. The part of you that does not like it is the part that is still tin.

—from *Mere Christianity*

As We Become Like Christ

And now we begin to see what it is that the New Testament is always talking about. It talks about Christians 'being born again'; it talks about them 'putting on Christ'; about Christ 'being formed in us'; about our coming to 'have the mind of Christ'.

Put right out of your head the idea that these are only fancy ways of saying that Christians are to read what Christ said and try to carry it out—as a man may read what Plato or Marx said and try to carry it out. They mean something much more than that. They mean that a real Person, Christ, here and now, in that very room where you are saying your prayers, is doing things to you. It is not a question of a good man who died two thousand years ago. It is a living Man, still as much a man as you, and still as much God as He was when He created the world, really coming and interfering with your very self; killing the old natural self in you and replacing it with the kind of self He has. At first, only for moments. Then for longer periods. Finally, if all goes well, turning you permanently into a different sort of thing; into a new little Christ, a being which, in its own small way, has the same kind of life as God; which shares in His power, joy, knowledge and eternity.

—from *Mere Christianity*

1946 Lewis receives an honorary Doctorate of Divinity from St. Andrew's University, Scotland.

Rats in the Cellar

We begin to notice, besides our particular sinful acts, our sinfulness; begin to be alarmed not only about what we do, but about what we are. This may sound rather difficult, so I will try to make it clear from my own case. When I come to my evening prayers and try to reckon up the sins of the day, nine times out of ten the most obvious one is some sin against charity; I have sulked or snapped or sneered or snubbed or stormed. And the excuse that immediately springs to my mind is that the provocation was so sudden and unexpected; I was caught off my guard, I had not time to collect myself. Now that may be an extenuating circumstance as regards those particular acts: they would obviously be worse if they had been deliberate and premeditated. On the other hand, surely what a man does when he is taken off his guard is the best evidence for what sort of a man he is? Surely what pops out before the man has time to put on a disguise is the truth? If there are rats in a cellar you are most likely to see them if you go in very suddenly. But the suddenness does not create the rats: it only prevents them from hiding. In the same way the suddenness of the provocation does not make me an ill-tempered man; it only shows me what an ill-tempered man I am. The rats are always there in the cellar, but if you go in shouting and noisily they will have taken cover before you switch on the light.

—from *Mere Christianity*

And More Rats Yet

Apparently the rats of resentment and vindictiveness are always there in the cellar of my soul. Now that cellar is out of reach of my conscious will. I can to some extent control my acts: I have no direct control over my temperament. And if (as I said before) what we are matters even more than what we do—if, indeed, what we do matters chiefly as evidence of what we are—then it follows that the change which I most need to undergo is a change that my own direct, voluntary efforts cannot bring about. And this applies to my good actions too. How many of them were done for the right motive? How many for fear of public opinion, or a desire to show off? How many from a sort of obstinacy or sense of superiority which, in different circumstances, might equally have led to some very bad act? But I cannot, by direct moral effort, give myself new motives. After the first few steps in the Christian life we realise that everything which really needs to be done in our souls can be done only by God.

—from *Mere Christianity*

JULY

Lead Them by the Nose

Screwtape sets out his proposition for managing moderns:

Democracy is the word with which you must lead them by the nose. The good work which our philological experts have already done in the corruption of human language makes it unnecessary to warn you that they should never be allowed to give this word a clear and definable meaning. They won't. It will never occur to them that *Democracy* is properly the name of a political system, even a system of voting, and that this has only the most remote and tenuous connection with what you are trying to sell them. . . . .

You are to use the word purely as an incantation; if you like, purely for its selling power. It is a name they venerate. And of course it is connected with the political ideal that men should be equally treated. You then make a stealthy transition in their minds from this political ideal to a factual belief that all men *are* equal. Especially the man you are working on. As a result you can use the word *Democracy* to sanction in his thought the most degrading (and also the least enjoyable) of all human feelings. You can get him to practise, not only without shame but with a positive glow of self-approval, conduct which, if undefended by the magic word, would be universally derided.

The feeling I mean is of course that which prompts a man to say *I'm as good as you.*

—from "Screwtape Proposes a Toast" *(The Screwtape Letters)*

July 1955 Lewis is elected a member of the British Academy.

"I'm as Good as You Are"

*Screwtape reveals the devilish genius behind getting humans to assert,
"I'm as good as you are":*

The first and most obvious advantage is that you thus induce him
to enthrone at the centre of his life a good, solid resounding lie. I don't
mean merely that his statement is false in fact, that he is no more
equal to everyone he meets in kindness, honesty, and good sense than
in height or waist-measurement. I mean that he does not believe it
himself. No man who says *I'm as good as you* believes it. He would
not say it if he did. The St Bernard never says it to the toy dog, nor the
scholar to the dunce, nor the employable to the bum, nor the pretty
woman to the plain. The claim to equality, outside the strictly political
field, is made only by those who feel themselves to be in some way
inferior. What it expresses is precisely the itching, smarting, writhing
awareness of an inferiority which the patient refuses to accept.

And therefore resents. Yes, and therefore resents every kind of
superiority in others; denigrates it; wishes its annihilation. Presently
he suspects every mere difference of being a claim to superiority. No
one must be different from himself in voice, clothes, manners, recre-
ations, choice of food. 'Here is someone who speaks English rather
more clearly and euphoniously than I—it must be a vile, upstage, lah-
di-dah affectation. Here's a fellow who says he doesn't like hot dogs—
thinks himself too good for them no doubt. Here's a man who hasn't
turned on the jukebox—he must be one of those highbrows and is
doing it to show off. If they were the right sort of chaps they'd be like
me. They've no business to be different. It's undemocratic.'

—from "Screwtape Proposes a Toast" *(The Screwtape Letters)*

July 1958 Lewis and Joy honeymoon in Ireland.

The Undemocratic Incantation

Screwtape shows the degeneration of thought:

Now this useful phenomenon [of thinking "I'm as good as you are"] is in itself by no means new. Under the name of Envy it has been known to the humans for thousands of years. But hitherto they always regarded it as the most odious, and also the most comical, of vices. Those who were aware of feeling it felt it with shame; those who were not gave it no quarter in others. The delightful novelty of the present situation is that you can sanction it—make it respectable and even laudable—by the incantatory use of the word *democratic.*

Under the influence of this incantation those who are in any or every way inferior can labour more wholeheartedly and successfully than ever before to pull down everyone else to their own level. But that is not all. Under the same influence, those who come, or could come, nearer to a full humanity, actually draw back from it for fear of being *undemocratic.* I am credibly informed that young humans now sometimes suppress an incipient taste for classical music or good literature because it might prevent their Being like Folks; that people who would really wish to be—and are offered the Grace which would enable them to be—honest, chaste, or temperate, refuse it. To accept might make them Different, might offend again the Way of Life, take them out of Togetherness, impair their Integration with the Group. They might (horror of horrors!) become individuals.

All is summed up in the prayer which a young female human is said to have uttered recently: 'Oh God, make me a normal twentieth-century girl!' Thanks to our labours, this will mean increasingly, 'Make me a minx, a moron, and a parasite'.

—from "Screwtape Proposes a Toast" *(The Screwtape Letters)*

The Tyranny of Democracy

Screwtape reveals the ultimate goal:

What I want to fix your attention on is the vast, overall movement towards the discrediting, and finally the elimination, of every kind of human excellence—moral, cultural, social, or intellectual. And is it not pretty to notice how *Democracy* (in the incantatory sense) is now doing for us the work that was once done by the most ancient Dictatorships, and by the same methods? You remember how one of the Greek Dictators (they called them 'tyrants' then) sent an envoy to another Dictator to ask his advice about the principles of government. The second Dictator led the envoy into a field of corn, and there he snicked off with his cane the top of every stalk that rose an inch or so above the general level. The moral was plain. Allow no pre-eminence among your subjects. Let no man live who is wiser, or better, or more famous, or even handsomer than the mass. Cut them all down to a level; all slaves, all ciphers, all nobodies. All equals. Thus Tyrants could practise, in a sense, 'democracy'. But now 'democracy' can do the same work without any other tyranny than her own. No one need now go through the field with a cane. The little stalks will now of themselves bite the tops off the big ones. The big ones are beginning to bite off their own in their desire to Be Like Stalks.

—from "Screwtape Proposes a Toast" *(The Screwtape Letters)*

The Democratic Imperative

I believe in political equality. But there are two opposite reasons for being a democrat. You may think all men so good that they deserve a share in the government of the commonwealth, and so wise that the commonwealth needs their advice. That is, in my opinion, the false, romantic doctrine of democracy. On the other hand, you may believe fallen men to be so wicked that not one of them can be trusted with any irresponsible power over his fellows.

That I believe to be the true ground of democracy. I do not believe that God created an egalitarian world. I believe the authority of parent over child, husband over wife, learned over simple to have been as much a part of the original plan as the authority of man over beast. I believe that if we had not fallen, ... patriarchal monarchy would be the sole lawful government. But since we have learned sin, we have found, as Lord Acton says, that "all power corrupts, and absolute power corrupts absolutely." The only remedy has been to take away the powers and substitute a legal fiction of equality. The authority of father and husband has been rightly abolished on the legal plane, not because this authority is in itself bad (on the contrary, it is, I hold, divine in origin), but because fathers and husbands are bad. Theocracy has been rightly abolished not because it is bad that learned priests should govern ignorant laymen, but because priests are wicked men like the rest of us. Even the authority of man over beast has had to be interfered with because it is constantly abused.

—from "Membership" *(The Weight of Glory)*

Medicine, Not Food

Equality is for me in the same position as clothes. It is a result of the Fall and the remedy for it. Any attempt to retrace the steps by which we have arrived at egalitarianism and to reintroduce the old authorities on the political level is for me as foolish as it would be to take off our clothes. The Nazi and the nudist make the same mistake. But it is the naked body, still there beneath the clothes of each one of us, which really lives. It is the hierarchical world, still alive and (very properly) hidden behind a façade of equal citizenship, which is our real concern.

Do not misunderstand me. I am not in the least belittling the value of this egalitarian fiction which is our only defence against one another's cruelty. I should view with the strongest disapproval any proposal to abolish manhood suffrage, or the Married Women's Property Act. But the function of equality is purely protective. It is medicine, not food. By treating human persons (in judicious defiance of the observed facts) as if they were all the same kind of thing, we avoid innumerable evils. But it is not on this that we were made to live.

—from "Membership" (*The Weight of Glory*)

New Perspective

Christianity asserts that every individual human being is going to live for ever, and this must be either true or false. Now there are a good many things which would not be worth bothering about if I were going to live only seventy years, but which I had better bother about very seriously if I am going to live for ever. Perhaps my bad temper or my jealousy are gradually getting worse—so gradually that the increase in seventy years will not be very noticeable. But it might be absolute hell in a million years: in fact, if Christianity is true, Hell is the precisely correct technical term for what it would be. And immortality makes this other difference, which, by the by, has a connection with the difference between totalitarianism and democracy. If individuals live only seventy years, then a state, or a nation, or a civilisation, which may last for a thousand years, is more important than an individual. But if Christianity is true, then the individual is not only more important but incomparably more important, for he is everlasting and the life of a state or a civilisation, compared with his, is only a moment.

—from *Mere Christianity*

1952 *Mere Christianity*, a revised and amplified edition of Lewis's *Broadcast Talks*, *Christian Behavior*, and *Beyond Personality*, is published by Geoffrey Bles, London.

Coming in Out of the Wind

The real problem of the Christian life comes where people do not usually look for it. It comes the very moment you wake up each morning. All your wishes and hopes for the day rush at you like wild animals. And the first job each morning consists simply in shoving them all back; in listening to that other voice, taking that other point of view, letting that other larger, stronger, quieter life come flowing in. And so on, all day. Standing back from all your natural fussings and frettings; coming in out of the wind.

We can only do it for moments at first. But from those moments the new sort of life will be spreading through our system: because now we are letting Him work at the right part of us. It is the difference between paint, which is merely laid on the surface, and a dye or stain which soaks right through. He never talked vague, idealistic gas. When He said, 'Be perfect,' He meant it. He meant that we must go in for the full treatment. It is hard; but the sort of compromise we are all hankering after is harder—in fact, it is impossible. It may be hard for an egg to turn into a bird: it would be a jolly sight harder for it to learn to fly while remaining an egg. We are like eggs at present. And you cannot go on indefinitely being just an ordinary, decent egg. We must be hatched or go bad.

—from *Mere Christianity*

The Full Treatment

I find a good many people have been bothered by .... Our Lord's words, 'Be ye perfect'. Some people seem to think this means 'Unless you are perfect, I will not help you'; and as we cannot be perfect, then, if He meant that, our position is hopeless. But I do not think He did mean that. I think He meant 'The only help I will give is help to become perfect. You may want something less: but I will give you nothing less.'

Let me explain. When I was a child I often had toothache, and I knew that if I went to my mother she would give me something which would deaden the pain for that night and let me get to sleep. But I did not go to my mother—at least, not till the pain became very bad. And the reason I did not go was this. I did not doubt she would give me the aspirin; but I knew she would also do something else. I knew she would take me to the dentist next morning. I could not get what I wanted out of her without getting something more, which I did not want. I wanted immediate relief from pain: but I could not get it without having my teeth set permanently right. And I knew those dentists: I knew they started fiddling about with all sorts of other teeth which had not yet begun to ache. They would not let sleeping dogs lie, if you gave them an inch they took an ell.

Now, if I may put it that way, Our Lord is like the dentists. If you give Him an inch, He will take an ell. Dozens of people go to Him to be cured of some one particular sin which they are ashamed of (like masturbation or physical cowardice) or which is obviously spoiling daily life (like bad temper or drunkenness). Well, He will cure it all right: but He will not stop there. That may be all you asked; but if once you call Him in, He will give you the full treatment.

—from *Mere Christianity*

"I Will Make You Perfect"

He warned people to 'count the cost' before becoming Christians. 'Make no mistake,' He says, 'if you let me, I will make you perfect. The moment you put yourself in My hands, that is what you are in for. Nothing less, or other, than that. You have free will, and if you choose, you can push Me away. But if you do not push Me away, understand that I am going to see this job through. Whatever suffering it may cost you in your earthly life, whatever inconceivable purification it may cost you after death, whatever it costs Me, I will never rest, nor let you rest, until you are literally perfect—until my Father can say without reservation that He is well pleased with you, as He said He was well pleased with me. This I can do and will do. But I will not do anything less.'

And yet—this is the other and equally important side of it—this Helper who will, in the long run, be satisfied with nothing less than absolute perfection, will also be delighted with the first feeble, stumbling effort you make tomorrow to do the simplest duty. As a great Christian writer (George MacDonald) pointed out, every father is pleased at the baby's first attempt to walk: no father would be satisfied with anything less than a firm, free, manly walk in a grown-up son. In the same way, he said, 'God is easy to please, but hard to satisfy.'

—from *Mere Christianity*

All or Nothing

On the one hand, God's demand for perfection need not discourage you in the least in your present attempts to be good, or even in your present failures. Each time you fall He will pick you up again. And He knows perfectly well that your own efforts are never going to bring you anywhere near perfection. On the other hand, you must realise from the outset that the goal towards which He is beginning to guide you is absolute perfection; and no power in the whole universe, except you yourself, can prevent Him from taking you to that goal. That is what you are in for. And it is very important to realise that. If we do not, then we are very likely to start pulling back and resisting Him after a certain point.

—from *Mere Christianity*

Faux Humility

I think that many of us, when Christ has enabled us to overcome one or two sins that were an obvious nuisance, are inclined to feel (though we do not put it into words) that we are now good enough. He has done all we wanted Him to do, and we should be obliged if He would now leave us alone. As we say 'I never expected to be a saint, I only wanted to be a decent ordinary chap.' And we imagine when we say this that we are being humble.

But this is the fatal mistake. Of course we never wanted, and never asked, to be made into the sort of creatures He is going to make us into. But the question is not what we intended ourselves to be, but what He intended us to be when He made us. He is the inventor, we are only the machine. He is the painter, we are only the picture. How should we know what He means us to be like? You see, He has already made us something very different from what we were. Long ago, before we were born, when we were inside our mothers' bodies, we passed through various stages. We were once rather like vegetables, and once rather like fish: it was only at a later stage that we became like human babies. And if we had been conscious at those earlier stages, I daresay we should have been quite contented to stay as vegetables or fish—should not have wanted to be made into babies. But all the time He knew His plan for us and was determined to carry it out. Something the same is now happening at a higher level. We may be content to remain what we call 'ordinary people': but He is determined to carry out a quite different plan. To shrink back from that plan is not humility: it is laziness and cowardice. To submit to it is not conceit or megalomania; it is obedience.

—from *Mere Christianity*

Simply a Phase

Lewis, grieving the death of his wife, Joy:

And then one or other dies. And we think of this as love cut short; like a dance stopped in mid-career or a flower with its head unluckily snapped off—something truncated and therefore, lacking its due shape. I wonder. If, as I can't help suspecting, the dead also feel the pains of separation (and this may be one of their purgatorial sufferings), then for both lovers, and for all pairs of lovers without exception, bereavement is a universal and integral part of our experience of love. It follows marriage as normally as marriage follows courtship or as autumn follows summer. It is not a truncation of the process but one of its phases; not the interruption of the dance, but the next figure. We are 'taken out of ourselves' by the loved one while she is here. Then comes the tragic figure of the dance in which we must learn to be still taken out of ourselves though the bodily presence is withdrawn, to love the very Her, and not fall back to loving our past, or our memory, or our sorrow, or our relief from sorrow, or our own love.

—from *A Grief Observed*

1942 *Broadcast Talks*, which includes Lewis's BBC talks "Right and Wrong: A Clue to the Meaning of the Universe" and "What Christians Believe" is published by Geoffrey Bles, London.

1960 Joy Davidman Lewis dies at the age of forty-five.

Cigars in Heaven

Lewis, grieving the death of his wife, Joy:

I know that the thing I want is exactly the thing I can never get. The old life, the jokes, the drinks, the arguments, the lovemaking, the tiny, heartbreaking commonplace. On any view whatever, to say, 'H. is dead,' is to say, 'All that is gone.' It is a part of the past. And the past is the past and that is what time means, and time itself is one more name for death, and Heaven itself is a state where 'the former things have passed away.'

Talk to me about the truth of religion and I'll listen gladly. Talk to me about the duty of religion and I'll listen submissively. But don't come talking to me about the consolations of religion or I shall suspect that you don't understand.

Unless, of course, you can literally believe all that stuff about family reunions 'on the further shore,' pictured in entirely earthly terms. But that is all unscriptural, all out of bad hymns and lithographs. There's not a word of it in the Bible. And it rings false. We *know* it couldn't be like that. Reality never repeats. The exact same thing is never taken away and given back. How well the spiritualists bait their hook! 'Things on this side are not so different after all.' There are cigars in Heaven. For that is what we should all like. The happy past restored.

And that, just that, is what I cry out for, with mad, midnight endearments and entreaties spoken into the empty air.

—from *A Grief Observed*

Tenderly, Tenderly

Lewis, grieving the death of his wife, Joy:
What does it matter how this grief of mine evolves or what I do with it? What does it matter how I remember her or whether I remember her at all? None of these alternatives will either ease or aggravate her past anguish.

Her past anguish. How do I know that all her anguish is past? I never believed before—I thought it immensely improbable—that the faithfulest soul could leap straight into perfection and peace the moment death has rattled in the throat. It would be wishful thinking with a vengeance to take up that belief now. H. was a splendid thing; a soul straight, bright, and tempered like a sword. But not a perfected saint. A sinful woman married to a sinful man; two of God's patients, not yet cured. I know there are not only tears to be dried but stains to be scoured. The sword will be made even brighter.

But oh God, tenderly, tenderly.

—from *A Grief Observed*

1963 Lewis suffers a heart attack during a medical procedure and is admitted to the Acland Nursing Home.

A Sword in God's Hand

Lewis, grieving the death of his wife, Joy:

Praise is the mode of love which always has some element of joy in it. Praise in due order; of Him as the giver, of her as the gift. Don't we in praise somehow enjoy what we praise, however far we are from it? I must do more of this. I have lost the fruition I once had of H. And I am far, far away in the valley of my unlikeness, from the fruition which, if His mercies are infinite, I may some time have of God. But by praising I can still, in some degree, enjoy her, and already, in some degree, enjoy Him. Better than nothing.

But perhaps I lack the gift. I see I've described H. as being like a sword. That's true as far as it goes. But utterly inadequate by itself, and misleading. I ought to have balanced it. I ought to have said, 'But also like a garden. Like a nest of gardens, wall within wall, hedge within hedge, more secret, more full of fragrant and fertile life, the further you entered.'

And then, of her, and of every created thing I praise, I should say, 'In some way, in its unique way, like Him who made it.'

Thus up from the garden to the Gardener, from the sword to the Smith. To the life-giving Life and the Beauty that makes beautiful.

'She is in God's hands.' That gains a new energy when I think of her as a sword. Perhaps the earthly life I shared with her was only part of the tempering. Now perhaps He grasps the hilt; weighs the new weapon; makes lightnings with it in the air. 'A right Jerusalem blade.'

—from *A Grief Observed*

1923 Lewis takes First in English Language and Literature.

Two Sides of the Truth

Here is another way of putting the two sides of the truth. On the one hand we must never imagine that our own unaided efforts can be relied on to carry us even through the next twenty-four hours as 'decent' people. If He does not support us, not one of us is safe from some gross sin. On the other hand, no possible degree of holiness or heroism which has ever been recorded of the greatest saints is beyond what He is determined to produce in every one of us in the end. The job will not be completed in this life; but He means to get us as far as possible before death.

That is why we must not be surprised if we are in for a rough time. When a man turns to Christ and seems to be getting on pretty well (in the sense that some of his bad habits are now corrected) he often feels that it would now be natural if things went fairly smoothly. When troubles come along—illnesses, money troubles, new kinds of temptation—he is disappointed. These things, he feels, might have been necessary to rouse him and make him repent in his bad old days; but why now? Because God is forcing him on, or up, to a higher level: putting him into situations where he will have to be very much braver, or more patient, or more loving, than he ever dreamed of being before. It seems to us all unnecessary: but that is because we have not yet had the slightest notion of the tremendous thing He means to make of us.

—from *Mere Christianity*

Transformed

I find I must borrow yet another parable from George MacDonald. Imagine yourself as a living house. God comes in to rebuild that house. At first, perhaps, you can understand what He is doing. He is getting the drains right and stopping the leaks in the roof and so on: you knew that those jobs needed doing and so you are not surprised. But presently he starts knocking the house about in a way that hurts abominably and does not seem to make sense. What on earth is He up to? The explanation is that He is building quite a different house from the one you thought of—throwing out a new wing here, putting on an extra floor there, running up towers, making courtyards. You thought you were going to be made into a decent little cottage: but He is building a palace. He intends to come and live in it Himself.

The command *Be ye perfect* is not idealistic gas. Nor is it a command to do the impossible. He is going to make us into creatures that can obey that command. He said (in the Bible) that we were 'gods' and He is going to make good His words. If we let Him—for we can prevent Him, if we choose—He will make the feeblest and filthiest of us into a god or goddess, a dazzling, radiant, immortal creature, pulsating all through with such energy and joy and wisdom and love as we cannot now imagine, a bright stainless mirror which reflects back to God perfectly (though, of course, on a smaller scale) His own boundless power and delight and goodness. The process will be long and in parts very painful, but that is what we are in for. Nothing less. He meant what He said.

—from *Mere Christianity*

The Real Self

There must be a real giving up of the self. You must throw it away
'blindly' so to speak. Christ will indeed give you a real personality: but
you must not go to Him for the sake of that. As long as your own personality is what you are bothering about you are not going to Him at
all. The very first step is to try to forget about the self altogether. Your
real, new self (which is Christ's and also yours, and yours just because
it is His) will not come as long as you are looking for it. It will come
when you are looking for Him. Does that sound strange? The same
principle holds, you know, for more everyday matters. Even in social
life, you will never make a good impression on other people until you
stop thinking about what sort of impression you are making. Even in
literature and art, no man who bothers about originality will ever be
original: whereas if you simply try to tell the truth (without caring
twopence how often it has been told before) you will, nine times out
of ten, become original without ever having noticed it. The principle
runs through all life from top to bottom. Give up yourself, and you
will find your real self. Lose your life and you will save it. Submit to
death, death of your ambitions and favourite wishes every day and
death of your whole body in the end: submit with every fibre of your
being, and you will find eternal life. Keep back nothing. Nothing that
you have not given away will be really yours. Nothing in you that has
not died will ever be raised from the dead. Look for yourself, and you
will find in the long run only hatred, loneliness, despair, rage, ruin,
and decay. But look for Christ and you will find Him, and with Him
everything else thrown in.

—from *Mere Christianity*

Defining Our Terms

The name *Christians* was first given at Antioch (Acts 11:26) to 'the disciples', to those who accepted the teaching of the apostles. There is no question of its being restricted to those who profited by that teaching as much as they should have. There is no question of its being extended to those who in some refined, spiritual, inward fashion were 'far closer to the spirit of Christ' than the less satisfactory of the disciples. The point is not a theological or moral one. It is only a question of using words so that we can all understand what is being said. When a man who accepts the Christian doctrine lives unworthily of it, it is much clearer to say he is a bad Christian than to say he is not a Christian.

—from *Mere Christianity*, Preface

Reflection of the Divine Life

Those Divine demands which sound to our natural ears most like those of a despot and least like those of a lover, in fact marshal us where we should want to go if we knew what we wanted. He demands our worship, our obedience, our prostration. Do we suppose that they can do Him any good, or fear, like the chorus in Milton, that human irreverence can bring about 'His glory's diminution'? A man can no more diminish God's glory by refusing to worship Him than a lunatic can put out the sun by scribbling the word 'darkness' on the walls of his cell. But God wills our good, and our good is to love Him (with that responsive love proper to creatures) and to love Him we must know Him: and if we know Him, we shall in fact fall on our faces. If we do not, that only shows that what we are trying to love is not yet God— though it may be the nearest approximation to God which our thought and fantasy can attain. Yet the call is not only to prostration and awe; it is to a reflection of the Divine life, a creaturely participation in the Divine attributes which is far beyond our present desires. We are bidden to 'put on Christ', to become like God. That is, whether we like it or not, God intends to give us what we need, not what we now think we want. Once more, we are embarrassed by the intolerable compliment, by too much love, not too little.

—from *The Problem of Pain*

1940 Lewis conceives the idea for *The Screwtape Letters.*

Judging by Results

If Christianity is true why are not all Christians obviously nicer than all non-Christians? What lies behind that question is partly something very reasonable and partly something that is not reasonable at all. The reasonable part is this. If conversion to Christianity makes no improvement in a man's outward actions—if he continues to be just as snobbish or spiteful or envious or ambitious as he was before—then I think we must suspect that his 'conversion' was largely imaginary; and after one's original conversion, every time one thinks one has made an advance, that is the test to apply. Fine feelings, new insights, greater interest in 'religion' mean nothing unless they make our actual behaviour better; just as in an illness 'feeling better' is not much good if the thermometer shows that your temperature is still going up. In that sense the outer world is quite right to judge Christianity by its results. Christ told us to judge by results. A tree is known by its fruit; or, as we say, the proof of the pudding is in the eating. When we Christians behave badly, or fail to behave well, we are making Christianity unbelievable to the outside world. The war-time posters told us that Careless Talk costs Lives. It is equally true that Careless Lives cost Talk. Our careless lives set the outer world talking; and we give them grounds for talking in a way that throws doubt on the truth of Christianity itself.

—from *Mere Christianity*

Out of Action

Screwtape's advice on wresting the Patient from Enemy hands:

It remains to consider how we can retrieve this disaster. The great thing is to prevent his doing anything. As long as he does not convert it into action, it does not matter how much he thinks about this new repentance. Let the little brute wallow in it. Let him, if he has any bent that way, write a book about it; that is often an excellent way of sterilising the seeds which the Enemy plants in a human soul. Let him do anything but act. No amount of piety in his imagination and affections will harm us if we can keep it out of his will. As one of the humans has said, active habits are strengthened by repetition but passive ones are weakened. The more often he feels without acting, the less he will be able ever to act, and, in the long run, the less he will be able to feel.

—from *The Screwtape Letters*

A Warning or an Encouragement?

There is either a warning or an encouragement here for every one of us. If you are a nice person—if virtue comes easily to you—beware! Much is expected from those to whom much is given. If you mistake for your own merits what are really God's gifts to you through nature, and if you are contented with simply being nice, you are still a rebel: and all those gifts will only make your fall more terrible, your corruption more complicated, your bad example more disastrous. The Devil was an archangel once; his natural gifts were as far above yours as yours are above those of a chimpanzee.

But if you are a poor creature—poisoned by a wretched upbringing in some house full of vulgar jealousies and senseless quarrels—saddled, by no choice of your own, with some loathsome sexual perversion—nagged day in and day out by an inferiority complex that makes you snap at your best friends—do not despair. He knows all about it. You are one of the poor whom He blessed. He knows what a wretched machine you are trying to drive. Keep on. Do what you can. One day (perhaps in another world, but perhaps far sooner than that) He will fling it on the scrap-heap and give you a new one. And then you may astonish us all—not least yourself: for you have learned your driving in a hard school. (Some of the last will be first and some of the first will be last).

—from *Mere Christianity*

Love Your Neighbour as Yourself

Well, how exactly do I love myself?

Now that I come to think of it, I have not exactly got a feeling of fondness or affection for myself, and I do not even always enjoy my own society. So apparently 'Love your neighbour' does not mean 'feel fond of him' or 'find him attractive'. I ought to have seen that before, because, of course, you cannot feel fond of a person by trying. Do I think well of myself, think myself a nice chap? Well, I am afraid I sometimes do (and those are, no doubt, my worst moments) but that is not why I love myself. In fact it is the other way round: my self-love makes me think myself nice, but thinking myself nice is not why I love myself. So loving my enemies does not apparently mean thinking them nice either. That is an enormous relief. For a good many people imagine that forgiving your enemies means making out that they are really not such bad fellows after all, when it is quite plain that they are. Go a step further. In my most clear-sighted moments not only do I not think myself a nice man, but I know that I am a very nasty one. I can look at some of the things I have done with horror and loathing. So apparently I am allowed to loathe and hate some of the things my enemies do.

—from *Mere Christianity*

1929 Lewis's father, Albert, is diagnosed with cancer.

Love the Sinner...

Now that I come to think of it, I remember Christian teachers telling me long ago that I must hate a bad man's actions, but not hate the bad man: or, as they would say, hate the sin but not the sinner.

For a long time I used to think this a silly, straw-splitting distinction: how could you hate what a man did and not hate the man? But years later it occurred to me that there was one man to whom I had been doing this all my life—namely myself. However much I might dislike my own cowardice or conceit or greed, I went on loving myself. There had never been the slightest difficulty about it. In fact the very reason why I hated the things was that I loved the man. Just because I loved myself, I was sorry to find that I was the sort of man who did those things. Consequently, Christianity does not want us to reduce by one atom the hatred we feel for cruelty and treachery. We ought to hate them. Not one word of what we have said about them needs to be unsaid. But it does want us to hate them in the same way in which we hate things in ourselves: being sorry that the man should have done such things, and hoping, if it is anyway possible, that somehow, sometime, somewhere he can be cured and made human again.

—from *Mere Christianity*

The Real Test

Suppose one reads a story of filthy atrocities in the paper. Then suppose that something turns up suggesting that the story might not be quite true, or not quite so bad as it was made out. Is one's first feeling, 'Thank God, even they aren't quite so bad as that,' or is it a feeling of disappointment, and even a determination to cling to the first story for the sheer pleasure of thinking your enemies as bad as possible? If it is the second then it is, I am afraid, the first step in a process which, if followed to the end, will make us into devils. You see, one is beginning to wish that black was a little blacker. If we give that wish its head, later on we shall wish to see grey as black, and then to see white itself as black. Finally, we shall insist on seeing everything—God and our friends and ourselves included—as bad, and not be able to stop doing it: we shall be fixed for ever in a universe of pure hatred.

—from Mere Christianity

Love Your Enemy

I imagine somebody will say, 'Well, if one is allowed to condemn the enemy's acts, and punish him, and kill him, what difference is left between Christian morality and the ordinary view?' All the difference in the world. Remember, we Christians think man lives for ever. Therefore, what really matters is those little marks or twists on the central, inside part of the soul which are going to turn it, in the long run, into a heavenly or a hellish creature. We may kill if necessary, but we must not hate and enjoy hating. We may punish if necessary, but we must not enjoy it. In other words, something inside us, the feeling of resentment, the feeling that wants to get one's own back, must be simply killed. I do not mean that anyone can decide this moment that he will never feel it any more. That is not how things happen. I mean that every time it bobs its head up, day after day, year after year, all our lives long, we must hit it on the head. It is hard work, but the attempt is not impossible. Even while we kill and punish we must try to feel about the enemy as we feel about ourselves—to wish that he were not bad, to hope that he may, in this world or another, be cured: in fact, to wish his good. That is what is meant in the Bible by loving him: wishing his good, not feeling fond of him nor saying he is nice when he is not.
—from *Mere Christianity*

The Thing Called Selves

I admit that this means loving people who have nothing lovable about them. But then, has oneself anything lovable about it? You love it simply because it is yourself. God intends us to love all selves in the same way and for the same reason: but He has given us the sum ready worked out in our own case to show us how it works. We have then to go on and apply the rule to all the other selves. Perhaps it makes it easier if we remember that that is how He loves us. Not for any nice, attractive qualities we think we have, but just because we are the things called selves. For really there is nothing else in us to love: creatures like us who actually find hatred such a pleasure that to give it up is like giving up beer or tobacco...

—from *Mere Christianity*

This Terrible Duty

[One of the most unpopular of the Christian virtues] is laid down in the Christian rule, 'Thou shalt love thy neighbour as thyself.' Because in Christian morals 'thy neighbour' includes 'thy enemy', and so we come up against this terrible duty of forgiving our enemies.

Every one says forgiveness is a lovely idea, until they have something to forgive, as we had during the war. And then, to mention the subject at all is to be greeted with howls of anger. It is not that people think this too high and difficult a virtue: it is that they think it hateful and contemptible. 'That sort of talk makes them sick,' they say. And half of you already want to ask me, 'I wonder how you'd feel about forgiving the Gestapo if you were a Pole or a Jew?'

So do I. I wonder very much. Just as when Christianity tells me that I must not deny my religion even to save myself from death by torture, I wonder very much what I should do when it came to the point. I am not trying to tell you in this book what I could do—I can do precious little—I am telling you what Christianity is. I did not invent it. And there, right in the middle of it, I find 'Forgive us our sins as we forgive those that sin against us.' There is no slightest suggestion that we are offered forgiveness on any other terms.

—from *Mere Christianity*

Start Small

It is made perfectly clear that if we do not forgive we shall not be forgiven. There are no two ways about it. What are we to do?

It is going to be hard enough, anyway, but I think there are two things we can do to make it easier. When you start mathematics you do not begin with the calculus; you begin with simple addition. In the same way, if we really want (but all depends on really wanting) to learn how to forgive, perhaps we had better start with something easier than the Gestapo. One might start with forgiving one's husband or wife, or parents or children, or the nearest N.C.O., for something they have done or said in the last week. That will probably keep us busy for the moment. And secondly, we might try to understand exactly what loving your neighbour as yourself means. I have to love him as I love myself.

—from *Mere Christianity*

AUGUST

Grieving, and Thinking About Grieving

Lewis, grieving the death of his wife, Joy:

Are these jottings morbid? I once read the sentence 'I lay awake all night with toothache, thinking about toothache and about lying awake.' That's true to life. Part of every misery is, so to speak, the misery's shadow or reflection: the fact that you don't merely suffer but have to keep on thinking about the fact that you suffer. I not only live each endless day in grief, but live each day thinking about living each day in grief.

—from *A Grief Observed*

August 1960 Following Joy's death in July 1960, Lewis writes *A Grief Observed*.

A Jab of Red-Hot Memory

Lewis, grieving the death of his wife, Joy:

No one ever told me that grief felt so like fear. I am not afraid, but the sensation is like being afraid. The same fluttering in the stomach, the same restlessness, the yawning. I keep on swallowing.

At other times it feels like being mildly drunk, or concussed. There is a sort of invisible blanket between the world and me. I find it hard to take in what anyone says. Or perhaps, hard to want to take it in. It is so uninteresting. Yet I want the others to be about me. I dread the moments when the house is empty. If only they would talk to one another and not to me.

There are moments, most unexpectedly, when something inside me tries to assure me that I don't really mind so much, not so very much, after all. Love is not the whole of a man's life. I was happy before I ever met H. I've plenty of what are called 'resources.' People get over these things. Come, I shan't do so badly. One is ashamed to listen to this voice but it seems for a little to be making out a good case. Then comes a sudden jab of red-hot memory and all this 'commonsense' vanishes like an ant in the mouth of a furnace.

—from *A Grief Observed*

August 1963 Due to ill health, Lewis resigns his teaching post at Cambridge and returns home to live full-time at The Kilns.

Alone into the Alone

Lewis, grieving the death of his wife, Joy:

There's a limit to the 'one flesh.' You can't really share someone else's weakness, or fear or pain. What you feel may be bad. It might conceivably be as bad as what the other felt, though I should distrust anyone who claimed that it was. But it would still be quite different. When I speak of fear, I mean the merely animal fear, the recoil of the organism from its destruction; the smothery feeling; the sense of being a rat in a trap. It can't be transferred. The mind can sympathize; the body, less. In one way the bodies of lovers can do it least. All their love passages have trained them to have, not identical, but complementary, correlative, even opposite, feelings about one another.

We both knew this. I had my miseries, not hers; she had hers, not mine. The end of hers would be the coming-of-age of mine. We were setting out on different roads. This cold truth, this terrible traffic-regulation ('You, Madam, to the right—you, Sir, to the left') is just the beginning of the separation which is death itself.

And this separation, I suppose, waits for all. I have been thinking of H. and myself as peculiarly unfortunate in being torn apart. But presumably all lovers are. She once said to me, 'Even if we both died at exactly the same moment, as we lie here side by side, it would be just as much a separation as the one you're so afraid of.' Of course she didn't *know*, any more than I do. But she was near death; near enough to make a good shot. She used to quote 'Alone into the Alone.' She said it felt like that. And how immensely improbable that it should be otherwise! Time and space and body were the very things that brought us together; the telephone wires by which we communicated. Cut one off, or cut both off simultaneously. Either way, mustn't the conversation stop?

—from *A Grief Observed*

Lament

Lewis, grieving the death of his wife, Joy:

I must think more about H. and less about myself.

Yes, that sounds very well. But there's a snag. I am thinking about her nearly always. Thinking of the H. facts—real words, looks, laughs, and actions of hers. But it is my own mind that selects and groups them. Already, less than a month after her death, I can feel the slow, insidious beginning of a process that will make the H. I think of into a more and more imaginary woman. Founded on fact, no doubt. I shall put in nothing fictitious (or I hope I shan't). But won't the composition inevitably become more and more my own? The reality is no longer there to check me, to pull me up short, as the real H. so often did, so unexpectedly, by being so thoroughly herself and not me.

The most precious gift that marriage gave me was this constant impact of something very close and intimate yet all the time unmistakably other, resistant—in a word, real. Is all that work to be undone? Is what I shall still call H. to sink back horribly into being not much more than one of my old bachelor pipe-dreams? Oh my dear, my dear, come back for one moment and drive that miserable phantom away. Oh God, God, why did you take such trouble to force this creature out of its shell if it is now doomed to crawl back—to be sucked back—into it?

—from *A Grief Observed*

1922 Lewis takes First in *Literae Humaniores* ("Greats")—classical philosophy.

Would I Wish Her Back?

Lewis, grieving the death of his wife, Joy:

What sort of a lover am I to think so much about my affliction and so much less about hers? Even the insane call, 'Come back,' is all for my own sake. I never even raised the question whether such a return, if it were possible, would be good for her. I want her back as an ingredient in the restoration of *my* past. Could I have wished her anything worse? Having got once through death, to come back and then, at some later date, have all her dying to do over again? They call Stephen the first martyr. Hadn't Lazarus the rawer deal?

—from *A Grief Observed*

Cherishing Our Unhappiness

Lewis, grieving the death of his wife, Joy:

Still, there's no denying that in some sense I 'feel better,' and with that comes at once a sort of shame, and a feeling that one is under a sort of obligation to cherish and foment and prolong one's unhappiness. . . . . What is behind it?

Partly, no doubt, vanity. We want to prove to ourselves that we are lovers on the grand scale, tragic heroes; not just ordinary privates in the huge army of the bereaved, slogging along and making the best of a bad job. But that's not the whole of the explanation.

I think there is also a confusion. We don't really want grief, in its first agonies, to be prolonged: nobody could. But we want something else of which grief is a frequent symptom, and then we confuse the symptom with the thing itself. I wrote the other night that bereavement is not the truncation of married love but one of its regular phases—like the honeymoon. What we want is to live our marriage well and faithfully through that phase too. If it hurts (and it certainly will) we accept the pains as a necessary part of this phase. We don't want to escape them at the price of desertion or divorce. Killing the dead a second time. We were one flesh. Now that it has been cut in two, we don't want to pretend that it is whole and complete. We will be still married, still in love. Therefore we shall still ache.

—from *A Grief Observed*

1941 Lewis delivers the first of four talks on "Right and Wrong" over the BBC. These talks are later published in *Broadcast Talks* (1942) and form Book 1 of *Mere Christianity*.

Holy Intentions

The Christian idea of marriage is based on Christ's words that a man and wife are to be regarded as a single organism—for that is what the words 'one flesh' would be in modern English. And the Christians believe that when He said this He was not expressing a sentiment but stating a fact—just as one is stating a fact when one says that a lock and its key are one mechanism, or that a violin and a bow are one musical instrument. The inventor of the human machine was telling us that its two halves, the male and the female, were made to be combined together in pairs, not simply on the sexual level, but totally combined. The monstrosity of sexual intercourse outside marriage is that those who indulge in it are trying to isolate one kind of union (the sexual) from all the other kinds of union which were intended to go along with it and make up the total union. The Christian attitude does not mean that there is anything wrong about sexual pleasure, any more than about the pleasure of eating. It means that you must not isolate that pleasure and try to get it by itself, any more than you ought to try to get the pleasures of taste without swallowing and digesting, by chewing things and spitting them out again.

—from *Mere Christianity*

Hell's Parody

Screwtape reveals Hell's intentions for human marriage:

The Enemy's demand on humans takes the form of a dilemma; *either* complete abstinence *or* unmitigated monogamy. Ever since our Father's first great victory, we have rendered the former very difficult to them. The latter, for the last few centuries, we have been closing up as a way of escape. We have done this through the poets and novelists by persuading the humans that a curious, and usually shortlived, experience which they call 'being in love' is the only respectable ground for marriage; that marriage can, and ought to, render this excitement permanent; and that a marriage which does not do so is no longer binding. This idea is our parody of an idea that came from the Enemy.

The whole philosophy of Hell rests on recognition of the axiom that one thing is not another thing, and, specially, that one self is not another self. My good is my good and your good is yours. What one gains another loses. Even an inanimate object is what it is by excluding all other objects from the space it occupies; if it expands, it does so by thrusting other objects aside or by absorbing them. A self does the same. With beasts the absorption takes the form of eating; for us, it means the sucking of will and freedom out of a weaker self into a stronger. 'To be' *means* 'to be in competition'.

—from *The Screwtape Letters*

One Flesh

Screwtape deconstructs the history of marriage:

Now comes the joke. The Enemy described a married couple as 'one flesh'. He did not say 'a happily married couple' or 'a couple who married because they were in love', but you can make the humans ignore that. You can also make them forget that the man they call Paul did not confine it to *married* couples. Mere copulation, for him, makes 'one flesh'. You can thus get the humans to accept as rhetorical eulogies of 'being in love' what were in fact plain descriptions of the real significance of sexual intercourse. The truth is that wherever a man lies with a woman, there, whether they like it or not, a transcendental relation is set up between them which must be eternally enjoyed or eternally endured. From the true statement that this transcendental relation was intended to produce, and, if obediently entered into, too often *will* produce, affection and the family, humans can be made to infer the false belief that the blend of affection, fear, and desire which they call 'being in love' is the only thing that makes marriage either happy or holy. The error is easy to produce because 'being in love' does very often, in Western Europe, precede marriages which are made in obedience to the Enemy's designs, that is, with the intention of fidelity, fertility and good will; just as religious emotion very often, but not always, attends conversion.

—from *The Screwtape Letters*

I Promise You

The idea that 'being in love' is the only reason for remaining married really leaves no room for marriage as a contract or promise at all. If love is the whole thing, then the promise can add nothing; and if it adds nothing, then it should not be made. The curious thing is that lovers themselves, while they remain really in love, know this better than those who talk about love. As Chesterton pointed out, those who are in love have a natural inclination to bind themselves by promises. Love songs all over the world are full of vows of eternal constancy. The Christian law is not forcing upon the passion of love something which is foreign to that passion's own nature: it is demanding that lovers should take seriously something which their passion of itself impels them to do.

And, of course, the promise, made when I am in love and because I am in love, to be true to the beloved as long as I live, commits me to being true even if I cease to be in love. A promise must be about things that I can do, about actions: no one can promise to go on feeling in a certain way. He might as well promise never to have a headache or always to feel hungry.

—from *Mere Christianity*

Falling in Love

What we call 'being in love' is a glorious state, and, in several ways, good for us. It helps to make us generous and courageous, it opens our eyes not only to the beauty of the beloved but to all beauty, and it subordinates (especially at first) our merely animal sexuality; in that sense, love is the great conqueror of lust. No one in his senses would deny that being in love is far better than either common sensuality or cold self-centredness. But, as I said before, 'the most dangerous thing you can do is to take any one impulse of our own nature and set it up as the thing you ought to follow at all costs'. Being in love is a good thing, but it is not the best thing. There are many things below it, but there are also things above it. You cannot make it the basis of a whole life. It is a noble feeling, but it is still a feeling. Now no feeling can be relied on to last in its full intensity, or even to last at all. Knowledge can last, principles can last, habits can last; but feelings come and go. And in fact, whatever people say, the state called 'being in love' usually does not last.

—from *Mere Christianity*

Being in Love

If the old fairy-tale ending 'They lived happily ever after' is taken to mean 'They felt for the next fifty years exactly as they felt the day before they were married', then it says what probably never was nor ever would be true, and would be highly undesirable if it were. Who could bear to live in that excitement for even five years? What would become of your work, your appetite, your sleep, your friendships? But, of course, ceasing to be 'in love' need not mean ceasing to love. Love in this second sense—love as distinct from 'being in love'—is not merely a feeling. It is a deep unity, maintained by the will and deliberately strengthened by habit; reinforced by (in Christian marriages) the grace which both partners ask, and receive, from God. They can have this love for each other even at those moments when they do not like each other; as you love yourself even when you do not like yourself. They can retain this love even when each would easily, if they allowed themselves, be 'in love' with someone else. 'Being in love' first moved them to promise fidelity: this quieter love enables them to keep the promise. It is on this love that the engine of marriage is run: being in love was the explosion that started it.

—from *Mere Christianity*

Romance Novels

People get from books the idea that if you have married the right person you may expect to go on 'being in love' for ever. As a result, when they find they are not, they think this proves they have made a mistake and are entitled to a change—not realising that, when they have changed, the glamour will presently go out of the new love just as it went out of the old one. In this department of life, as in every other, thrills come at the beginning and do not last. The sort of thrill a boy has at the first idea of flying will not go on when he has joined the R.A.F. and is really learning to fly. The thrill you feel on first seeing some delightful place dies away when you really go to live there. . . . .

Another notion we get from novels and plays is that 'falling in love' is something quite irresistible; something that just happens to one, like measles. And because they believe this, some married people throw up the sponge and give in when they find themselves attracted by a new acquaintance. But I am inclined to think that these irresistible passions are much rarer in real life than in books, at any rate when one is grown up. When we meet someone beautiful and clever and sympathetic, of course we ought, in one sense, to admire and love these good qualities. But is it not very largely in our own choice whether this love shall, or shall not, turn into what we call 'being in love'? No doubt, if our minds are full of novels and plays and sentimental songs, and our bodies full of alcohol, we shall turn any love we feel into that kind of love: just as if you have a rut in your path all the rainwater will run into that rut, and if you wear blue spectacles everything you see will turn blue. But that will be our own fault.

—from *Mere Christianity*

1929 Lewis returns to Belfast to nurse his father, Albert, in his final illness.

Love Then Marriage—
or Marriage Then Love?

Screwtape details Hell's lies about marriage:

In other words, the humans are to be encouraged to regard as the basis for marriage a highly-coloured and distorted version of something the Enemy really promises as its result. Two advantages follow. In the first place, humans who have not the gift of continence can be deterred from seeking marriage as a solution because they do not find themselves 'in love', and, thanks to us, the idea of marrying with any other motive seems to them low and cynical. Yes, they think that. They regard the intention of loyalty to a partnership for mutual help, for the preservation of chastity, and for the transmission of life, as something lower than a storm of emotion. (Don't neglect to make your man think the marriage-service very offensive.) In the second place any sexual infatuation whatever, so long as it intends marriage, will be regarded as 'love', and 'love' will be held to excuse a man from all the guilt, and to protect him from all the consequences, of marrying a heathen, a fool, or a wanton.

—from *The Screwtape Letters*

That Love May Find a Foothold

Screwtape rails against the impossibility of Love:

He [the Enemy] aims at a contradiction. Things are to be many, yet somehow also one. The good of one self is to be the good of another. This impossibility He calls *love*, and this same monotonous panacea can be detected under all He does and even all He is—or claims to be. Thus He is not content, even Himself, to be a sheer arithmetical unity; He claims to be three as well as one, in order that this nonsense about Love may find a foothold in His own nature. At the other end of the scale, He introduces into matter that obscene invention the organism, in which the parts are perverted from their natural destiny of competition and made to co-operate.

His real motive for fixing on sex as the method of reproduction among humans is only too apparent from the use He has made of it. Sex might have been, from our point of view, quite innocent. It might have been merely one more mode in which a stronger self preyed upon a weaker—as it is, indeed, among the spiders where the bride concludes her nuptials by eating the groom. But in the humans the Enemy has gratuitously associated affection between the parties with sexual desire. He has also made the offspring dependent on the parents and given the parents an impulse to support it—thus producing the Family, which is like the organism, only worse; for the members are more distinct, yet also united in a more conscious and responsible way. The whole thing, in fact, turns out to be simply one more device for dragging in Love.

—from *The Screwtape Letters*

1932 Lewis begins to write *The Pilgrim's Regress*.

The Least Bad of All Sins

If anyone thinks that Christians regard unchastity as the supreme vice, he is quite wrong. The sins of the flesh are bad, but they are the least bad of all sins. All the worst pleasures are purely spiritual: the pleasure of putting other people in the wrong, of bossing and patronising and spoiling sport, and back-biting, the pleasures of power, of hatred. For there are two things inside me, competing with the human self which I must try to become. They are the Animal self, and the Diabolical self. The Diabolical self is the worse of the two. That is why a cold, self-righteous prig who goes regularly to church may be far nearer to hell than a prostitute. But, of course, it is better to be neither.

—from *Mere Christianity*

1945 *That Hideous Strength* (the final volume of Lewis's *Space Trilogy*) is published by The Bodley Head, London.

Bent Appetites

Chastity is the most unpopular of the Christian virtues. There is no getting away from it; the Christian rule is, 'Either marriage, with complete faithfulness to your partner, or else total abstinence.' Now this is so difficult and so contrary to our instincts, that obviously either Christianity is wrong or our sexual instinct, as it now is, has gone wrong. One or the other. Of course, being a Christian, I think it is the instinct which has gone wrong.

But I have other reasons for thinking so. The biological purpose of sex is children, just as the biological purpose of eating is to repair the body. Now if we eat whenever we feel inclined and just as much as we want, it is quite true most of us will eat too much: but not terrifically too much. One man may eat enough for two, but he does not eat enough for ten. The appetite goes a little beyond its biological purpose, but not enormously. But if a healthy young man indulged his sexual appetite whenever he felt inclined, and if each act produced a baby, then in ten years he might easily populate a small village. This appetite is in ludicrous and preposterous excess of its function.

Or take it another way. You can get a large audience together for a strip-tease act—that is, to watch a girl undress on the stage. Now suppose you come to a country where you could fill a theatre by simply bringing a covered plate on to the stage and then slowly lifting the cover so as to let every one see, just before the lights went out, that it contained a mutton chop or a bit of bacon, would you not think that in that country something had gone wrong with the appetite for food? And would not anyone who had grown up in a different world think there was something equally queer about the state of the sex instinct among us?

—from *Mere Christianity*

One Reason We Don't Desire Chastity

Our warped natures, the devils who tempt us, and all the contemporary propaganda for lust, combine to make us feel that the desires we are resisting are so 'natural', so 'healthy', and so reasonable, that it is almost perverse and abnormal to resist them. Poster after poster, film after film, novel after novel, associate the idea of sexual indulgence with the ideas of health, normality, youth, frankness, and good humour. Now this association is a lie. Like all powerful lies, it is based on a truth—the truth, acknowledged above, that sex in itself (apart from the excesses and obsessions that have grown round it) is 'normal' and 'healthy', and all the rest of it. The lie consists in the suggestion that any sexual act to which you are tempted at the moment is also healthy and normal. Now this, on any conceivable view, and quite apart from Christianity, must be nonsense. Surrender to all our desires obviously leads to impotence, disease, jealousies, lies, concealment, and everything that is the reverse of health, good humour, and frankness.

—from *Mere Christianity*

Another Reason We Don't Desire Chastity

Many people are deterred from seriously attempting Christian chastity because they think (before trying) that it is impossible. But when a thing has to be attempted, one must never think about possibility or impossibility. Faced with an optional question in an examination paper, one considers whether one can do it or not: faced with a compulsory question, one must do the best one can. You may get some marks for a very imperfect answer: you will certainly get none for leaving the question alone. Not only in examinations but in war, in mountain climbing, in learning to skate, or swim, or ride a bicycle, even in fastening a stiff collar with cold fingers, people quite often do what seemed impossible before they did it. It is wonderful what you can do when you have to.

We may, indeed, be sure that perfect chastity—like perfect charity—will not be attained by any merely human efforts. You must ask for God's help. Even when you have done so, it may seem to you for a long time that no help, or less help than you need, is being given. Never mind. After each failure, ask forgiveness, pick yourself up, and try again. Very often what God first helps us towards is not the virtue itself but just this power of always trying again. For however important chastity (or courage, or truthfulness, or any other virtue) may be, this process trains us in habits of the soul which are more important still. It cures our illusions about ourselves and teaches us to depend on God. We learn, on the one hand, that we cannot trust ourselves even in our best moments, and, on the other, that we need not despair even in our worst, for our failures are forgiven. The only fatal thing is to sit down content with anything less than perfection.

—from *Mere Christianity*

A Final Reason We Don't Desire Chastity

People often misunderstand what psychology teaches about 'repressions'. It teaches us that 'repressed' sex is dangerous. But 'repressed' is here a technical term: it does not mean 'suppressed' in the sense of 'denied' or 'resisted'. A repressed desire or thought is one which has been thrust into the subconscious (usually at a very early age) and can now come before the mind only in a disguised and unrecognisable form. Repressed sexuality does not appear to the patient to be sexuality at all. When an adolescent or an adult is engaged in resisting a conscious desire, he is not dealing with a repression nor is he in the least danger of creating a repression. On the contrary, those who are seriously attempting chastity are more conscious, and soon know a great deal more about their own sexuality than anyone else. They come to know their desires as Wellington knew Napoleon, or as Sherlock Holmes knew Moriarty; as a rat-catcher knows rats or a plumber knows about leaky pipes. Virtue—even attempted virtue—brings light; indulgence brings fog.

—from *Mere Christianity*

Gluttony of Delicacy

Screwtape demonstrates the value of gluttony:

The contemptuous way in which you spoke of gluttony as a means of catching souls, in your last letter, only shows your ignorance. One of the great achievements of the last hundred years has been to deaden the human conscience on that subject, so that by now you will hardly find a sermon preached or a conscience troubled about it in the whole length and breadth of Europe. This has largely been effected by concentrating all our efforts on gluttony of Delicacy, not gluttony of Excess. Your patient's mother, as I learn from the dossier and you might have learned from Glubose, is a good example. She would be astonished—one day, I hope, *will* be—to learn that her whole life is enslaved to this kind of sensuality, which is quite concealed from her by the fact that the quantities involved are small. But what do quantities matter, provided we can use a human belly and palate to produce querulousness, impatience, uncharitableness, and self-concern?

—from *The Screwtape Letters*

Profile of a Glutton: The Demure Little Smile

Screwtape profiles gluttony in action:

Glubose has this old woman well in hand. She is a positive terror to hostesses and servants. She is always turning from what has been offered her to say with a demure little sigh and a smile 'Oh please, please... *all* I want is a cup of tea, weak but not too weak, and the teeniest weeniest bit of really crisp toast.' You see? Because what she wants is smaller and less costly than what has been set before her, she never recognises as gluttony her determination to get what she wants, however troublesome it may be to others. At the very moment of indulging her appetite she believes that she is practising temperance. In a crowded restaurant she gives a little scream at the plate which some overworked waitress has set before her and says, 'Oh, that's far, far too much! Take it away and bring me about a quarter of it.' If challenged, she would say she was doing this to avoid waste; in reality she does it because the particular shade of delicacy to which we have enslaved her is offended by the sight of more food than she happens to want.

—from *The Screwtape Letters*

Profile of a Glutton: "All I Want..."

Screwtape continues his profile of gluttony in action:

The real value of the quiet, unobtrusive work which Glubose has been doing for years on this old woman can be gauged by the way in which her belly now dominates her whole life. The woman is in what may be called the 'All-I-want' state of mind. *All* she wants is a cup of tea properly made, or an egg properly boiled, or a slice of bread properly toasted. But she never finds any servant or any friend who can do these simple things 'properly'—because her 'properly' conceals an insatiable demand for the exact, and almost impossible, palatal pleasures which she imagines she remembers from the past; a past described by her as 'the days when you could get good servants' but known to us as the days when her senses were more easily pleased and she had pleasures of other kinds which made her less dependent on those of the table. Meanwhile, the daily disappointment produces daily ill temper: cooks give notice and friendships are cooled. If ever the Enemy introduces into her mind a faint suspicion that she is too interested in food, Glubose counters it by suggesting to her that she doesn't mind what she eats herself but 'does like to have things nice for her boy'. In fact, of course, her greed has been one of the chief sources of his domestic discomfort for many years.

—from *The Screwtape Letters*

1863 Albert James Lewis, father of C. S. Lewis, is born in Cork, County Cork, Ireland.

1908 Flora Hamilton Lewis (age forty-six) dies of cancer on her husband Albert's forty-fifth birthday, leaving two young sons, Warren, thirteen, and Jack, nine. During this year Albert Lewis's father and brother also die.

In the Know

Screwtape adds a new spin to gluttony:

Now your patient is his mother's son. While working your hardest, quite rightly, on other fronts, you must not neglect a little quiet infiltration in respect of gluttony. Being a male, he is not so likely to be caught by the '*All* I want' camouflage. Males are best turned into gluttons with the help of their vanity. They ought to be made to think themselves very knowing about food, to pique themselves on having found the only restaurant in the town where steaks are really 'properly' cooked. What begins as vanity can then be gradually turned into habit. But, however you approach it, the great thing is to bring him into the state in which the denial of any one indulgence—it matters not which, champagne or tea, *sole colbert* or cigarettes—'puts him out', for then his charity, justice, and obedience are all at your mercy.

—from *The Screwtape Letters*

Deadly Annoyances

Screwtape offers more advice on using daily annoyances to entrap a Patient:

It is, no doubt, impossible to prevent his praying for his mother, but we have means of rendering the prayers innocuous. Make sure that they are always very 'spiritual', that he is always concerned with the state of her soul and never with her rheumatism. Two advantages will follow. In the first place, his attention will be kept on what he regards as her sins, by which, with a little guidance from you, he can be induced to mean any of her actions which are inconvenient or irritating to himself. Thus you can keep rubbing the wounds of the day a little sorer even while he is on his knees; the operation is not at all difficult and you will find it very entertaining. In the second place, since his ideas about her soul will be very crude and often erroneous, he will, in some degree, be praying for an imaginary person, and it will be your task to make that imaginary person daily less and less like the real mother—the sharp-tongued old lady at the breakfast table. In time, you may get the cleavage so wide that no thought or feeling from his prayers for the imagined mother will ever flow over into his treatment of the real one. I have had patients of my own so well in hand that they could be turned at a moment's notice from impassioned prayer for a wife's or son's 'soul' to beating or insulting the real wife or son without a qualm.

—from *The Screwtape Letters*

Under the Same Roof

Screwtape offers more advice on the value of daily annoyances in trapping a Patient:

When two humans have lived together for many years it usually happens that each has tones of voice and expressions of face which are almost unendurably irritating to the other. Work on that. Bring fully into the consciousness of your patient that particular lift of his mother's eyebrows which he learned to dislike in the nursery, and let him think how much he dislikes it. Let him assume that she knows how annoying it is and does it to annoy—if you know your job he will not notice the immense improbability of the assumption. And, of course, never let him suspect that he has tones and looks which similarly annoy her. As he cannot see or hear himself, this is easily managed.

—from *The Screwtape Letters*

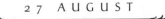

"All I Said..."

Screwtape's last advice on using daily annoyances to distract a Patient:

In civilised life domestic hatred usually expresses itself by saying things which would appear quite harmless on paper (the *words* are not offensive) but in such a voice, or at such a moment, that they are not far short of a blow in the face. To keep this game up you and Glubose must see to it that each of these two fools has a sort of double standard. Your patient must demand that all his own utterances are to be taken at their face value and judged simply on the actual words, while at the same time judging all his mother's utterances with the fullest and most over-sensitive interpretation of the tone and the context and the suspected intention. She must be encouraged to do the same to him. Hence from every quarrel they can both go away convinced, or very nearly convinced, that they are quite innocent. You know the kind of thing: 'I simply ask her what time dinner will be and she flies into a temper.' Once this habit is well established you have the delightful situation of a human saying things with the express purpose of offending and yet having a grievance when offence is taken.

—from *The Screwtape Letters*

I Believe in the Forgiveness of Sins

We say a great many things in church (and out of church too) without thinking of what we are saying. For instance, we say in the Creed "I believe in the forgiveness of sins." I had been saying it for several years before I asked myself why it was in the Creed. At first sight it seems hardly worth putting in. "If one is a Christian," I thought, "of course one believes in the forgiveness of sins. It goes without saying." But the people who compiled the Creed apparently thought that this was a part of our belief which we needed to be reminded of every time we went to church. And I have begun to see that, as far as I am concerned, they were right. To believe in the forgiveness of sins is not nearly so easy as I thought. Real belief in it is the sort of thing that very easily slips away if we don't keep on polishing it up.

We believe that God forgives us our sins; but also that He will not do so unless we forgive other people their sins against us. There is no doubt about the second part of this statement. It is in the Lord's Prayer; was emphatically stated by our Lord. If you don't forgive you will not be forgiven. No part of His teaching is clearer, and there are no exceptions to it. He doesn't say that we are to forgive other people's sins provided they are not too frightful, or provided there are extenuating circumstances, or anything of that sort. We are to forgive them all, however spiteful, however mean, however often they are repeated. If we don't, we shall be forgiven none of our own.

—from "On Forgiveness" *(The Weight of Glory)*

1947 Lewis writes "On Forgiveness" at the request of Father Patrick Kevin Irwin for inclusion in the parish magazine of the Church of St. Mary, Sawston, Cambridgeshire.

Forgiving Versus Excusing

I find that when I think I am asking God to forgive me I am often in reality (unless I watch myself very carefully) asking Him to do something quite different. I am asking Him not to forgive me but to excuse me. But there is all the difference in the world between forgiving and excusing. Forgiveness says "Yes, you have done this thing, but I accept your apology; I will never hold it against you and everything between us two will be exactly as it was before." But excusing says "I see that you couldn't help it or didn't mean it; you weren't really to blame." If one was not really to blame then there is nothing to forgive. In that sense forgiveness and excusing are almost opposites. Of course, in dozens of cases, either between God and man, or between one man and another, there may be a mixture of the two. Part of what seemed at first to be the sins turns out to be really nobody's fault and is excused; the bit that is left over is forgiven. .... But the trouble is that what we call "asking God's forgiveness" very often really consists in asking God to accept our excuses. What leads us into this mistake is the fact that there usually is some amount of excuse, some "extenuating circumstances." We are so very anxious to point these out to God (and to ourselves) that we are apt to forget the really important thing; that is, the bit left over, the bit which the excuses don't cover, the bit which is inexcusable but not, thank God, unforgivable. And if we forget this, we shall go away imagining that we have repented and been forgiven when all that has really happened is that we have satisfied ourselves with our own excuses. They may be very bad excuses; we are all too easily satisfied about ourselves.

—from "On Forgiveness" *(The Weight of Glory)*

1894 Albert James Lewis and Florence Augusta ("Flora") Hamilton are married at St. Mark's, Dundela, Belfast.

Two Remedies for Excuses

There are two remedies for this danger. One is to remember that God knows all the real excuses very much better than we do. If there are real "extenuating circumstances" there is no fear that He will overlook them. Often He must know many excuses that we have never thought of, and therefore humble souls will, after death, have the delightful surprise of discovering that on certain occasions they sinned much less than they had thought. All the real excusing He will do. What we have got to take to Him is the inexcusable bit, the sin. We are only wasting time by talking about all the parts which can (we think) be excused. When you go to a doctor you show him the bit of you that is wrong—say, a broken arm. It would be a mere waste of time to keep on explaining that your legs and eyes and throat are all right. You may be mistaken in thinking so, and anyway, if they are really all right, the doctor will know that.

The second remedy is really and truly to believe in the forgiveness of sins. A great deal of our anxiety to make excuses comes from not really believing in it, from thinking that God will not take us to Himself again unless He is satisfied that some sort of case can be made out in our favour. But that would not be forgiveness at all. Real forgiveness means looking steadily at the sin, the sin that is left over without any excuse, after all allowances have been made, and seeing it in all its horror, dirt, meanness, and malice, and nevertheless being wholly reconciled to the man who has done it. That, and only that, is forgiveness, and that we can always have from God if we ask for it.

—from "On Forgiveness" (*The Weight of Glory*)

As We Forgive Others

When it comes to a question of our forgiving other people, it is partly the same and partly different. It is the same because, here also, forgiving does not mean excusing. Many people seem to think it does. They think that if you ask them to forgive someone who has cheated or bullied them you are trying to make out that there was really no cheating or no bullying. But if that were so, there would be nothing to forgive. They keep on replying, "But I tell you the man broke a most solemn promise." Exactly: that is precisely what you have to forgive. (This doesn't mean that you must necessarily believe his next promise. It does mean that you must make every effort to kill every taste of resentment in your own heart—every wish to humiliate or hurt him or to pay him out.) The difference between this situation and the one in which you are asking God's forgiveness is this. In our own case we accept excuses too easily; in other people's we do not accept them easily enough.

—from "On Forgiveness" (*The Weight of Glory*)

SEPTEMBER

No Exceptions

As regards my own sins it is a safe bet (though not a certainty) that the excuses are not really so good as I think; as regards other men's sins against me it is a safe bet (though not a certainty) that the excuses are better than I think. One must therefore begin by attending to everything which may show that the other man was not so much to blame as we thought. But even if he is absolutely fully to blame we still have to forgive him; and even if ninety-nine per cent of his apparent guilt can be explained away by really good excuses, the problem of forgiveness begins with the one per cent of guilt which is left over. To excuse what can really produce good excuses is not Christian charity; it is only fairness. To be a Christian means to forgive the inexcusable, because God has forgiven the inexcusable in you.

This is hard. It is perhaps not so hard to forgive a single great injury. But to forgive the incessant provocations of daily life—to keep on forgiving the bossy mother-in-law, the bullying husband, the nagging wife, the selfish daughter, the deceitful son—how can we do it? Only, I think, by remembering where we stand, by meaning our words when we say in our prayers each night "forgive us our trespasses as we forgive those that trespass against us." We are offered forgiveness on no other terms. To refuse it is to refuse God's mercy for ourselves. There is no hint of exceptions and God means what He says.

—from "On Forgiveness" (*The Weight of Glory*)

September 1910 Lewis (age eleven) is enrolled at Campbell College, Belfast, for a period of four months.

September 1913 Warren begins private studies with his father's former teacher, William T. Kirkpatrick, in Great Bookham, Surrey.

Past, Present, and Future

Screwtape strategizes with Wormwood, using Time as a weapon:

I had noticed, of course, that the humans were having a lull in their European war—what they naïvely call *'The War'!*—and am not surprised that there is a corresponding lull in the patient's anxieties. Do we want to encourage this, or to keep him worried? Tortured fear and stupid confidence are both desirable states of mind. Our choice between them raises important questions.

The humans live in time but our Enemy destines them to eternity. He therefore, I believe, wants them to attend chiefly to two things, to eternity itself, and to that point of time which they call the Present. For the Present is the point at which time touches eternity. Of the present moment, and of it only, humans have an experience analogous to the experience which our Enemy has of reality as a whole; in it alone freedom and actuality are offered them. He would therefore have them continually concerned either with eternity (which means being concerned with Him) or with the Present—either meditating on their eternal union with, or separation from, Himself, or else obeying the present voice of conscience, bearing the present cross, receiving the present grace, giving thanks for the present pleasure.

—from *The Screwtape Letters*

1939 The first children evacuated from war-time London arrive at The Kilns.

1973 J. R. R. Tolkien, Lewis's lifelong friend, colleague, and fellow Inkling, dies at age eighty-one.

Life on the Edge of a Precipice

War creates no absolutely new situation; it simply aggravates the permanent human situation so that we can no longer ignore it. Human life has always been lived on the edge of a precipice. Human culture has always had to exist under the shadow of something infinitely more important than itself. If men had postponed the search for knowledge and beauty until they were secure, the search would never have begun. We are mistaken when we compare war with "normal life." Life has never been normal. Even those periods which we think most tranquil, like the nineteenth century, turn out, on closer inspection, to be full of crises, alarms, difficulties, emergencies. Plausible reasons have never been lacking for putting off all merely cultural activities until some imminent danger has been averted or some crying injustice put right. But humanity long ago chose to neglect those plausible reasons. They wanted knowledge and beauty now, and would not wait for the suitable moment that never comes. Periclean Athens leaves us not only the Parthenon but, significantly, the Funeral Oration. The insects have chosen a different line: they have sought first the material welfare and security of the hive, and presumably they have their reward. Men are different. They propound mathematical theorems in beleaguered cities, conduct metaphysical arguments in condemned cells, make jokes on scaffolds, discuss the last new poem while advancing to the walls of Quebec, and comb their hair at Thermopylae. This is not *panache;* it is our nature.

—from "Learning in War-Time" *(The Weight of Glory)*

1939 Britain and France declare war on Germany.

The Imaginary Claims of War and Religion

Before I became a Christian I do not think I fully realised that one's life, after conversion, would inevitably consist in doing most of the same things one had been doing before, one hopes, in a new spirit, but still the same things. Before I went to the last war I certainly expected that my life in the trenches would, in some mysterious sense, be all war. In fact, I found that the nearer you got to the front line the less everyone spoke and thought of the allied cause and the progress of the campaign; and I am pleased to find that Tolstoi, in the greatest war book ever written, records the same thing—and so, in its own way, does the *Iliad*. Neither conversion nor enlistment in the army is really going to obliterate our human life. Christians and soldiers are still men; the infidel's idea of a religious life and the civilian's idea of active service are fantastic. If you attempted, in either case, to suspend your whole intellectual and aesthetic activity, you would only succeed in substituting a worse cultural life for a better. You are not, in fact, going to read nothing, either in the Church or in the line: if you don't read good books, you will read bad ones. If you don't go on thinking rationally, you will think irrationally. If you reject aesthetic satisfactions, you will fall into sensual satisfactions.

There is therefore this analogy between the claims of our religion and the claims of the war: neither of them, for most of us, will simply cancel or remove from the slate the merely human life which we were leading before we entered them.

—from "Learning in War-Time" *(The Weight of Glory)*

The Claims of War: Render unto Caesar

The war will fail to absorb our whole attention because it is a finite object and, therefore, intrinsically unfitted to support the whole attention of a human soul. In order to avoid misunderstanding I must here make a few distinctions. I believe our cause to be, as human causes go, very righteous, and I therefore believe it to be a duty to participate in this war. And every duty is a religious duty, and our obligation to perform every duty is therefore absolute. Thus we may have a duty to rescue a drowning man and, perhaps, if we live on a dangerous coast, to learn lifesaving so as to be ready for any drowning man when he turns up. It may be our duty to lose our own lives in saving him. But if anyone devoted himself to lifesaving in the sense of giving it his total attention—so that he thought and spoke of nothing else and demanded the cessation of all other human activities until everyone had learned to swim—he would be a monomaniac. The rescue of drowning men is, then, a duty worth dying for, but not worth living for. It seems to me that all political duties (among which I include military duties) are of this kind. A man may have to die for our country, but no man must, in any exclusive sense, live for his country. He who surrenders himself without reservation to the temporal claims of a nation, or a party, or a class is rendering to Caesar that which, of all things, most emphatically belongs to God: himself.

—from "Learning in War-Time" (*The Weight of Glory*)

The Claims of Religion:
Do All to the Glory of God

It is for a very different reason that religion cannot occupy the whole of life in the sense of excluding all our natural activities. For, of course, in some sense, it must occupy the whole of life. There is no question of a compromise between the claims of God and the claims of culture, or politics, or anything else. God's claim is infinite and inexorable. You can refuse it, or you can begin to try to grant it. There is no middle way. Yet in spite of this it is clear that Christianity does not exclude any of the ordinary human activities. St. Paul tells people to get on with their jobs. He even assumes that Christians may go to dinner parties, and, what is more, dinner parties given by pagans. Our Lord attends a wedding and provides miraculous wine. Under the aegis of His Church, and in the most Christian ages, learning and the arts flourish. The solution of this paradox is, of course, well known to you. "Whether ye eat or drink or whatsoever ye do, do all to the glory of God."

All our merely natural activities will be accepted, if they are offered to God, even the humblest, and all of them, even the noblest, will be sinful if they are not. Christianity does not simply replace our natural life and substitute a new one; it is rather a new organisation which exploits, to its own supernatural ends, these natural materials.

—from "Learning in War-Time" *(The Weight of Glory)*

1954 *The Horse and His Boy* (the fifth book written in *The Chronicles of Narnia*) is published by Geoffrey Bles, London.

Learning as Vocation

A man's upbringing, his talents, his circumstances, are usually a tolerable index of his vocation. If our parents have sent us to Oxford, if our country allows us to remain there, this is *prima facie* evidence that the life which we, at any rate, can best lead to the glory of God at present is the learned life. By leading that life to the glory of God I do not, of course, mean any attempt to make our intellectual inquiries work out to edifying conclusions. That would be, as Bacon says, to offer to the author of truth the unclean sacrifice of a lie. I mean the pursuit of knowledge and beauty, in a sense, for their own sake, but in a sense which does not exclude their being for God's sake. An appetite for these things exists in the human mind, and God makes no appetite in vain. We can therefore pursue knowledge as such, and beauty as such, in the sure confidence that by so doing we are either advancing to the vision of God ourselves or indirectly helping others to do so. Humility, no less than the appetite, encourages us to concentrate simply on the knowledge or the beauty, not too much concerning ourselves with their ultimate relevance to the vision of God. That relevance may not be intended for us but for our betters—for men who come after and find the spiritual significance of what we dug out in blind and humble obedience to our vocation. .... The intellectual life is not the only road to God, nor the safest, but we find it to be a road, and it may be the appointed road for us.

—from "Learning in War-Time" *(The Weight of Glory)*

1953 *The Silver Chair* (the fourth book written in *The Chronicles of Narnia*) is published by Geoffrey Bles, London.

Learning as a Necessary Weapon

If all the world were Christian, it might not matter if all the world were uneducated. But, as it is, a cultural life will exist outside the Church whether it exists inside or not. To be ignorant and simple now—not to be able to meet the enemies on their own ground—would be to throw down our weapons, and to betray our uneducated brethren who have, under God, no defence but us against the intellectual attacks of the heathen. Good philosophy must exist, if for no other reason, because bad philosophy needs to be answered. The cool intellect must work not only against cool intellect on the other side, but against the muddy heathen mysticisms which deny intellect altogether. Most of all, perhaps, we need intimate knowledge of the past. Not that the past has any magic about it, but because we cannot study the future, and yet need something to set against the present, to remind us that the basic assumptions have been quite different in different periods and that much which seems certain to the uneducated is merely temporary fashion. A man who has lived in many places is not likely to be deceived by the local errors of his native village; the scholar has lived in many times and is therefore in some degree immune from the great cataract of nonsense that pours from the press and the microphone of his own age.

—from "Learning in War-Time" *(The Weight of Glory)*

1947 Lewis appears on the cover of *Time* magazine, with the caption "Oxford's C. S. Lewis, His Heresy: Christianity"

1958 *Reflections on the Psalms* is published by Geoffrey Bles, London.

What Is Charity?

'Charity' now means simply what used to be called 'alms'—that is, giving to the poor. Originally it had a much wider meaning. (You can see how it got the modern sense. If a man has 'charity', giving to the poor is one of the most obvious things he does, and so people came to talk as if that were the whole of charity. In the same way, 'rhyme' is the most obvious thing about poetry, and so people come to mean by 'poetry' simply rhyme and nothing more.) Charity means 'Love, in the Christian sense'. But love, in the Christian sense, does not mean an emotion. It is a state not of the feelings but of the will; that state of the will which we have naturally about ourselves, and must learn to have about other people.

—from *Mere Christianity*

1960 *Studies in Words* is published by Cambridge University Press.

The Rule of Love

The rule for all of us is perfectly simple. Do not waste time bothering whether you 'love' your neighbour; act as if you did. As soon as we do this we find one of the great secrets. When you are behaving as if you loved someone, you will presently come to love him. If you injure someone you dislike, you will find yourself disliking him more. If you do him a good turn, you will find yourself disliking him less. There is, indeed, one exception. If you do him a good turn, not to please God and obey the law of charity, but to show him what a fine forgiving chap you are, and to put him in your debt, and then sit down to wait for his 'gratitude', you will probably be disappointed. (People are not fools: they have a very quick eye for anything like showing off, or patronage.) But whenever we do good to another self, just because it is a self, made (like us) by God, and desiring its own happiness as we desire ours, we shall have learned to love it a little more or, at least, to dislike it less.

—from *Mere Christianity*

1905 George MacDonald, whose writings greatly influenced Lewis, dies at age eighty.

1956 *Till We Have Faces: A Myth Retold* is published by Geoffrey Bles, London.

Compound Interest

Though Christian charity sounds a very cold thing to people whose heads are full of sentimentality, and though it is quite distinct from affection, yet it leads to affection. The difference between a Christian and a worldly man is not that the worldly man has only affections or 'likings' and the Christian has only 'charity'. The worldly man treats certain people kindly because he 'likes' them: the Christian, trying to treat every one kindly, finds himself liking more and more people as he goes on—including people he could not even have imagined himself liking at the beginning.

This same spiritual law works terribly in the opposite direction. The Germans, perhaps, at first ill-treated the Jews because they hated them: afterwards they hated them much more because they had ill-treated them. The more cruel you are, the more you will hate; and the more you hate, the more cruel you will become—and so on in a vicious circle for ever.

Good and evil both increase at compound interest. That is why the little decisions you and I make every day are of such infinite importance. The smallest good act today is the capture of a strategic point from which, a few months later, you may be able to go on to victories you never dreamed of. An apparently trivial indulgence in lust or anger today is the loss of a ridge or railway line or bridgehead from which the enemy may launch an attack otherwise impossible.

—from *Mere Christianity*

No Manufactured Feelings

Some writers use the word charity to describe not only Christian love between human beings, but also God's love for man and man's love for God. About the second of these two, people are often worried. They are told they ought to love God. They cannot find any such feeling in themselves. What are they to do? The answer is the same as before. Act as if you did. Do not sit trying to manufacture feelings. Ask yourself, 'If I were sure that I loved God, what would I do?' When you have found the answer, go and do it.

On the whole, God's love for us is a much safer subject to think about than our love for Him. Nobody can always have devout feelings: and even if we could, feelings are not what God principally cares about. Christian Love, either towards God or towards man, is an affair of the will. If we are trying to do His will we are obeying the commandment, 'Thou shalt love the Lord thy God.' He will give us feelings of love if He pleases. We cannot create them for ourselves, and we must not demand them as a right. But the great thing to remember is that, though our feelings come and go, His love for us does not. It is not wearied by our sins, or our indifference; and, therefore, it is quite relentless in its determination that we shall be cured of those sins, at whatever cost to us, at whatever cost to Him.

—from *Mere Christianity*

On Giving

In the passage where the New Testament says that every one must work, it gives as a reason 'in order that he may have something to give to those in need'. Charity—giving to the poor—is an essential part of Christian morality: in the frightening parable of the sheep and the goats it seems to be the point on which everything turns. Some people nowadays say that charity ought to be unnecessary and that instead of giving to the poor we ought to be producing a society in which there were no poor to give to. They may be quite right in saying that we ought to produce this kind of society. But if anyone thinks that, as a consequence, you can stop giving in the meantime, then he has parted company with all Christian morality. I do not believe one can settle how much we ought to give. I am afraid the only safe rule is to give more than we can spare. In other words, if our expenditure on comforts, luxuries, amusements, etc., is up to the standard common among those with the same income as our own, we are probably giving away too little. If our charities do not at all pinch or hamper us, I should say they are too small. There ought to be things we should like to do and cannot do because our charities expenditure excludes them. I am speaking now of 'charities' in the common way. Particular cases of distress among your own relatives, friends, neighbours or employees, which God, as it were, forces upon your notice, may demand much more: even to the crippling and endangering of your own position. For many of us the great obstacle to charity lies not in our luxurious living or desire for more money, but in our fear—fear of insecurity. This must often be recognised as a temptation. Sometimes our pride also hinders our charity; we are tempted to spend more than we ought on the showy forms of generosity (tipping, hospitality) and less than we ought on those who really need our help.
—from *Mere Christianity*

Is It Really Kindness?

For about a hundred years we have so concentrated on one of the virtues—'kindness' or mercy—that most of us do not feel anything except kindness to be really good or anything but cruelty to be really bad. Such lopsided ethical developments are not uncommon, and other ages too have had their pet virtues and curious insensibilities. And if one virtue must be cultivated at the expense of all the rest, none has a higher claim than mercy—for every Christian must reject with detestation that covert propaganda for cruelty which tries to drive mercy out of the world by calling it names such as 'Humanitarianism' and 'Sentimentality'. The real trouble is that 'kindness' is a quality fatally easy to attribute to ourselves on quite inadequate grounds. Everyone *feels* benevolent if nothing happens to be annoying him at the moment. Thus a man easily comes to console himself for all his other vices by a conviction that 'his heart's in the right place' and 'he wouldn't hurt a fly', though in fact he has never made the slightest sacrifice for a fellow creature. We think we are kind when we are only happy: it is not so easy, on the same grounds, to imagine oneself temperate, chaste, or humble.

—from *The Problem of Pain*

Wise as Serpents

Prudence means practical common sense, taking the trouble to think out what you are doing and what is likely to come of it. Nowadays most people hardly think of Prudence as one of the 'virtues'. In fact, because Christ said we could only get into His world by being like children, many Christians have the idea that, provided you are 'good', it does not matter being a fool. But that is a misunderstanding. In the first place, most children show plenty of 'prudence' about doing the things they are really interested in, and think them out quite sensibly. In the second place, as St Paul points out, Christ never meant that we were to remain children in *intelligence:* on the contrary. He told us to be not only 'as harmless as doves', but also 'as wise as serpents'. He wants a child's heart, but a grown-up's head. He wants us to be simple, single-minded, affectionate, and teachable, as good children are; but He also wants every bit of intelligence we have to be alert at its job, and in first-class fighting trim. The fact that you are giving money to a charity does not mean that you need not try to find out whether that charity is a fraud or not. The fact that what you are thinking about is God Himself (for example, when you are praying) does not mean that you can be content with the same babyish ideas which you had when you were a five-year-old. It is, of course, quite true that God will not love you any the less, or have less use for you, if you happen to have been born with a very second-rate brain. He has room for people with very little sense, but He wants every one to use what sense they have.

—from *Mere Christianity*

1952 *The Voyage of the "Dawn Treader"* (the third volume written in *The Chronicles of Narnia*) is published by Geoffrey Bles, London.

Not Just About Falling Down

Temperance is, unfortunately, one of those words that has changed its meaning. It now usually means teetotalism. But in the days when the second Cardinal virtue was christened 'Temperance', it meant nothing of the sort. Temperance referred not specially to drink, but to all pleasures; and it meant not abstaining, but going the right length and no further. It is a mistake to think that Christians ought all to be teetotallers; Mohammedanism, not Christianity, is the teetotal religion. Of course it may be the duty of a particular Christian, or of any Christian, at a particular time, to abstain from strong drink, either because he is the sort of man who cannot drink at all without drinking too much, or because he is with people who are inclined to drunkenness and must not encourage them by drinking himself. But the whole point is that he is abstaining, for a good reason, from something which he does not condemn and which he likes to see other people enjoying. One of the marks of a certain type of bad man is that he cannot give up a thing himself without wanting every one else to give it up. That is not the Christian way. . . . .

One great piece of mischief has been done by the modern restriction of the word Temperance to the question of drink. It helps people to forget that you can be just as intemperate about lots of other things. A man who makes his golf or his motor-bicycle the centre of his life, or a woman who devotes all her thoughts to clothes or bridge or her dog, is being just as 'intemperate' as someone who gets drunk every evening. Of course, it does not show on the outside so easily: bridge-mania or golf-mania do not make you fall down in the middle of the road. But God is not deceived by externals.

—from *Mere Christianity*

1954 *English Literature in the Sixteenth Century Excluding Drama* is published by Clarendon Press, Oxford.

When Worlds Collide

The word Faith seems to be used by Christians in two senses. .... In the first sense it means simply Belief—accepting or regarding as true the doctrines of Christianity. That is fairly simple. But what does puzzle people—at least it used to puzzle me—is the fact that Christians regard faith in this sense as a virtue. I used to ask how on earth it can be a virtue—what is there moral or immoral about believing or not believing a set of statements? Obviously, I used to say, a sane man accepts or rejects any statement, not because he wants to or does not want to, but because the evidence seems to him good or bad. ....

Well, I think I still take that view. But what I did not see then—and a good many people do not see still—was this. I was assuming that if the human mind once accepts a thing as true it will automatically go on regarding it as true, until some real reason for reconsidering it turns up. In fact, I was assuming that the human mind is completely ruled by reason. But that is not so. For example, my reason is perfectly convinced by good evidence that anaesthetics do not smother me and that properly trained surgeons do not start operating until I am unconscious. But that does not alter the fact that when they have me down on the table and clap their horrible mask over my face, a mere childish panic begins inside me. I start thinking I am going to choke, and I am afraid they will start cutting me up before I am properly under. In other words, I lose my faith in anaesthetics. It is not reason that is taking away my faith: on the contrary, my faith is based on reason. It is my imagination and emotions. The battle is between faith and reason on one side and emotion and imagination on the other.

—from *Mere Christianity*

Faith in Training

Now Faith, in the sense in which I am here using the word, is the art of holding on to things your reason has once accepted, in spite of your changing moods. For moods will change, whatever view your reason takes. I know that by experience. Now that I am a Christian I do have moods in which the whole thing looks very improbable: but when I was an atheist I had moods in which Christianity looked terribly probable. This rebellion of your moods against your real self is going to come anyway. That is why Faith is such a necessary virtue: unless you teach your moods 'where they get off', you can never be either a sound Christian or even a sound atheist, but just a creature dithering to and fro, with its beliefs really dependent on the weather and the state of its digestion. Consequently one must train the habit of Faith.

The first step is to recognise the fact that your moods change. The next is to make sure that, if you have once accepted Christianity, then some of its main doctrines shall be deliberately held before your mind for some time every day. That is why daily prayers and religious readings and churchgoing are necessary parts of the Christian life. We have to be continually reminded of what we believe. Neither this belief nor any other will automatically remain alive in the mind. It must be fed. And as a matter of fact, if you examined a hundred people who had lost their faith in Christianity, I wonder how many of them would turn out to have been reasoned out of it by honest argument? Do not most people simply drift away?

—from *Mere Christianity*

1908 Lewis (age nine) is enrolled at Wynyard School, Watford, England.

1913 Lewis (age fourteen) is enrolled at Malvern College with scholarship.

Real Temptation

You may remember I said that the first step towards humility was to realise that one is proud. I want to add now that the next step is to make some serious attempt to practise the Christian virtues. A week is not enough. Things often go swimmingly for the first week. Try six weeks. By that time, having, as far as one can see, fallen back completely or even fallen lower than the point one began from, one will have discovered some truths about oneself. No man knows how bad he is till he has tried very hard to be good. A silly idea is current that good people do not know what temptation means. This is an obvious lie. Only those who try to resist temptation know how strong it is. After all, you find out the strength of the German army by fighting against it, not by giving in. You find out the strength of a wind by trying to walk against it, not by lying down. A man who gives in to temptation after five minutes simply does not know what it would have been like an hour later. That is why bad people, in one sense, know very little about badness. They have lived a sheltered life by always giving in. We never find out the strength of the evil impulse inside us until we try to fight it: and Christ, because He was the only man who never yielded to temptation, is also the only man who knows to the full what temptation means—the only complete realist.

—from *Mere Christianity*

1914 Lewis (age fifteen) is sent to William T. Kirkpatrick at Great Bookham, Surrey, to be tutored by him until March 1917. Kirkpatrick becomes the most influential teacher in Lewis's education.

1955 *Surprised by Joy: The Shape of My Early Life* is published by Geoffrey Bles, London.

Not Really So Bad

Screwtape offers more techniques for confusing the Patient:

I have been writing hitherto on the assumption that the people in the next pew afford no *rational* ground for disappointment. Of course if they do—if the patient knows that the woman with the absurd hat is a fanatical bridge-player or the man with squeaky boots a miser and an extortioner—then your task is so much the easier. All you then have to do is to keep out of his mind the question 'If I, being what I am, can consider that I am in some sense a Christian, why should the different vices of those people in the next pew prove that their religion is mere hypocrisy and convention?' You may ask whether it is possible to keep such an obvious thought from occurring even to a human mind. It is, Wormwood, it is! Handle him properly and it simply won't come into his head. He has not been anything like long enough with the Enemy to have any real humility yet. What he says, even on his knees, about his own sinfulness is all parrot talk. At bottom, he still believes he has run up a very favourable credit-balance in the Enemy's ledger by allowing himself to be converted, and thinks that he is showing great humility and condescension in going to church with these 'smug', commonplace neighbours at all. Keep him in that state of mind as long as you can.

—from *The Screwtape Letters*

1926 *Dymer* is published by J. M. Dent, London, under the pseudonym of Clive Hamilton.

1942 Lewis delivers the first of nine talks on "Christian Behavior" over BBC. These talks are later expanded and become Book 3 of *Mere Christianity*.

Lessons from Practising Christian Virtues

The main thing we learn from a serious attempt to practise the Christian virtues is that we fail. If there was any idea that God had set us a sort of exam. and that we might get good marks by deserving them, that has to be wiped out. If there was any idea of a sort of bargain—any idea that we could perform our side of the contract and thus put God in our debt so that it was up to Him, in mere justice, to perform His side—that has to be wiped out.

I think every one who has some vague belief in God, until he becomes a Christian, has the idea of an exam. or of a bargain in his mind. The first result of real Christianity is to blow that idea into bits. When they find it blown into bits, some people think this means that Christianity is a failure and give up. They seem to imagine that God is very simple-minded. In fact, of course, He knows all about this. One of the very things Christianity was designed to do was to blow this idea to bits. God has been waiting for the moment at which you discover that there is no question of earning a pass mark in this exam. or putting Him in your debt.

Then comes another discovery. Every faculty you have, your power of thinking or of moving your limbs from moment to moment, is given you by God. If you devoted every moment of your whole life exclusively to His service you could not give Him anything that was not in a sense His own already. So that when we talk of a man doing anything for God or giving anything to God, I will tell you what it is really like. It is like a small child going to its father and saying, 'Daddy, give me sixpence to buy you a birthday present.' Of course, the father does, and he is pleased with the child's present. It is all very nice and proper, but only an idiot would think that the father is sixpence to the good on the transaction.

—from *Mere Christianity*

Like the Spokes of a Wheel

What God cares about is not exactly our actions. What he cares about is that we should be creatures of a certain kind or quality—the kind of creatures He intended us to be—creatures related to Himself in a certain way. I do not add 'and related to one another in a certain way', because that is included: if you are right with Him you will inevitably be right with all your fellow-creatures, just as if all the spokes of a wheel are fitted rightly into the hub and the rim they are bound to be in the right positions to one another. And as long as a man is thinking of God as an examiner who has set him a sort of paper to do, or as the opposite party in a sort of bargain—as long as he is thinking of claims and counter-claims between himself and God—he is not yet in the right relation to Him. He is misunderstanding what he is and what God is. And he cannot get into the right relation until he has discovered the fact of our bankruptcy.

When I say 'discovered', I mean really discovered: not simply said it parrot-fashion. Of course, any child, if given a certain kind of religious education, will soon learn to say that we have nothing to offer to God that is not already His own and that we find ourselves failing to offer even that without keeping something back. But I am talking of really discovering this: really finding out by experience that it is true.

—from *Mere Christianity*

Leaving It to God

Now we cannot .... discover our failure to keep God's law except by trying our very hardest (and then failing). Unless we really try, whatever we say there will always be at the back of our minds the idea that if we try harder next time we shall succeed in being completely good. Thus, in one sense, the road back to God is a road of moral effort, of trying harder and harder. But in another sense it is not trying that is ever going to bring us home. All this trying leads up to the vital moment at which you turn to God and say, 'You must do this. I can't.' Do not, I implore you, start asking yourselves, 'Have I reached that moment?' Do not sit down and start watching your own mind to see if it is coming along. That puts a man quite on the wrong track. When the most important things in our life happen we quite often do not know, at the moment, what is going on. A man does not always say to himself, 'Hullo! I'm growing up.' It is often only when he looks back that he realises what has happened and recognises it as what people call 'growing up'. You can see it even in simple matters. A man who starts anxiously watching to see whether he is going to sleep is very likely to remain wide awake. As well, the thing I am talking of now may not happen to every one in a sudden flash—as it did to St Paul or Bunyan: it may be so gradual that no one could ever point to a particular hour or even a particular year. And what matters is the nature of the change in itself, not how we feel while it is happening. It is the change from being confident about our own efforts to the state in which we despair of doing anything for ourselves and leave it to God.

—from *Mere Christianity*

1938 *Out of the Silent Planet* (the first volume of his Lewis's *Space Trilogy*) is published by The Bodley Head, London.

A First Faint Gleam of Heaven

I know the words 'leave it to God' can be misunderstood, but they must stay for the moment. The sense in which a Christian leaves it to God is that he puts all his trust in Christ: trusts that Christ will some-how share with him the perfect human obedience which He carried out from His birth to His crucifixion: that Christ will make the man more like Himself and, in a sense, make good his deficiencies. In Christian language, He will share His 'sonship' with us, will make us, like Himself, 'Sons of God'. . . . . If you like to put it that way, Christ offers something for nothing: He even offers everything for nothing. In a sense, the whole Christian life consists in accepting that very remarkable offer. But the difficulty is to reach the point of recognising that all we have done and can do is nothing. What we should have liked would be for God to count our good points and ignore our bad ones. Again, in a sense, you may say that no temptation is ever over-come until we stop trying to overcome it—throw up the sponge. But then you could not 'stop trying' in the right way and for the right rea-son until you had tried your very hardest. And, in yet another sense, handing everything over to Christ does not, of course, mean that you stop trying. To trust Him means, of course, trying to do all that He says. There would be no sense in saying you trusted a person if you would not take his advice. Thus if you have really handed yourself over to Him, it must follow that you are trying to obey Him. But trying in a new way, a less worried way. Not doing these things in order to be saved, but because He has begun to save you already. Not hoping to get to Heaven as a reward for your actions, but inevitably wanting to act in a certain way because a first faint gleam of Heaven is already inside you.

—from *Mere Christianity*

1952 Lewis meets Joy Gresham for the first time, over lunch at the Eastgate Hotel, Oxford.

Faith or Works

Christians have often disputed as to whether what leads the Christian home is good actions, or Faith in Christ. I have no right really to speak on such a difficult question, but it does seem to me like asking which blade in a pair of scissors is most necessary. A serious moral effort is the only thing that will bring you to the point where you throw up the sponge. Faith in Christ is the only thing to save you from despair at that point: and out of that Faith in Him good actions must inevitably come. There are two parodies of the truth which different sets of Christians have, in the past, been accused by other Christians of believing: perhaps they may make the truth clearer. One set were accused of saying, 'Good actions are all that matters. The best good action is charity. The best kind of charity is giving money. The best thing to give money to is the Church. So hand us over £10,000 and we will see you through.' The answer to that nonsense, of course, would be that good actions done for that motive, done with the idea that Heaven can be bought, would not be good actions at all, but only commercial speculations. The other set were accused of saying, 'Faith is all that matters. Consequently, if you have faith, it doesn't matter what you do. Sin away, my lad, and have a good time and Christ will see that it makes no difference in the end.' The answer to that nonsense is that, if what you call your 'faith' in Christ does not involve taking the slightest notice of what He says, then it is not Faith at all—not faith or trust in Him, but only intellectual acceptance of some theory about Him.

—from *Mere Christianity*

1929 Lewis's father, Albert, dies at age sixty-six.

God in Tandem

The Bible really seems to clinch the matter when it puts the two things together into one amazing sentence. The first half is, 'Work out your own salvation with fear and trembling'—which looks as if everything depended on us and our good actions: but the second half goes on, 'For it is God who worketh in you'—which looks as if God did everything and we nothing. I am afraid that is the sort of thing we come up against in Christianity. I am puzzled, but I am not surprised. You see, we are now trying to understand, and to separate into water-tight compartments, what exactly God does and what man does when God and man are working together. And, of course, we begin by thinking it is like two men working together, so that you could say, 'He did this bit and I did that.' But this way of thinking breaks down. God is not like that. He is inside you as well as outside: even if we could understand who did what, I do not think human language could properly express it. In the attempt to express it different Churches say different things. But you will find that even those who insist most strongly on the importance of good actions tell you you need Faith; and even those who insist most strongly on Faith tell you to do good actions.

—from *Mere Christianity*

Follow Thou Me

There are questions at issue between Christians to which I do not think we have been told the answer. There are some to which I may never know the answer: if I asked them, even in a better world, I might (for all I know) be answered as a far greater questioner was answered: 'What is that to thee? Follow thou Me.'

—from *Mere Christianity*, Preface

Fantasy Virtues

Screwtape offers a helpful image:

Think of your man as a series of concentric circles, his will being the innermost, his intellect coming next, and finally his fantasy. You can hardly hope, at once, to exclude from all the circles everything that smells of the Enemy: but you must keep on shoving all the virtues outward till they are finally located in the circle of fantasy, and all the desirable qualities inward into the Will. It is only in so far as they reach the Will and are there embodied in habits that the virtues are really fatal to us. (I don't, of course, mean what the patient mistakes for his Will, the conscious fume and fret of resolutions and clenched teeth, but the real centre, what the Enemy calls the Heart.) All sorts of virtues painted in the fantasy or approved by the intellect or even, in some measure, loved and admired, will not keep a man from Our Father's house: indeed they may make him more amusing when he gets there.

—from *The Screwtape Letters*

1931 Lewis returns to a belief "that Jesus Christ is the Son of God" while riding to Whipsnade Zoo in the sidecar of brother Warren's motorcycle.

Where Is God?

Lewis, grieving the death of his wife, Joy:

Meanwhile, where is God? This is one of the most disquieting symptoms. When you are happy, so happy that you have no sense of needing Him, so happy that you are tempted to feel His claims upon you as an interruption, if you remember yourself and turn to Him with gratitude and praise, you will be— or so it feels—welcomed with open arms. But go to Him when your need is desperate, when all other help is vain, and what do you find? A door slammed in your face, and a sound of bolting and double bolting on the inside. After that, silence. You may as well turn away. The longer you wait, the more emphatic the silence will become. There are no lights in the windows. It might be an empty house. Was it ever inhabited? It seemed so once. And that seeming was as strong as this. What can this mean? Why is He so present a commander in our time of prosperity and so very absent a help in time of trouble?

I tried to put some of these thoughts to C. this afternoon. He reminded me that the same thing seems to have happened to Christ: 'Why hast thou forsaken me?' I know. Does that make it easier to understand?

Not that I am (I think) in much danger of ceasing to believe in God. The real danger is of coming to believe such dreadful things about Him. The conclusion I dread is not 'So there's no God after all,' but 'So this is what God's really like. Deceive yourself no longer.'

—from *A Grief Observed*

1961 *A Grief Observed* is published by Faber and Faber, London, under the pseudonym N. W. Clerk.

At Peace

Lewis, grieving the death of his wife, Joy:

They tell me H. is happy now, they tell me she is at peace. What makes them so sure of this? I don't mean that I fear the worst of all. Nearly her last words were, 'I am at peace with God.' She had not always been. And she never lied. And she wasn't easily deceived, least of all, in her own favour. I don't mean that. But why are they so sure that all anguish ends with death? More than half the Christian world, and millions in the East, believe otherwise. How do they know she is 'at rest'? Why should the separation (if nothing else) which so agonizes the lover who is left behind be painless to the lover who departs?

'Because she is in God's hands.' But if so, she was in God's hands all the time, and I have seen what they did to her here. Do they suddenly become gentler to us the moment we are out of the body? And if so, why? If God's goodness is inconsistent with hurting us, then either God is not good or there is no God: for in the only life we know He hurts us beyond our worst fears and beyond all we can imagine. If it is consistent with hurting us, then He may hurt us after death as unendurably as before it.

Sometimes it is hard not to say, 'God forgive God.' Sometimes it is hard to say so much. But if our faith is true, He didn't. He crucified Him.

—from *A Grief Observed*

OCTOBER

Blurred Vision

Lewis, grieving the death of his wife, Joy:

Why has no one told me these things? How easily I might have misjudged another man in the same situation? I might have said, 'He's got over it. He's forgotten his wife,' when the truth was, 'He remembers her better *because* he has partly got over it.'

Such was the fact. And I believe I can make sense out of it. You can't see anything properly while your eyes are blurred with tears. You can't, in most things, get what you want if you want it too desperately: anyway, you can't get the best out of it. 'Now! Let's have a real good talk' reduces everyone to silence. 'I *must* get a good sleep tonight' ushers in hours of wakefulness. Delicious drinks are wasted on a really ravenous thirst. Is it similarly the very intensity of the longing that draws the iron curtain, that makes us feel we are staring into a vacuum when we think about our dead? 'Them as asks' (at any rate 'as asks too importunately') don't get. Perhaps can't.

And so, perhaps, with God. I have gradually been coming to feel that the door is no longer shut and bolted. Was it my own frantic need that slammed it in my face? The time when there is nothing at all in your soul except a cry for help may be just the time when God can't give it: you are like the drowning man who can't be helped because he clutches and grabs. Perhaps your own reiterated cries deafen you to the voice you hoped to hear.

—from *A Grief Observed*

October 1922 Lewis begins reading English Language and Literature at Oxford University.

October 1959 Joy Lewis's X rays show that her cancer has returned.

Mustn't Grumble

Lewis, grieving the death of his wife, Joy:

How far have I got? Just as far, I think, as a widower of another sort who would stop, leaning on his spade, and say in answer to our inquiry, 'Thank'ee. Mustn't grumble. I do miss her something dreadful. But they say these things are sent to try us.' We have come to the same point; he with his spade, and I, who am not now much good at digging, with my own instrument. But of course one must take 'sent to try us' the right way. God has not been trying an experiment on my faith or love in order to find out their quality. He knew it already. It was I who didn't. In this trial He makes us occupy the dock, the witness box, and the bench all at once. He always knew that my temple was a house of cards. His only way of making me realize the fact was to knock it down.

—from *A Grief Observed*

October 1961 Lewis is too ill to return to teaching.

The Great Iconoclast

Lewis, grieving the death of his wife, Joy:

It doesn't matter that all the photographs of H. are bad. It doesn't matter—not much—if my memory of her is imperfect. Images, whether on paper or in the mind, are not important for themselves. Merely links. Take a parallel from an infinitely higher sphere. Tomorrow morning a priest will give me a little round, thin, cold, tasteless wafer. Is it a disadvantage—is it not in some ways an advantage—that it can't pretend the least *resemblance* to that with which it unites me?

I need Christ, not something that resembles Him. I want H., not something that is like her. A really good photograph might become in the end a snare, a horror, and an obstacle.

Images, I must suppose, have their use or they would not have been so popular. (It makes little difference whether they are pictures and statues outside the mind or imaginative constructions within it.) To me, however, their danger is more obvious. Images of the Holy easily become holy images—sacrosanct. My idea of God is not a divine idea. It has to be shattered time after time. He shatters it Himself. He is the great iconoclast. Could we not almost say that this shattering is one of the marks of His presence? The Incarnation is the supreme example; it leaves all previous ideas of the Messiah in ruins. And most are 'offended' by the iconoclasm; and blessed are those who are not. But the same thing happens in our private prayers.

All reality is iconoclastic. The earthly beloved, even in this life, incessantly triumphs over your mere idea of her. And you want her to; you want her with all her resistances, all her faults, all her unexpectedness. That is, in her foursquare and independent reality. And this, not any image or memory, is what we are to love still, after she is dead.

—from *A Grief Observed*

A Chuckle in the Darkness

Lewis, grieving the death of his wife, Joy:

Can a mortal ask questions which God finds unanswerable? Quite easily, I should think. All nonsense questions are unanswerable. How many hours are there in a mile? Is yellow square or round? Probably half the questions we ask—half our great theological and metaphysical problems—are like that.

And now that I come to think of it, there's no practical problem before me at all. I know the two great commandments, and I'd better get on with them. Indeed, H.'s death has ended the practical problem. While she was alive I could, in practice, have put her before God; that is, could have done what she wanted instead of what He wanted; if there'd been a conflict. What's left is not a problem about anything I could *do*. It's all about weights of feelings and motives and that sort of thing. It's a problem I'm setting myself. I don't believe God set it me at all. . . . .

The mystical union on the one hand. The resurrection of the body, on the other. I can't reach the ghost of an image, a formula, or even a feeling, that combines them. But the reality, we are given to understand, does. Reality the iconoclast once more. Heaven will solve our problems, but not, I think, by showing us subtle reconciliations between all our apparently contradictory notions. The notions will all be knocked from under our feet. We shall see that there never was any problem.

And, more than once, that impression which I can't describe except by saying that it's like the sound of a chuckle in the darkness. The sense that some shattering and disarming simplicity is the real answer.

—from *A Grief Observed*

Reconciling Human Suffering
with a God Who Loves

The problem of reconciling human suffering with the existence of a God who loves, is only insoluble so long as we attach a trivial meaning to the word 'love', and look on things as if man were the centre of them. Man is not the centre. God does not exist for the sake of man. Man does not exist for his own sake. 'Thou hast created all things, and for thy pleasure they are and were created' [Revelation 4:11]. We were made not primarily that we may love God (though we were made for that too) but that God may love us, that we may become objects in which the Divine love may rest 'well pleased'. To ask that God's love should be content with us as we are is to ask that God should cease to be God: because He is what He is, His love must, in the nature of things, be impeded and repelled, by certain stains in our present character, and because He already loves us He must labour to make us lovable. We cannot even wish, in our better moments, that He could reconcile Himself to our present impurities—no more than the beggar maid could wish that King Cophetua should be content with her rags and dirt, or a dog, once having learned to love man, could wish that man were such as to tolerate in his house the snapping, verminous, polluting creature of the wild pack. What we would here and now call our 'happiness' is not the end God chiefly has in view: but when we are such as He can love without impediment, we shall in fact be happy.

—from *The Problem of Pain*

The Source of Pain

The possibility of pain is inherent in the very existence of a world where souls can meet. When souls become wicked they will certainly use this possibility to hurt one another; and this, perhaps, accounts for four-fifths of the sufferings of men. It is men, not God, who have produced racks, whips, prisons, slavery, guns, bayonets, and bombs; it is by human avarice or human stupidity, not by the churlishness of nature, that we have poverty and overwork. But there remains, none the less, much suffering which cannot thus be traced to ourselves. Even if all suffering were man-made, we should like to know the reason for the enormous permission to torture their fellows which God gives to the worst of men. To say.... that good, for such creatures as we now are, means primarily corrective or remedial good, is an incomplete answer. Not all medicine tastes nasty: or if it did, that is itself one of the unpleasant facts for which we should like to know the reason.

—from *The Problem of Pain*

Surrender

Now the proper good of a creature is to surrender itself to its Creator—to enact intellectually, volitionally, and emotionally, that relationship which is given in the mere fact of its being a creature. When it does so, it is good and happy. Lest we should think this a hardship, this kind of good begins on a level far above the creatures, for God Himself, as Son, from all eternity renders back to God as Father by filial obedience the being which the Father by paternal love eternally generates in the Son. This is the pattern which man was made to imitate—which Paradisal man did imitate—and wherever the will conferred by the Creator is thus perfectly offered back in delighted and delighting obedience by the creature, there, most undoubtedly, is Heaven, and there the Holy Ghost proceeds. In the world as we now know it, the problem is how to recover this self-surrender. We are not merely imperfect creatures who must be improved: we are, as Newman said, rebels who must lay down our arms.

The first answer, then, to the question why our cure should be painful, is that to render back the will which we have so long claimed for our own, is in itself, wherever and however it is done, a grievous pain. Even in Paradise I have supposed a minimal self-adherence to be overcome, though the overcoming, and the yielding, would there be rapturous. But to surrender a self-will inflamed and swollen with years of usurpation is a kind of death.

—from *The Problem of Pain*

The Rebellious Self

We all remember this self-will as it was in childhood: the bitter, prolonged rage at every thwarting, the burst of passionate tears, the black, Satanic wish to kill or die rather than to give in. Hence the older type of nurse or parent was quite right in thinking that the first step in education is 'to break the child's will'. Their methods were often wrong: but not to see the necessity is, I think, to cut oneself off from all understanding of spiritual laws. And if, now that we are grown up, we do not howl and stamp quite so much, that is partly because our elders began the process of breaking or killing our self-will in the nursery, and partly because the same passions now take more subtle forms and have grown clever at avoiding death by various 'compensations'. Hence the necessity to die daily: however often we think we have broken the rebellious self we shall still find it alive.

—from *The Problem of Pain*

1942 *A Preface to Paradise Lost* is published by Oxford University Press.

God's Megaphone

The human spirit will not even begin to try to surrender self-will as long as all seems to be well with it. Now error and sin both have this property, that the deeper they are the less their victim suspects their existence; they are masked evil. Pain is unmasked, unmistakable evil; every man knows that something is wrong when he is being hurt. .... And pain is not only immediately recognisable evil, but evil impossible to ignore. We can rest contentedly in our sins and in our stupidities; and anyone who has watched gluttons shovelling down the most exquisite foods as if they did not know what they were eating, will admit that we can ignore even pleasure. But pain insists upon being attended to. God whispers to us in our pleasures, speaks in our conscience, but shouts in our pain: it is His megaphone to rouse a deaf world.

—from *The Problem of Pain*

1944 *Beyond Personality* (later Book 4 of *Mere Christianity*) is published by Geoffrey Bles/The Centenary Press, London.

Clinging to Our Own Lives

If the first and lowest operation of pain shatters the illusion that all is well, the second shatters the illusion that what we have, whether good or bad in itself, is our own and enough for us. Everyone has noticed how hard it is to turn our thoughts to God when everything is going well with us. We 'have all we want' is a terrible saying when 'all' does not include God. We find God an interruption. As St Augustine says somewhere, 'God wants to give us something, but cannot, because our hands are full—there's nowhere for Him to put it.' Or as a friend of mine said, 'We regard God as an airman regards his parachute; it's there for emergencies but he hopes he'll never have to use it.' Now God, who has made us, knows what we are and that our happiness lies in Him. Yet we will not seek it in Him as long as he leaves us any other resort where it can even plausibly be looked for. While what we call 'our own life' remains agreeable we will not surrender it to Him. What then can God do in our interests but make 'our own life' less agreeable to us, and take away the plausible source of false happiness?

—from *The Problem of Pain*

Tender Words

It is just here, where God's providence seems at first to be most cruel, that the Divine humility, the stooping down of the Highest, most deserves praise. We are perplexed to see misfortune falling upon decent, inoffensive, worthy people—on capable, hard-working mothers of families or diligent, thrifty little tradespeople, on those who have worked so hard, and so honestly, for their modest stock of happiness and now seem to be entering on the enjoyment of it with the fullest right. How can I say with sufficient tenderness what here needs to be said? It does not matter that I know I must become, in the eyes of every hostile reader, as it were, personally responsible for all the sufferings I try to explain—just as, to this day, everyone talks as if St Augustine wanted unbaptised infants to go to Hell. But it matters enormously if I alienate anyone from the truth. Let me implore the reader to try to believe, if only for the moment, that God, who made these deserving people, may really be right when He thinks that their modest prosperity and the happiness of their children are not enough to make them blessed: that all this must fall from them in the end, and that if they have not learned to know Him they will be wretched. And therefore He troubles them, warning them in advance of an insufficiency that one day they will have to discover. The life to themselves and their families stands between them and the recognition of their need; He makes that life less sweet to them.

—from *The Problem of Pain*

1930 Lewis, his brother Warren, Mrs. Janie Moore, her daughter Maureen, and Mr. Papworth the dog move into their new home, The Kilns, near Oxford. This will be Lewis's home until his death.

Surrender in Obedience

But when we have said that God commands things only because they are good, we must add that one of the things intrinsically good is that rational creatures should freely surrender themselves to their Creator in obedience. The content of our obedience—the thing we are commanded to do—will always be something intrinsically good, something we ought to do even if (by an impossible supposition) God had not commanded it. But in addition to the content, the mere obeying is also intrinsically good, for, in obeying, a rational creature consciously enacts its creaturely role, reverses the act by which we fell, treads Adam's dance backward, and returns.

—from *The Problem of Pain*

Collaborators in Creation

If pain sometimes shatters the creature's false sufficiency, yet in supreme 'Trial' or 'Sacrifice' it teaches him the self-sufficiency which really ought to be his—the 'strength, which, if Heaven gave it, may be called his own': for then, in the absence of all merely natural motives and supports, he acts in that strength, and that alone, which God confers upon him through his subjected will. Human will becomes truly creative and truly our own when it is wholly God's, and this is one of the many senses in which he that loses his soul shall find it. In all other acts our will is fed through nature, that is, through created things other than the self—through the desires which our physical organism and our heredity supply to us. When we act from ourselves alone—that is, from God *in* ourselves—we are collaborators in, or live instruments of, creation: and that is why such an act undoes with 'backward mutters of disscvering power' the uncreative spell which Adam laid upon his species. Hence as suicide is the typical expression of the stoic spirit, and battle of the warrior spirit, martyrdom always remains the supreme enacting and perfection of Christianity. This great action has been initiated for us, done on our behalf, exemplified for our imitation, and inconceivably communicated to all believers, by Christ on Calvary. There the degree of accepted Death reaches the utmost bounds of the imaginable and perhaps goes beyond them; not only all natural supports, but the presence of the very Father to whom the sacrifice is made deserts the victim, and surrender to God does not falter though God 'forsakes' it.

—from *The Problem of Pain*

1961 *An Experiment in Criticism* is published by Cambridge University Press, Cambridge.

Don't Stone the Messenger

All arguments in justification of suffering provoke bitter resentment against the author. You would like know how I behave when I am experiencing pain, not writing books about it. You need not guess, for I will tell you; I am a great coward. But what is that to the purpose? When I think of pain—of anxiety that gnaws like fire and loneliness that spreads out like a desert, and the heartbreaking routine of monotonous misery, or again of dull aches that blacken our whole landscape or sudden nauseating pains that knock a man's heart out at one blow, of pains that seem already intolerable and then are suddenly increased, of infuriating scorpion-stinging pains that startle into maniacal movement a man who seemed half dead with his previous tortures—it 'quite o'ercrows my spirit'. If I knew any way of escape I would crawl through sewers to find it. But what is the good of telling you about my feelings? You know them already: they are the same as yours. I am not arguing that pain is not painful. Pain hurts. That is what the word means. I am only trying to show that the old Christian doctrine of being made 'perfect through suffering' [Hebrews 2:10] is not incredible. To prove it palatable is beyond my design.

—from *The Problem of Pain*

1924 Lewis gives his first lecture at the University of Oxford, on "The Good: Its Position Among Values."

One Man's Tale of Tribulation

My own experience is something like this. I am progressing along the path of life in my ordinary contentedly fallen and godless condition, absorbed in a merry meeting with my friends for the morrow or a bit of work that tickles my vanity today, a holiday or a new book, when suddenly a stab of abdominal pain that threatens serious disease, or a headline in the newspapers that threatens us all with destruction, sends this whole pack of cards tumbling down. At first I am overwhelmed, and all my little happinesses look like broken toys. Then, slowly and reluctantly, bit by bit, I try to bring myself into the frame of mind that I should be in at all times. I remind myself that all these toys were never intended to possess my heart, that my true good is in another world and my only real treasure is Christ. And perhaps, by God's grace, I succeed, and for a day or two become a creature consciously dependent on God and drawing its strength from the right sources. But the moment the threat is withdrawn, my whole nature leaps back to the toys: I am even anxious, God forgive me, to banish from my mind the only thing that supported me under the threat because it is now associated with the misery of those few days. Thus the terrible necessity of tribulation is only too clear. God has had me for but forty-eight hours and then only by dint of taking everything else away from me. Let Him but sheathe that sword for a moment and I behave like a puppy when the hated bath is over—I shake myself as dry as I can and race off to reacquire my comfortable dirtiness, if not in the nearest manure heap, at least in the nearest flower bed. And that is why tribulations cannot cease until God either sees us remade or sees that our remaking is now hopeless.

—from *The Problem of Pain*

1951 *Prince Caspian* (the second volume written in *The Chronicles of Narnia*) is published by Geoffrey Bles, London.

The Products of Suffering

The tendency of this or that novelist or poet may represent suffering as wholly bad in its effects, as producing, and justifying, every kind of malice and brutality in the sufferer. And, of course, pain, like pleasure, can be so received: all that is given to a creature with free will must be two-edged, not by the nature of the giver or of the gift, but by the nature of the recipient. And, again, the evil results of pain can be multiplied if sufferers are persistently taught by the bystanders that such results are the proper and manly results for them to exhibit. Indignation at others' sufferings, though a generous passion, needs to be well managed lest it steal away patience and humanity from those who suffer and plant anger and cynicism in their stead. But I am not convinced that suffering, if spared such officious vicarious indignation, has any natural tendency to produce such evils. I did not find the front-line trenches or the C.C.S. [battlefield Casualty Clearing Stations] more full than any other place of hatred, selfishness, rebellion, and dishonesty. I have seen great beauty of spirit in some who were great sufferers. I have seen men, for the most part, grow better not worse with advancing years, and I have seen the last illness produce treasures of fortitude and meekness from most unpromising subjects. I see in loved and revered historical figures, such as Johnson and Cowper, traits which might scarcely have been tolerable if the men had been happier. If the world is indeed a 'vale of soul making' it seems on the whole to be doing its work.

—from *The Problem of Pain*

1950 *The Lion, the Witch and the Wardrobe* (the first volume written in *The Chronicles of Narnia*) is published by Geoffrey Bles, London.

To Produce the Complex Good

A merciful man aims at his neighbour's good and so does 'God's will', consciously co-operating with 'the simple good'. A cruel man oppresses his neighbour, and so does simple evil. But in doing such evil, he is used by God, without his own knowledge or consent, to produce the complex good—so that the first man serves God as a son, and the second as a tool. For you will certainly carry out God's purpose, however you act, but it makes a difference to you whether you serve like Judas or like John. The whole system is, so to speak, calculated for the clash between good men and bad men, and the good fruits of fortitude, patience, pity and forgiveness for which the cruel man is permitted to be cruel, presuppose that the good man ordinarily continues to seek simple good. I say 'ordinarily' because a man is sometimes entitled to hurt (or even, in my opinion, to kill) his fellow, but only where the necessity is urgent and the good to be attained obvious, and usually (though not always) when he who inflicts the pain has a definite authority to do so—a parent's authority derived from nature, a magistrate's or soldier's derived from civil society, or a surgeon's derived, most often, from the patient. To turn this into a general charter for afflicting humanity 'because affliction is good for them'....is not indeed to break the Divine scheme but to volunteer for the post of Satan within that scheme. If you do his work, you must be prepared for his wages.

—from *The Problem of Pain*

Some Pleasant Inns

The Christian doctrine of suffering explains, I believe, a very curious fact about the world we live in. The settled happiness and security which we all desire, God withholds from us by the very nature of the world: but joy, pleasure, and merriment, He has scattered broadcast. We are never safe, but we have plenty of fun, and some ecstasy. It is not hard to see why. The security we crave would teach us to rest our hearts in this world and oppose an obstacle to our return to God: a few moments of happy love, a landscape, a symphony, a merry meeting with our friends, a bathe or a football match, have no such tendency. Our Father refreshes us on the journey with some pleasant inns, but will not encourage us to mistake them for home.

—from *The Problem of Pain*

1940 *The Problem of Pain* is published by Centenary Press, London.

To Stop One Tooth from Aching

It may be asked whether, faint as the hope is of abolishing war by Pacifism, there is any other hope. But the question belongs to a mode of thought which I find quite alien to me. It consists in assuming that the great permanent miseries in human life must be curable if only we can find the right cure; and it then proceeds by elimination and concludes that whatever is left, however unlikely to prove a cure, must nevertheless do so. Hence the fanaticism of Marxists, Freudians, Eugenists, Spiritualists, Douglasites, Federal Unionists, Vegetarians, and all the rest. But I have received no assurance that anything we can do will eradicate suffering. I think the best results are obtained by people who work quietly away at limited objectives, such as the abolition of the slave trade, or prison reform, or factory acts, or tuberculosis, not by those who think they can achieve universal justice, or health, or peace. I think the art of life consists in tackling each immediate evil as well as we can. To avert or postpone one particular war by wise policy, or to render one particular campaign shorter by strength and skill or less terrible by mercy to the conquered and the civilians is more useful than all the proposals for universal peace that have ever been made; just as the dentist who can stop one toothache has deserved better of humanity than all the men who think they have some scheme for producing a perfectly healthy race.

—from "Why I Am Not a Pacifist" *(The Weight of Glory)*

1956 Joy Gresham Lewis is admitted to Wingfield-Morris Hospital with a broken femur, where she is subsequently diagnosed with multiple cancers.

Heaven Will Work Backwards

The Teacher explains Time:

'Son,' he said, 'ye cannot in your present state understand eternity: when Anodos looked through the door of the Timeless he brought no message back. But ye can get some likeness of it if ye say that both good and evil, when they are full grown, become retrospective. Not only this valley but all their earthly past will have been Heaven to those who are saved. Not only the twilight in that town, but all their life on Earth too, will then be seen by the damned to have been Hell. That is what mortals misunderstand. They say of some temporal suffering, "No future bliss can make up for it," not knowing that Heaven, once attained, will work backwards and turn even that agony into a glory. And of some sinful pleasure they say "Let me have but *this* and I'll take the consequences": little dreaming how damnation will spread back and back into their past and contaminate the pleasure of the sin. Both processes begin even before death. The good man's past begins to change so that his forgiven sins and remembered sorrows take on the quality of Heaven: the bad man's past already conforms to his badness and is filled only with dreariness. And that is why, at the end of all things, when the sun rises here and the twilight turns to blackness down there, the Blessed will say "We have never lived anywhere except in Heaven," and the Lost, "We were always in Hell." And both will speak truly.'

—from *The Great Divorce*

1949 The Inklings hold their last recorded Thursday night meeting in Lewis's rooms in Magdalen College. The Tuesday morning meetings in the back room at the Eagle and Child ("Bird and Baby") pub continue.

Present at the Creation of the World

Most of our prayers if fully analysed, ask either for a miracle or for events whose foundation will have to have been laid before I was born, indeed, laid when the universe began. But then to God (though not to me) I and the prayer I make in 1945 were just as much present at the creation of the world as they are now and will be a million years hence. God's creative act is timeless and timelessly adapted to the 'free' elements within it: but this timeless adaptation meets our consciousness as a sequence and prayer and answer.

—from *Miracles*

A Defence Against the Enemy of Excitement

The first enemy [of the scholar in war-time] is excitement—the tendency to think and feel about the war when we had intended to think about our work. The best defence is a recognition that in this, as in everything else, the war has not really raised up a new enemy but only aggravated an old one. There are always plenty of rivals to our work. We are always falling in love or quarrelling, looking for jobs or fearing to lose them, getting ill and recovering, following public affairs. If we let ourselves, we shall always be waiting for some distraction or other to end before we can really get down to our work. The only people who achieve much are those who want knowledge so badly that they seek it while the conditions are still unfavourable. Favourable conditions never come. There are, of course, moments when the pressure of the excitement is so great that only superhuman self-control could resist it. They come both in war and peace. We must do the best we can.

—from "Learning in War-Time" *(The Weight of Glory)*

1939 Lewis preaches "Learning in War-Time" at Evensong in Oxford University Church of St. Mary the Virgin.

A Defence Against the Enemy of Frustration

The second enemy [of the scholar in war-time] is frustration—the feeling that we shall not have time to finish. If I say to you that no one has time to finish, that the longest human life leaves a man, in any branch of learning, a beginner, I shall seem to you to be saying something quite academic and theoretical. You would be surprised if you knew how soon one begins to feel the shortness of the tether, of how many things, even in middle life, we have to say "No time for that," "Too late now," and "Not for me." But Nature herself forbids you to share that experience. A more Christian attitude, which can be attained at any age, is that of leaving futurity in God's hands. We may as well, for God will certainly retain it whether we leave it to Him or not. Never, in peace or war, commit your virtue or your happiness to the future. Happy work is best done by the man who takes his long-term plans somewhat lightly and works from moment to moment "as to the Lord." It is only our *daily* bread that we are encouraged to ask for. The present is the only time in which any duty can be done or any grace received.

—from "Learning in War-Time" *(The Weight of Glory)*

A Defence Against the Enemy of Fear

The third enemy [of the scholar in war-time] is fear. War threatens us with death and pain. No man—and specially no Christian who remembers Gethsemane—need try to attain a stoic indifference about these things, but we can guard against the illusions of the imagination. We think of the streets of Warsaw and contrast the deaths there suffered with an abstraction called Life. But there is no question of death or life for any of us, only a question of this death or of that—of a machine gun bullet now or a cancer forty years later. What does war do to death? It certainly does not make it more frequent; 100 percent of us die, and the percentage cannot be increased. It puts several deaths earlier, but I hardly suppose that that is what we fear. Certainly when the moment comes, it will make little difference how many years we have behind us. Does it increase our chances of a painful death? I doubt it. As far as I can find out, what we call natural death is usually preceded by suffering, and a battlefield is one of the very few places where one has a reasonable prospect of dying with no pain at all. Does it decrease our chances of dying at peace with God? I cannot believe it. If active service does not persuade a man to prepare for death, what conceivable concatenation of circumstances would? Yet war does do something to death. It forces us to remember it. The only reason why the cancer at sixty or the paralysis at seventy-five do not bother us is that we forget them.

—from "Learning in War-Time" *(The Weight of Glory)*

Death Is Real

War makes death real to us, and that would have been regarded as one of its blessings by most of the great Christians of the past. They thought it good for us to be always aware of our mortality. I am inclined to think they were right. All the animal life in us, all schemes of happiness that centred in this world, were always doomed to a final frustration. In ordinary times only a wise man can realise it. Now the stupidest of us knows. We see unmistakably the sort of universe in which we have all along been living, and must come to terms with it. If we had foolish un-Christian hopes about human culture, they are now shattered. If we thought we were building up a heaven on earth, if we looked for something that would turn the present world from a place of pilgrimage into a permanent city satisfying the soul of man, we are disillusioned, and not a moment too soon. But if we thought that for some souls, and at some times, the life of learning, humbly offered to God, was, in its own small way, one of the appointed approaches to the Divine reality and the Divine beauty which we hope to enjoy hereafter, we can think so still.

—from "Learning in War-Time" *(The Weight of Glory)*

How God Can Answer Prayer

Screwtape offers a short lesson on Time and Eternity:

But you must remember that he takes Time for an ultimate reality. He supposes that the Enemy, like himself, sees some things as present, remembers others as past, and anticipates others as future; or even if he believes that the Enemy does not see things that way, yet, in his heart of hearts, he regards this as a peculiarity of the Enemy's mode of perception—he doesn't really think (though he would say he did) that things as the Enemy sees them are things as they are! If you tried to explain to him that men's prayers today are one of the innumerable co-ordinates with which the Enemy harmonises the weather of tomorrow, he would reply that then the Enemy always knew men were going to make those prayers and, if so, they did not pray freely but were predestined to do so. And he would add that the weather on a given day can be traced back through its causes to the original creation of matter itself—so that the whole thing, both on the human and on the material side, is given 'from the word go'. What he ought to say, of course, is obvious to us; that the problem of adapting the particular weather to the particular prayers is merely the appearance, at two points in his temporal mode of perception, of the total problem of adapting the whole spiritual universe to the whole corporeal universe; that creation in its entirety operates at every point of space and time, or rather that their kind of consciousness forces them to encounter the whole, self-consistent creative act as a series of successive events. *Why* that creative act leaves room for their free will is the problem of problems, the secret behind the Enemy's nonsense about 'Love'. *How* it does so is no problem at all; for the Enemy does not *foresee* the humans making their free contributions in a future, but *sees* them doing so in His unbounded Now. And obviously to watch a man doing something is not to make him do it.

—from *The Screwtape Letters*

Time Reconsidered

I should like to deal with a difficulty that some people find about the whole idea of prayer. A man put it to me by saying 'I can believe in God all right, but what I cannot swallow is the idea of Him attending to several hundred million human beings who are all addressing Him at the same moment.' And I have found that quite a lot of people feel this.

Now, the first thing to notice is that the whole sting of it comes in the words *at the same moment.* Most of us can imagine God attending to any number of applicants if only they came one by one and He had an endless time to do it in. So what is really at the back of this difficulty is the idea of God having to fit too many things into one moment of time.

Well that is of course what happens to us. Our life comes to us moment by moment. One moment disappears before the next comes along: and there is room for very little in each. That is what Time is like. And of course you and I tend to take it for granted that this Time series—this arrangement of past, present and future—is not simply the way life comes to us but the way all things really exist. We tend to assume that the whole universe and God Himself are always moving on from past to future just as we do.

—from *Mere Christianity*

Our Contribution to the Cosmic Shape

When we are praying about the result, say, of a battle or a medical consultation the thought will often cross our minds that (if only we knew it) the event is already decided one way or the other. I believe this to be no good reason for ceasing our prayers. The event certainly has been decided—in a sense it was decided 'before all worlds'. But one of the things taken into account in deciding it, and therefore one of the things that really cause it to happen, may be this very prayer that we are now offering. Thus, shocking as it may sound, I conclude that we can at noon become part causes of an event occurring at ten a.m. (Some scientists would find this easier than popular thought does.) The imagination will, no doubt, try to play all sorts of tricks on us at this point. It will ask, 'Then if I stop praying can God go back and alter what has already happened?' No. The event has already happened and one of its causes has been the fact that you are asking such questions instead of praying. It will ask, 'Then if I begin to pray can God go back and alter what has already happened?' No. The event has already happened and one of its causes is your present prayer. Thus something does really depend on my choice. My free act contributes to the cosmic shape. That contribution is made in eternity or 'before all worlds'; but my consciousness of contributing reaches me at a particular point in the time-series.

—from *Miracles*

Not a Film Unrolling

We must not picture destiny as a film unrolling for the most part on its own, but in which our prayers are sometimes allowed to insert additional items. On the contrary; what the film displays to us as it unrolls already contains the results of our prayers and of all our other acts. There is no question *whether* an event has happened because of your prayer. When the event you prayed for occurs your prayer has always contributed to it. When the opposite event occurs your prayer has never been ignored; it has been considered and refused, for your ultimate good and the good of the whole universe. (For example, because it is better for you and for everyone else in the long run that other people, including wicked ones, should exercise free will than that you should be protected from cruelty or treachery by turning the human race into automata.) But this is, and must remain, a matter of faith. You will, I think, only deceive yourself by trying to find special evidence for it in some cases more than in others.

—from *Miracles*

Our Keenest Pleasure

Paradisal man always chose to follow God's will. In following it he also gratified his own desire, both because all the actions demanded of him were, in fact, agreeable to his blameless inclination, and also because the service of God was itself his keenest pleasure, without which as their razor edge all joys would have been insipid to him. The question 'Am I doing this for God's sake or only because I happen to like it?' did not then arise, since doing things for God's sake was what he chiefly 'happened to like'. His God-ward will rode his happiness like a well-managed horse, whereas our will, when we are happy, is carried away in the happiness as in a ship racing down a swift stream. Pleasure was then an acceptable offering to God because offering was a pleasure.

—from *The Problem of Pain*

On Enemy Ground

Screwtape twists the gift of pleasure:

Never forget that when we are dealing with any pleasure in its healthy and normal and satisfying form, we are, in a sense, on the Enemy's ground. I know we have won many a soul through pleasure. All the same, it is His invention, not ours. He made the pleasures: all our research so far has not enabled us to produce one. All we can do is to encourage the humans to take the pleasures which our Enemy has produced, at times, or in ways, or in degrees, which He has forbidden. Hence we always try to work away from the natural condition of any pleasure to that in which it is least natural, least redolent of its Maker, and least pleasurable. An ever increasing craving for an ever diminishing pleasure is the formula. It is more certain; and it's better *style*. To get the man's soul and give him *nothing* in return—that is what really gladdens Our Father's heart. And the troughs are the time for beginning the process.

—from *The Screwtape Letters*

NOVEMBER

Real Pleasure

When the Patient repents, Screwtape outlines Wormwood's blunders:

On your own showing you first of all allowed the patient to read a book he really enjoyed, because he enjoyed it and not in order to make clever remarks about it to his new friends. In the second place, you allowed him to walk down to the old mill and have tea there—a walk through country he really likes, and taken alone. In other words you allowed him two real positive Pleasures. Were you so ignorant as not to see the danger of this? The characteristic of Pains and Pleasures is that they are unmistakably real, and therefore, as far as they go, give the man who feels them a touchstone of reality. Thus if you had been trying to damn your man by the Romantic method—by making him a kind of Childe Harold or Werther submerged in self-pity for imaginary distresses—you would try to protect him at all costs from any real pain; because, of course, five minutes' genuine toothache would reveal the romantic sorrows for the nonsense they were and unmask your whole stratagem. But you were trying to damn your patient by the World, that is by palming off vanity, bustle, irony, and expensive tedium as pleasures. How can you have failed to see that a *real* pleasure was the last thing you ought to have let him meet? Didn't you foresee that it would just kill by contrast all the trumpery which you have been so laboriously teaching him to value? And that the sort of pleasure which the book and the walk gave him was the most dangerous of all? That it would peel off from his sensibility the kind of crust you have been forming on it, and make him feel that he was coming home, recovering himself? As a preliminary to detaching him from the Enemy, you wanted to detach him from himself, and had made some progress in doing so. Now, all that is undone.

—from *The Screwtape Letters*

Raw Material

Screwtape warns of the danger of permitting small personal pleasures:
The deepest likings and impulses of any man are the raw material, the starting-point, with which the Enemy has furnished him. To get him away from those is therefore always a point gained; even in things indifferent it is always desirable to substitute the standards of the World, or convention, or fashion, for a human's own real likings and dislikings. I myself would carry this very far. I would make it a rule to eradicate from my patient any strong personal taste which is not actually a sin, even if it is something quite trivial such as a fondness for county cricket or collecting stamps or drinking cocoa. Such things, I grant you, have nothing of virtue in them; but there is a sort of innocence and humility and self-forgetfulness about them which I distrust. The man who truly and disinterestedly enjoys any one thing in the world, for its own sake, and without caring two-pence what other people say about it, is by that very fact forearmed against some of our subtlest modes of attack. You should always try to make the patient abandon the people or food or books he really likes in favour of the 'best' people, the 'right' food, the 'important' books. I have known a human defended from strong temptations to social ambition by a still stronger taste for tripe and onions.

—from *The Screwtape Letters*

Scientific Theories

Has it come to that? Does the whole vast structure of modern natural-ism depend not on positive evidence but simply on an *a priori* meta-physical prejudice? Was it devised not to get in facts but to keep out God? Even, however, if Evolution in the strict biological sense has some better grounds than [this]....—and I can't help thinking it must—we should distinguish Evolution in this strict sense from what may be called the universal evolutionism of modern thought. By uni-versal evolutionism I mean the belief that the very formula of univer-sal process is from imperfect to perfect, from small beginnings to great endings, from the rudimentary to the elaborate, the belief which makes people find it natural to think that morality springs from savage taboos, adult sentiment from infantile sexual maladjustments, thought from instinct, mind from matter, organic from inorganic, cosmos from chaos. This is perhaps the deepest habit of mind in the contemporary world. It seems to me immensely unplausible, because it makes the general course of nature so very unlike those parts of nature we can observe.

—from "Is Theology Poetry?" *(The Weight of Glory)*

Scientific Observation

You remember the old puzzle as to whether the owl came from the egg or the egg from the owl. The modern acquiescence in universal evolutionism is a kind of optical illusion, produced by attending exclusively to the owl's emergence from the egg. We are taught from childhood to notice how the perfect oak grows from the acorn and to forget that the acorn itself was dropped by a perfect oak. We are reminded constantly that the adult human being was an embryo, never that the life of the embryo came from two adult human beings. We love to notice that the express engine of today is the descendant of the "Rocket"; we do not equally remember that the "Rocket" springs not from some even more rudimentary engine, but from something much more perfect and complicated than itself—namely, a man of genius. The obviousness or naturalness which most people seem to find in the idea of emergent evolution thus seems to be a pure hallucination.

—from "Is Theology Poetry?" *(The Weight of Glory)*

1914 Warren Lewis is sent to France with the 4th Company 7th
Divisional Train, British Expeditionary Force.

Science or Magic?

I have described as a 'magician's bargain' that process whereby man surrenders object after object, and finally himself, to Nature in return for power. And I meant what I said. The fact that the scientist has succeeded where the magician failed has put such a wide contrast between them in popular thought that the real story of the birth of Science is misunderstood. You will even find people who write about the sixteenth century as if Magic were a medieval survival and Science the new thing that came in to sweep it away. Those who have studied the period know better. There was very little magic in the Middle Ages: the sixteenth and seventeenth centuries are the high noon of magic. The serious magical endeavour and the serious scientific endeavour are twins: one was sickly and died, the other strong and throve. But they were twins. They were born of the same impulse. I allow that some (certainly not all) of the early scientists were actuated by a pure love of knowledge. But if we consider the temper of that age as a whole we can discern the impulse of which I speak.

There is something which unites magic and applied science while separating both from the 'wisdom' of earlier ages. For the wise men of old the cardinal problem had been how to conform the soul to reality, and the solution had been knowledge, self-discipline, and virtue. For magic and applied science alike the problem is how to subdue reality to the wishes of men: the solution is a technique; and both, in the practice of this technique, are ready to do things hitherto regarded as disgusting and impious—such as digging up and mutilating the dead.

—from *The Abolition of Man*

From Dream to Waking

This is how I distinguish dreaming and waking. When I am awake I can, in some degree, account for and study my dream. The dragon that pursued me last night can be fitted into my waking world. I know that there are such things as dreams; I know that I had eaten an indigestible dinner; I know that a man of my reading might be expected to dream of dragons. But while in the nightmare I could not have fitted in my waking experience. The waking world is judged more real because it can thus contain the dreaming world; the dreaming world is judged less real because it cannot contain the waking one. For the same reason I am certain that in passing from the scientific points of view to the theological, I have passed from dream to waking. Christian theology can fit in science, art, morality, and the sub-Christian religions. The scientific point of view cannot fit in any of these things, not even science itself. I believe in Christianity as I believe that the Sun has risen, not only because I see it, but because by it I see everything else.

—from "Is Theology Poetry?" (*The Weight of Glory*)

1944 Lewis reads "Is Theology Poetry?" to the Oxford University Socratic Club; it is later published in *The Socratic Digest,* vol. 3 (1945).

Turn the Other Cheek?

There are three ways of taking the command to turn the other cheek. One is the Pacifist interpretation; it means what it says and imposes a duty of nonresistance on all men in all circumstances. Another is the minimising interpretation; it does not mean what it says but is merely an orientally hyperbolical way of saying that you should put up with a lot and be placable. Both you and I agree in rejecting this view. The conflict is therefore between the Pacifist interpretation and a third one which I am now going to propound. I think the text means exactly what it says, but with an understood reservation in favour of those obviously exceptional cases which every hearer would naturally assume to be exceptions without being told. .... That is, insofar as the only relevant factors in the case are an injury to me by my neighbour and a desire on my part to retaliate, then I hold that Christianity commands the absolute mortification of that desire. No quarter whatever is given to the voice within us which says, "He's done it to me, so I'll do the same to him."

—from "Why I Am Not a Pacifist" *(The Weight of Glory)*

What "Turn the Other Cheek" *Doesn't* Mean

But the moment you introduce other factors, of course, the problem is altered. Does anyone suppose that Our Lord's hearers understood Him to mean that if a homicidal maniac, attempting to murder a third party, tried to knock me out of the way, I must stand aside and let him get his victim? I at any rate think it impossible they could have so understood Him. I think it equally impossible that they supposed Him to mean that the best way of bringing up a child was to let it hit its parents whenever it was in a temper, or, when it had grabbed at the jam, to give it the honey also. I think the meaning of the words was perfectly clear— "Insofar as you are simply an angry man who has been hurt, mortify your anger and do not hit back"—even, one would have assumed that insofar as you are a magistrate struck by a private person, a parent struck by a child, a teacher by a scholar, a sane man by a lunatic, or a soldier by the public enemy, your duties may be very different, different because [there] may be then other motives than egoistic retaliation for hitting back.

—from "Why I Am Not a Pacifist" *(The Weight of Glory)*

Virtue's Testing Point

Screwtape weighs his options:

Now this is a ticklish business. We have made men proud of most vices, but not of cowardice. Whenever we have almost succeeded in doing so, the Enemy permits a war or an earthquake or some other calamity, and at once courage becomes so obviously lovely and important even in human eyes that all our work is undone, and there is still at least one vice of which they feel genuine shame. The danger of inducing cowardice in our patients, therefore, is lest we produce real self-knowledge and self-loathing with consequent repentance and humility. And in fact, in the last war, thousands of humans, by discovering their own cowardice, discovered the whole moral world for the first time. In peace we can make many of them ignore good and evil entirely; in danger, the issue is forced upon them in a guise to which even we cannot blind them. There is here a cruel dilemma before us. If we promoted justice and charity among men, we should be playing directly into the Enemy's hands; but if we guide them to the opposite behaviour, this sooner or later produces (for He permits it to produce) a war or a revolution, and the undisguisable issue of cowardice or courage awakes thousands of men from moral stupor.

This, indeed, is probably one of the Enemy's motives for creating a dangerous world—a world in which moral issues really come to the point. He sees as well as you do that courage is not simply *one* of the virtues, but the form of every virtue at the testing point, which means, at the point of highest reality. A chastity or honesty, or mercy, which yields to danger will be chaste or honest or merciful only on conditions. Pilate was merciful till it became risky.

—from *The Screwtape Letters*

How to Create a Coward

Screwtape explains the techniques of temptation to cowardice:
The main point is that precautions have a tendency to increase fear. The precautions publicly enjoined on your patient, however, soon become a matter of routine and this effect disappears. What you must do is to keep running in his mind (side by side with the conscious intention of doing his duty) the vague idea of all sorts of things he can do or not do, *inside* the framework of the duty, which seem to make him a little safer. Get his mind off the simple rule ('I've got to stay here and do so-and-so') into a series of imaginary life lines ('If A happened—though I very much hope it won't—I could do B—and if the worst came to the worst, I could always do C'). Superstitions, if not recognised as such, can be awakened. The point is to keep him feeling that he has *something,* other than the Enemy and courage the Enemy supplies, *to fall back on,* so that what was intended to be a total commitment to duty becomes honeycombed all through with little unconscious reservations. By building up a series of imaginary expedients to prevent 'the worst coming to the worst' you may produce, at that level of his will which he is not aware of, a determination that the worst *shall not* come to the worst. Then, at the moment of real terror, rush it out into his nerves and muscles and you may get the fatal act done before he knows what you're about. For remember, the *act* of cowardice is all that matters; the emotion of fear is, in itself, no sin and, though we enjoy it, does us no good.

—from *The Screwtape Letters*

1944 Lewis's *The Great Divorce* debuts in the *Guardian,* the first of fifteen weekly installments.

A Logical Conclusion to Pacifist Politics

If not the greatest evil, yet war is a great evil. Therefore, we should all like to remove it if we can. But every war leads to another war. The removal of war must therefore be attempted. We must increase by propaganda the number of Pacifists in each nation until it becomes great enough to deter that nation from going to war. This seems to me wild work. Only liberal societies tolerate Pacifists. In the liberal society, the number of Pacifists will either be large enough to cripple the state as a belligerent, or not. If not, you have done nothing. If it is large enough, then you have handed over the state which does tolerate Pacifists to its totalitarian neighbour who does not. Pacifism of this kind is taking the straight road to a world in which there will be no Pacifists.
—from "Why I Am Not a Pacifist" *(The Weight of Glory)*

1918 The Armistice is signed, marking the end of World War I.

Weighing the Costs

It remains to inquire whether, if I still remain a Pacifist, I ought to suspect the secret influence of any passion. .... Let me say at the outset that I think it unlikely there is anyone present less courageous than myself. But let me also say that there is no man alive so virtuous that he need feel himself insulted at being asked to consider the possibility of a warping passion when the choice is one between so much happiness and so much misery. For let us make no mistake. All that we fear from all the kinds of adversity, severally, is collected together in the life of a soldier on active service. Like sickness, it threatens pain and death. Like poverty, it threatens ill lodging, cold, heat, thirst, and hunger. Like slavery, it threatens toil, humiliation, injustice, and arbitrary rule. Like exile, it separates you from all you love. Like the gallies, it imprisons you at close quarters with uncongenial companions. It threatens *every* temporal evil—every evil except dishonour and final perdition, and those who bear it like it no better than you would like it. On the other side, though it may not be your fault, it is certainly a fact that Pacifism threatens you with almost nothing. Some public opprobrium, yes, from people whose opinion you discount and whose society you do not frequent, soon recompensed by the mutual approval which exists, inevitably, in any minority group. For the rest it offers you a continuance of the life you know and love, among the people and in the surroundings you know and love. It offers you time to lay the foundations of a career; for whether you will or no, you can hardly help getting the jobs for which the discharged soldiers will one day look in vain. You do not even have to fear, as Pacifists may have had to fear in the last war, that public opinion will punish you when the peace comes. For we have learned now that though the world is slow to forgive, it is quick to forget.
—from "Why I Am Not a Pacifist" *(The Weight of Glory)*

Weighing Hell's Miseries

The Teacher offers perspective to Hell's miseries and Heaven's joys:

'All Hell is smaller than one pebble of your earthly world: but it is smaller than one atom of *this* world, the Real World. Look at yon butterfly. If it swallowed all Hell, Hell would not be big enough to do it any harm or to have any taste.'

'It seems big enough when you're in it, Sir.'

'And yet all loneliness, angers, hatreds, envies and itchings that it contains, if rolled into one single experience and put into the scale against the least moment of the joy that is felt by the least in Heaven, would have no weight that could be registered at all. Bad cannot succeed even in being bad as truly as good is good. If all Hell's miseries together entered the consciousness of yon wee yellow bird on the bough there, they would be swallowed up without trace, as if one drop of ink had been dropped into that Great Ocean to which your terrestrial Pacific itself is only a molecule.'

—from *The Great Divorce*

Of Heaven and Earth

I believe, to be sure, that any man who reaches Heaven will find that what he abandoned (even in plucking out his right eye) has not been lost: that the kernel of what he was really seeking even in his most depraved wishes will be there, beyond expectation, waiting for him in 'the High Countries'. In that sense it will be true for those who have completed the journey (and for no others) to say that good is everything and Heaven everywhere. But we, at this end of the road, must not try to anticipate that retrospective vision. If we do, we are likely to embrace the false and disastrous converse and fancy that everything is good and everywhere is Heaven.

But what, you ask, of earth? Earth, I think, will not be found by anyone to be in the end a very distinct place. I think earth, if chosen instead of Heaven, will turn out to have been, all along, only a region in Hell: and earth, if put second to Heaven, to have been from the beginning a part of Heaven itself.

—from *The Great Divorce*, Preface

No Chocolates?

The letter and spirit of scripture, and of all Christianity, forbid us to suppose that life in the New Creation will be a sexual life; and this reduces our imagination to the withering alternative either of bodies which are hardly recognisable as human bodies at all or else of a perpetual fast. As regards the fast, I think our present outlook might be like that of a small boy who, on being told that the sexual act was the highest bodily pleasure should immediately ask whether you ate chocolates at the same time. On receiving the answer 'No,' he might regard absence of chocolates as the chief characteristic of sexuality. In vain would you tell him that the reason why lovers in their carnal raptures don't bother about chocolates is that they have something better to think of. The boy knows chocolate: he does not know the positive thing that excludes it. We are in the same position. We know the sexual life; we do not know, except in glimpses, the other thing which, in Heaven, will leave no room for it. Hence where fullness awaits us we anticipate fasting. In denying that sexual life, as we now understand it, makes any part of the final beatitude, it is not of course necessary to suppose that the distinction of sexes will disappear. What is no longer needed for biological purposes may be expected to survive for splendour. Sexuality is the instrument both of virginity and of conjugal virtue; neither men nor women will be asked to throw away weapons they have used victoriously. It is the beaten and the fugitives who throw away their swords. The conquerors sheathe theirs and retain them. 'Trans-sexual' would be a better word than 'sexless' for the heavenly life.

—from *Miracles*

A Gradual Change

Those who have attained everlasting life in the vision of God doubtless know very well that it is no mere bribe, but the very consummation of their earthly discipleship; but we who have not yet attained it cannot know this in the same way, and cannot even begin to know it at all except by continuing to obey and finding the first reward of our obedience in our increasing power to desire the ultimate reward. Just in proportion as the desire grows, our fear lest it should be a mercenary desire will die away and finally be recognised as an absurdity. But probably this will not, for most of us, happen in a day; poetry replaces grammar, gospel replaces law, longing transforms obedience, as gradually as the tide lifts a grounded ship.

—from "The Weight of Glory" *(The Weight of Glory)*

The Sweet, Secret Desire

In speaking of this desire for our own far-off country, which we find in ourselves even now, I feel a certain shyness. I am almost committing an indecency. I am trying to rip open the inconsolable secret in each one of you—the secret which hurts so much that you take your revenge on it by calling it names like Nostalgia and Romanticism and Adolescence; the secret also which pierces with such sweetness that when, in very intimate conversation, the mention of it becomes imminent, we grow awkward and affect to laugh at ourselves; the secret we cannot hide and cannot tell, though we desire to do both. We cannot tell it because it is a desire for something that has never actually appeared in our experience. We cannot hide it because our experience is constantly suggesting it, and we betray ourselves like lovers at the mention of a name. Our commonest expedient is to call it beauty and behave as if that had settled the matter. .... The books or the music in which we thought the beauty was located will betray us if we trust to them; it was not *in* them, it only came *through* them, and what came through them was longing. These things—the beauty, the memory of our own past—are good images of what we really desire; but if they are mistaken for the thing itself, they turn into dumb idols, breaking the hearts of their worshippers. For they are not the thing itself; they are only the scent of a flower we have not found, the echo of a tune we have not heard, news from a country we have never yet visited. Do you think I am trying to weave a spell? Perhaps I am; but remember your fairy tales. Spells are used for breaking enchantments as well as for inducing them.
    —from "The Weight of Glory" *(The Weight of Glory)*

1917 Lewis (age eighteen) is deployed to France with his regiment, the Somerset Light Infantry.

Well Done

I turn next to the idea of glory. There is no getting away from the fact that this idea is very prominent in the New Testament and in early Christian writings. Salvation is constantly associated with palms, crowns, white robes, thrones, and splendour like the sun and stars. All this makes no immediate appeal to me at all, and in that respect I fancy I am a typical modern. Glory suggests two ideas to me, of which one seems wicked and the other ridiculous. Either glory means to me fame, or it means luminosity. As for the first, since to be famous means to be better known than other people, the desire for fame appears to me as a competitive passion and therefore of hell rather than heaven. As for the second, who wishes to become a kind of living electric light bulb?

When I began to look into this matter I was shocked to find such different Christians as Milton, Johnson, and Thomas Aquinas taking heavenly glory quite frankly in the sense of fame or good report. But not fame conferred by our fellow creatures—fame with God, approval or (I might say) "appreciation" by God. And then, when I had thought it over, I saw that this view was scriptural; nothing can eliminate from the parable the divine *accolade*, "Well done, thou good and faithful servant." With that, a good deal of what I had been thinking all my life fell down like a house of cards.

—from "The Weight of Glory" *(The Weight of Glory)*

Perfect Humility

I suddenly remembered that no one can enter heaven except as a child; and nothing is so obvious in a child—not in a conceited child, but in a good child—as its great and undisguised pleasure in being praised. Not only in a child, either, but even in a dog or a horse. Apparently what I had mistaken for humility had, all these years, prevented me from understanding what is in fact the humblest, the most childlike, the most creaturely of pleasures—nay, the specific pleasure of the inferior: the pleasure of a beast before men, a child before its father, a pupil before his teacher, a creature before its Creator. I am not forgetting how horribly this most innocent desire is parodied in our human ambitions, or how very quickly, in my own experience, the lawful pleasure of praise from those whom it was my duty to please turns into the deadly poison of self-admiration. But I thought I could detect a moment—a very, very short moment—before this happened, during which the satisfaction of having pleased those whom I rightly loved and rightly feared was pure. And that is enough to raise our thoughts to what may happen when the redeemed soul, beyond all hope and nearly beyond belief, learns at last that she has pleased Him whom she was created to please. There will be no room for vanity then. She will be free from the miserable illusion that it is her doing. With no taint of what we should now call self-approval she will most innocently rejoice in the thing that God has made her to be, and the moment which heals her old inferiority complex forever will also drown her pride deeper than Prospero's book. Perfect humility dispenses with modesty. If God is satisfied with the work, the work may be satisfied with itself; "it is not for her to bandy compliments with her Sovereign."

—from "The Weight of Glory" (*The Weight of Glory*)

The Promise of Glory

I can imagine someone saying that he dislikes my idea of heaven as a place where we are patted on the back. But proud misunderstanding is behind that dislike. In the end that Face which is the delight or the terror of the universe must be turned upon each of us either with one expression or with the other, either conferring glory inexpressible or inflicting shame that can never be cured or disguised. I read in a periodical the other day that the fundamental thing is how we think of God. By God Himself, it is not! How God thinks of us is not only more important, but infinitely more important. Indeed, how we think of Him is of no importance except insofar as it is related to how He thinks of us. It is written that we shall "stand before" Him, shall appear, shall be inspected. The promise of glory is the promise, almost incredible and only possible by the work of Christ, that some of us, that any of us who really chooses, shall actually survive that examination, shall find approval, shall please God. To please God...to be a real ingredient in the divine happiness...to be loved by God, not merely pitied, but delighted in as an artist delights in his work or a father in a son—it seems impossible, a weight or burden of glory which our thoughts can hardly sustain. But so it is.

—from "The Weight of Glory" *(The Weight of Glory)*

Overheard Messages

When I attempted....to describe our spiritual longings, I was omitting one of their most curious characteristics. We usually notice it just as the moment of vision dies away, as the music ends, or as the landscape loses the celestial light. .... For a few minutes we have had the illusion of belonging to that world. Now we wake to find that it is no such thing. We have been mere spectators. Beauty has smiled, but not to welcome us; her face was turned in our direction, but not to see us. We have not been accepted, welcomed, or taken into the dance. We may go when we please, we may stay if we can: "Nobody marks us." A scientist may reply that since most of the things we call beautiful are inanimate, it is not very surprising that they take no notice of us. That, of course, is true. It is not the physical objects that I am speaking of, but that indescribable something of which they become for a moment the messengers. And part of the bitterness which mixes with the sweetness of that message is due to the fact that it so seldom seems to be a message intended for us, but rather something we have overheard. By bitterness I mean pain, not resentment. We should hardly dare to ask that any notice be taken of ourselves. But we pine. The sense that in this universe we are treated as strangers, the longing to be acknowledged, to meet with some response, to bridge some chasm that yawns between us and reality, is part of our inconsolable secret. And surely, from this point of view, the promise of glory, in the sense described, becomes highly relevant to our deep desire. For glory means good report with God, acceptance by God, response, acknowledgement, and welcome into the heart of things. The door on which we have been knocking all our lives will open at last.

—from "The Weight of Glory" *(The Weight of Glory)*

To Be at Last Summoned Inside

Perhaps it seems rather crude to describe glory as the fact of being "noticed" by God. But this is almost the language of the New Testament. St. Paul promises to those who love God not, as we should expect, that they will know Him, but that they will be known by Him (I Cor. 8:3). It is a strange promise. Does not God know all things at all times? But it is dreadfully reechoed in another passage of the New Testament. There we are warned that it may happen to any one of us to appear at last before the face of God and hear only the appalling words, "I never knew you. Depart from Me." In some sense, as dark to the intellect as it is unendurable to the feelings, we can be both banished from the presence of Him who is present everywhere and erased from the knowledge of Him who knows all. We can be left utterly and absolutely *outside*—repelled, exiled, estranged, finally and unspeakably ignored. On the other hand, we can be called in, welcomed, received, acknowledged. We walk every day on the razor edge between these two incredible possibilities. Apparently, then, our lifelong nostalgia, our longing to be reunited with something in the universe from which we now feel cut off, to be on the inside of some door which we have always seen from the outside, is no mere neurotic fancy, but the truest index of our real situation. And to be at last summoned inside would be both glory and honour beyond all our merits and also the healing of that old ache.

—from "The Weight of Glory" (*The Weight of Glory*)

1963 Lewis dies at 5:30 P.M. at The Kilns, one week short of his sixty-fifth birthday. He is buried in the yard of Holy Trinity Church in Headington Quarry, Oxford.

Is It Wrong to Want Heaven?

We are very shy nowadays of even mentioning heaven. We are afraid of the jeer about 'pie in the sky', and of being told that we are trying to 'escape' from the duty of making a happy world here and now into dreams of a happy world elsewhere. But either there is 'pie in the sky' or there is not. If there is not, then Christianity is false, for this doctrine is woven into its whole fabric. If there is, then this truth, like any other, must be faced, whether it is useful at political meetings or no. Again, we are afraid that heaven is a bribe, and that if we make it our goal we shall no longer be disinterested. It is not so. Heaven offers nothing that a mercenary soul can desire. It is safe to tell the pure in heart that they shall see God, for only the pure in heart want to. There are rewards that do not sully motives. A man's love for a woman is not mercenary because he wants to marry her, nor his love for poetry mercenary because he wants to read it, nor his love of exercise less disinterested because he wants to run and leap and walk. Love, by definition, seeks to enjoy its object.

—from *The Problem of Pain*

Aim at Heaven

Hope is one of the Theological virtues. This means that a continual looking forward to the eternal world is not (as some modern people think) a form of escapism or wishful thinking, but one of the things a Christian is meant to do. It does not mean that we are to leave the present world as it is. If you read history you will find that the Christians who did most for the present world were just those who thought most of the next. The Apostles themselves, who set on foot the conversion of the Roman Empire, the great men who built up the Middle Ages, the English Evangelicals who abolished the Slave Trade, all left their mark on Earth, precisely because their minds were occupied with Heaven. It is since Christians have largely ceased to think of the other world that they have become so ineffective in this. Aim at Heaven and you will get earth 'thrown in': aim at earth and you will get neither. It seems a strange rule, but something like it can be seen at work in other matters. Health is a great blessing, but the moment you make health one of your main, direct objects you start becoming a crank and imagining there is something wrong with you. You are only likely to get health provided you want other things more—food, games, work, fun, open air. In the same way, we shall never save civilisation as long as civilisation is our main object. We must learn to want something else even more.

—from *Mere Christianity*

Books for Grown-Ups

There is no need to be worried by facetious people who try to make
the Christian hope of 'Heaven' ridiculous by saying they do not want
'to spend eternity playing harps'. The answer to such people is that if
they cannot understand books written for grown-ups, they should not
talk about them. All the scriptural imagery (harps, crowns, gold, etc.)
is, of course, a merely symbolical attempt to express the inexpressible.
Musical instruments are mentioned because for many people (not all)
music is the thing known in the present life which most strongly suggests ecstasy and infinity. Crowns are mentioned to suggest the fact
that those who are united with God in eternity share His splendour
and power and joy. Gold is mentioned to suggest the timelessness of
Heaven (gold does not rust) and the preciousness of it. People who
take these symbols literally might as well think that when Christ told
us to be like doves, He meant that we were to lay eggs.

—from *Mere Christianity*

Comparing Cats and Dogs

The world does not consist of 100 per cent. Christians and 100 per cent. non-Christians. There are people (a great many of them) who are slowly ceasing to be Christians but who still call themselves by that name: some of them are clergymen. There are other people who are slowly becoming Christians though they do not yet call themselves so. There are people who do not accept the full Christian doctrine about Christ but who are so strongly attracted by Him that they are His in a much deeper sense than they themselves understand. There are people in other religions who are being led by God's secret influence to concentrate on those parts of their religion which are in agreement with Christianity, and who thus belong to Christ without knowing it. For example, a Buddhist of good will may be led to concentrate more and more on the Buddhist teaching about mercy and to leave in the background (though he might still say he believed) the Buddhist teaching on certain other points. Many of the good Pagans long before Christ's birth may have been in this position. And always, of course, there are a great many people who are just confused in mind and have a lot of inconsistent beliefs all jumbled up together. Consequently, it is not much use trying to make judgments about Christians and non-Christians in the mass. It is some use comparing cats and dogs, or even men and women, in the mass, because there one knows definitely which is which. Also, an animal does not turn (either slowly or suddenly) from a dog into a cat. But when we are comparing Christians in general with non-Christians in general, we are usually not thinking about real people whom we know at all, but only about two vague ideas which we have got from novels and newspapers.

—from *Mere Christianity*

Sooner or Later They Fell

We do not know how many of these creatures God made, nor how long they continued in the Paradisal state. But sooner or later they fell. Someone or something whispered that they could become as gods—that they could cease directing their lives to their Creator and taking all their delights as uncovenanted mercies, as 'accidents' (in the logical sense) which arose in the course of a life directed not to those delights but to the adoration of God. As a young man wants a regular allowance from his father which he can count on as his own, within which he makes his own plans (and rightly, for his father is after all a fellow creature), so they desired to be on their own, to take care for their own future, to plan for pleasure and for security, to have a *meum* from which, no doubt, they would pay some reasonable tribute to God in the way of time, attention, and love, but which, nevertheless, was theirs not His. They wanted, as we say, to 'call their souls their own'. But that means to live a lie, for our souls are not, in fact, our own. They wanted some corner in the universe of which they could say to God, 'This is our business, not yours.' But there is no such corner. They wanted to be nouns, but they were, and eternally must be, mere adjectives.

—from *The Problem of Pain*

The Place of Finality and Darkness

[One] objection [to the conception of Hell as punishment inflicted by God] is that no charitable man could himself be blessed in heaven while he knew that even one human soul was still in hell; and if so, are we more merciful than God? At the back of this objection lies a mental picture of heaven and hell co-existing in unilinear time as the histories of England and America co-exist: so that at each moment the blessed could say 'The miseries of hell are *now* going on.' But I notice that Our Lord, while stressing the terror of hell with unsparing severity, usually emphasises the idea not of duration but of *finality*. Consignment to the destroying fire is usually treated as the end of the story—not as the beginning of a new story. That the lost soul is eternally fixed in its diabolical attitude we cannot doubt: but whether this eternal fixity implies endless duration—or duration at all—we cannot say. .... We know much more about heaven than hell, for heaven is the home of humanity and therefore contains all that is implied in a glorified human life: but hell was not made for men. It is in no sense *parallel* to heaven: it is 'the darkness outside', the outer rim where being fades away into nonentity.

—from *The Problem of Pain*

Shall Hell Veto Heaven?

The Teacher exposes the blackmail scheme:

'What some people say on Earth is that the final loss of one soul gives the lie to all the joy of those who are saved.'

'Ye see it does not.'

'I feel in a way that it ought to.'

'That sounds very merciful. but see what lurks behind it.'

'What?'

'The demand of the loveless and the self-imprisoned that they should be allowed to blackmail the universe: that till they consent to be happy (on their own terms) no one else shall taste joy: that theirs should be the final power; that Hell should be able to *veto* Heaven.'

'I don't know what I want, Sir.'

'Son, son, it must be one way or the other. Either the day must come when joy prevails and all the makers of misery are no longer able to infect it: or else for ever and ever the makers of misery can destroy in others the happiness they reject for themselves. I know it has a grand sound to say ye'll accept no salvation which leaves even one creature in the dark outside. But watch that sophistry or ye'll make a Dog in a Manger the tyrant of the universe.'

—from *The Great Divorce*

1898 Clive Staples ("Jack") Lewis is born in Belfast, Northern Ireland, to Albert J. Lewis (1863–1929) and Florence Augusta Hamilton Lewis (1862–1908).

1917 Lewis arrives at the front-line trenches in France.

Must Pity Die?

The Teacher reveals the evil aspects of Pity:

'But dare one say—it is horrible to say—that Pity must ever die?'

'Ye must distinguish. The action of Pity will live for ever: but the passion of Pity will not. The passion of Pity, the Pity we merely suffer, the ache that draws men to concede what should not be conceded and to flatter when they should speak truth, the pity that has cheated many a woman out of her virginity and many a statesman out of his honesty—that will die. It was used as a weapon by bad men against good ones: their weapon will be broken.'

'And what is the other kind—the action?'

'It's a weapon on the other side. It leaps quicker than light from the highest place to the lowest to bring healing and joy, whatever the cost to itself. It changes darkness into light and evil into good. But it will not, at the cunning tears of Hell, impose on good the tyranny of evil. Every disease that submits to a cure shall be cured: but we will not call blue yellow to please those who insist on still having jaundice, nor make a midden of the world's garden for the sake of some who cannot abide the smell of roses.'

—from *The Great Divorce*

November 1954 Lewis delivers his Inaugural Lecture, *"De Descriptione Temporum,"* at Cambridge University.

DECEMBER

Hell's Doors

It is objected that the ultimate loss of a single soul means the defeat of omnipotence. And so it does. In creating beings with free will, omnipotence from the outset submits to the possibility of such defeat. What you call defeat, I call miracle: for to make things which are not Itself, and thus to become, in a sense, capable of being resisted by its own handiwork, is the most astonishing and unimaginable of all the feats we attribute to the Deity. I willingly believe that the damned are, in one sense, successful, rebels to the end; that the doors of hell are locked on the *inside*. I do not mean that the ghosts may not *wish* to come out of hell, in the vague fashion wherein an envious man 'wishes' to be happy: but they certainly do not will even the first preliminary stages of that self-abandonment through which alone the soul can reach any good. They enjoy forever the horrible freedom they have demanded, and are therefore self-enslaved: just as the blessed, forever submitting to obedience, become through all eternity more and more free.

—from *The Problem of Pain*

December 1957 Joy's health continues to improve after her cancer goes into remission, and by Christmas, she is able to walk around the house and garden.

Left Alone

In the long run the answer to all those who object to the doctrine of hell, is itself a question: 'What are you asking God to do?' To wipe out their past sins and, at all costs, to give them a fresh start, smoothing every difficulty and offering every miraculous help? But He has done so, on Calvary. To forgive them? They will not be forgiven. To leave them alone? Alas, I am afraid that is what He does.

One caution, and I have done. In order to rouse modern minds to an understanding of the issues, I ventured to introduce in this chapter a picture of the sort of bad man whom we most easily perceive to be truly bad. But when the picture has done that work, the sooner it is forgotten the better. In all discussions of Hell we should keep steadily before our eyes the possible damnation, not of our enemies nor our friends (since both these disturb the reason) but of ourselves. This chapter is not about your wife or son, nor about Nero or Judas Iscariot; it is about you and me.

—from *The Problem of Pain*

December 1932 Warren Lewis retires from the Royal Army Service Corps after an eighteen-year career and moves into The Kilns, Oxford.

A Detestable Doctrine

Some will not be redeemed. There is no doctrine which I would more willingly remove from Christianity than this, if it lay in my power. But it has the full support of Scripture and, specially, of Our Lord's own words; it has always been held by Christendom; and it has the support of reason. If a game is played, it must be possible to lose it. If the happiness of a creature lies in self-surrender, no one can make that surrender but himself (though many can help him to make it) and he may refuse. I would pay any price to be able to say truthfully 'All will be saved.' But my reason retorts 'Without their will, or with it?' If I say 'Without their will,' I at once perceive a contradiction; how can the supreme voluntary act of self-surrender be involuntary? If I say 'With their will,' my reason replies 'How if they *will not* give in?'

—from *The Problem of Pain*

1954 Lewis completes his last tutorial at Magdalen College, Oxford, after accepting a chair at Cambridge.

You Be the Judge

Let us try to be honest with ourselves. Picture to yourself a man who has risen to wealth or power by a continued course of treachery and cruelty, by exploiting for purely selfish ends the noble motions of his victims, laughing the while at their simplicity; who, having thus attained success, uses it for the gratification of lust and hatred and finally parts with the last rag of honour among thieves by betraying his own accomplices and jeering at their last moments of bewildered disillusionment. Suppose, further, that he does all this, not (as we like to imagine) tormented by remorse or even misgiving, but eating like a schoolboy and sleeping like a healthy infant—a jolly, ruddy-cheeked man, without a care in the world, unshakably confident to the very end that he alone has found the answer to the riddle of life, that God and man are fools whom he has got the better of, that his way of life is utterly successful, satisfactory, unassailable. We must be careful at this point. The least indulgence of the passion for revenge is very deadly sin. Christian charity counsels us to make every effort for the conversion of such a man: to prefer his conversion, at the peril of our own lives, perhaps of our own souls, to his punishment; to prefer it infinitely. But that is not the question. Supposing he *will* not be converted, what destiny in the eternal world can you regard as proper for him? Can you really desire that such a man, *remaining what he is* (and he must be able to do that if he has free will) should be confirmed forever in his present happiness—should continue, for all eternity, to be perfectly convinced that the laugh is on his side?

—from *The Problem of Pain*

Viewing the Remains

You will remember that in the parable, the saved go to a place prepared for *them*, while the damned go to a place never made for men at all [Matthew 25:34, 41]. To enter heaven is to become more human than you ever succeeded in being on earth; to enter hell, is to be banished from humanity. What is cast (or casts itself) into hell is not a man: it is 'remains'. To be a complete man means to have the passions obedient to the will and the will offered to God: to *have been* a man—to be an ex-man or 'damned ghost'—would presumably mean to consist of a will utterly centred in its self and passions utterly uncontrolled by the will.

—from *The Problem of Pain*

Either-Or

I do not think that all who choose wrong roads perish; but their rescue consists in being put back on the right road. A sum can be put right: but only by going back till you find the error and working it afresh from that point, never by simply *going on*. Evil can be undone, but it cannot 'develop' into good. Time does not heal it. The spell must be unwound, bit by bit, 'with backward mutters of dissevering power'—or else not. It is still 'either-or'. If we insist on keeping Hell (or even Earth) we shall not see Heaven: if we accept Heaven we shall not be able to retain even the smallest and most intimate souvenirs of Hell.

—from *The Great Divorce*, Preface

Choose Now, Choose Well

Why is God landing in this enemy-occupied world in disguise and starting a sort of secret society to undermine the devil? Why is He not landing in force, invading it? Is it that He is not strong enough? Well, Christians think He is going to land in force; we do not know when. But we can guess why He is delaying. He wants to give us the chance of joining His side freely. I do not suppose you and I would have thought much of a Frenchman who waited till the Allies were marching into Germany and then announced he was on our side. God will invade. But I wonder whether people who ask God to interfere openly and directly in our world quite realise what it will be like when He does. When that happens, it is the end of the world. When the author walks on to the stage the play is over. God is going to invade, all right: but what is the good of saying you are on His side then, when you see the whole natural universe melting away like a dream and something else—something it never entered your head to conceive—comes crashing in; something so beautiful to some of us and so terrible to others that none of us will have any choice left? For this time it will be God without disguise; something so overwhelming that it will strike either irresistible love or irresistible horror into every creature. It will be too late then to choose your side. There is no use saying you choose to lie down when it has become impossible to stand up. That will not be the time for choosing: it will be the time when we discover which side we really have chosen, whether we realised it before or not. Now, today, this moment, is our chance to choose the right side. God is holding back to give us that chance. It will not last for ever. We must take it or leave it.

—from *Mere Christianity*

Thy Will Be Done

The Teacher explains our power to choose:

'There are only two kinds of people in the end: those who say to God, "Thy will be done," and those to whom God says, in the end, "*Thy* will be done." All that are in Hell, choose it. Without that self-choice there could be no Hell. No soul that seriously and constantly desires joy will ever miss it. Those who seek find. To those who knock it is opened.'

—from *The Great Divorce*

Better to Reign in Hell

The Teacher exposes the true nature of sin:

'What do they choose, these souls who go back (I have yet seen no others)? And how can they choose it?'

'Milton was right,' said my Teacher. 'The choice of every lost soul can be expressed in the words "Better to reign in Hell than serve in Heaven." There is always something they insist on keeping even at the price of misery. There is always something they prefer to joy— that is, to reality. Ye see it easily enough in a spoiled child that would sooner miss its play and its supper than say it was sorry and be friends. Ye call it the Sulks. But in adult life it has a hundred fine names— Achilles' wrath and Coriolanus' grandeur, Revenge and Injured Merit and Self-Respect and Tragic Greatness and Proper Pride.'

'Then is no one lost through the undignified vices, Sir? Through mere sensuality?'

'Some are, no doubt. The sensualist, I'll allow ye, begins by pursuing a real pleasure, though a small one. His sin is the less. But the time comes on when, though the pleasure becomes less and less and the craving fiercer and fiercer, and though he knows that joy can never come that way, yet he prefers to joy the mere fondling of unappeasable lust and would not have it taken from him. He'd fight to the death to keep it. He'd like well to be able to scratch; but even when he can scratch no more he'd rather itch than not.'

—from *The Great Divorce*

The Man Who Mistook the Means for the End

The Teacher tells a story:

'There was a creature came here not long ago and went back—Sir Archibald they called him. In his earthly life he'd been interested in nothing but Survival. He'd written a whole shelf-full of books about it. .... It grew to be his only occupation—experimenting, lecturing, running a magazine. And travelling too: digging out queer stories among Tibetan lamas and being initiated into brotherhoods in Central Africa. Proofs—and more proofs—and then more proofs again—were what he wanted. .... Well, in good time, the poor creature died and came here: and there was no power in the universe would have prevented him staying and going on to the mountains. But do ye think that did him any good? This country was no use to him at all. Everyone here had "survived" already. Nobody took the least interest in the question. There was nothing more to prove. His occupation was clean gone. Of course if he would only have admitted that he'd mistaken the means for the end and had a good laugh at himself he could have begun all over again like a little child and entered into joy. But he would not do that. He cared nothing about joy. In the end he went away.'

'How fantastic!' said I.

'Do ye think so?' said the Teacher with a piercing glance. .... 'There have been men before now who got so interested in proving the existence of God that they came to care nothing for God Himself... as if the good Lord had nothing to do but *exist!* There have been some who were so occupied in spreading Christianity that they never gave a thought to Christ.'

—from *The Great Divorce*

1824 George MacDonald (d. 1905), of whose writing Lewis would later say, "What it did to me was to convert, even to baptize...my imagination," is born in Aberdeenshire, Scotland.

To the Extreme

Screwtape explains the usefulness of extremism:

I had not forgotten my promise to consider whether we should make the patient an extreme patriot or an extreme pacifist. All extremes, except extreme devotion to the Enemy, are to be encouraged. Not always, of course, but at this period. Some ages are lukewarm and complacent, and then it is our business to soothe them yet faster asleep. Other ages, of which the present is one, are unbalanced and prone to faction, and it is our business to inflame them. Any small coterie, bound together by some interest which other men dislike or ignore, tends to develop inside itself a hothouse mutual admiration, and towards the outer world, a great deal of pride and hatred which is entertained without shame because the 'Cause' is its sponsor and it is thought to be impersonal. Even when the little group exists originally for the Enemy's own purposes, this remains true. We want the Church to be small not only that fewer men may know the Enemy but also that those who do may acquire the uneasy intensity and the defensive self-righteousness of a secret society or a clique. The Church herself is, of course, heavily defended and we have never yet quite succeeded in giving her *all* the characteristics of a faction; but subordinate factions within her have often produced admirable results, from the parties of Paul and of Apollos at Corinth down to the High and Low parties in the Church of England.

—from *The Screwtape Letters*

From Outsider to Insider

Screwtape instructs Wormwood to foster a sense of entitlement:

Here is your chance. While the Enemy, by means of sexual love and of some very agreeable people far advanced in His service, is drawing the young barbarian up to levels he could never otherwise have reached, you must make him feel that he is finding his *own* level—that these people are 'his sort' and that, coming among them, he has come home. When he turns from them to other society he will find it dull; partly because almost any society within his reach is, in fact, much less entertaining, but still more because he will miss the enchantment of the young woman. You must teach him to mistake this contrast between the circle that delights and the circle that bores him for the contrast between Christians and unbelievers. He must be made to feel (he'd better not put it into words) 'how different we Christians are'; and by 'we Christians' he must really, but unknowingly, mean 'my set'; and by 'my set' he must mean not 'The people who, in their charity and humility, have accepted me', but 'The people with whom I associate by right'.

—from *The Screwtape Letters*

From Vanity into Pride

Screwtape shows Wormwood how to transform a minor trespass into a major sin:

Success here depends on confusing him. If you try to make him explicitly and professedly proud of being a Christian, you will probably fail; the Enemy's warnings are too well known. If, on the other hand, you let the idea of 'we Christians' drop out altogether and merely make him complacent about 'his set', you will produce not true spiritual pride but mere social vanity which, by comparison, is a trumpery, puny little sin. What you want is to keep a sly self-congratulation mixing with all his thoughts and never allow him to raise the question 'What, precisely, am I congratulating myself *about?*' The idea of belonging to an inner ring, of being in a secret, is very sweet to him. Play on that nerve. Teach him, using the influence of this girl when she is silliest, to adopt an air of *amusement* at the things the unbelievers say. Some theories which he may meet in modern Christian circles may here prove helpful; theories, I mean, that place the hope of society in some inner ring of 'clerks', some trained minority of theocrats. It is no affair of yours whether those theories are true or false; the great thing is to make Christianity a mystery religion in which he feels himself one of the initiates.

—from *The Screwtape Letters*

1916 Lewis (age eighteen) receives a scholarship to University College, Oxford.

To Be on the Inside

I believe that in all men's lives at certain periods, and in many men's lives at all periods between infancy and extreme old age, one of the most dominant elements is the desire to be inside the local Ring and the terror of being left outside. This desire, in one of its forms, has indeed had ample justice done to it in literature. I mean, in the form of snobbery. Victorian fiction is full of characters who are hagridden by the desire to get inside that particular Ring which is, or was, called Society. But it must be clearly understood that "Society," in that sense of the word, is merely one of a hundred Rings and snobbery, there-fore, only one form of the longing to be inside. People who believe themselves to be free, and indeed are free, from snobbery, and who read satires on snobbery with tranquil superiority, may be devoured by the desire in another form. It may be the very intensity of their desire to enter some quite different Ring which renders them immune from the allurements of high life. An invitation from a duchess would be very cold comfort to a man smarting under the sense of exclusion from some artistic or communist coterie. Poor man—it is not large, lighted rooms, or champagne, or even scandals about peers and Cabi-net Ministers that he wants; it is the sacred little attic or studio, the heads bent together, the fog of tobacco smoke, and the delicious knowl-edge that we—we four or five all huddled beside this stove—are the people who *know*.

—from "The Inner Ring" *(The Weight of Glory)*

1944 Lewis delivers "The Inner Ring" as the annual "Commemoration Oration" given at King's College, University of London.

The Sly Impulse

Often the desire [to be part of the Inner Ring] conceals itself so well that we hardly recognise the pleasures of fruition. Men tell not only their wives but themselves that it is a hardship to stay late at the office or the school on some bit of important extra work which they have been let in for because they and So-and-so and the two others are the only people left in the place who really know how things are run. But it is not quite true. It is a terrible bore, of course, when old Fatty Smithson draws you aside and whispers, "Look here, we've got to get you in on this examination somehow" or "Charles and I saw at once that you've got to be on this committee." A terrible bore...ah, but how much more terrible if you were left out! It is tiring and unhealthy to lose your Saturday afternoons, but to have them free because you don't matter, that is much worse.

Freud would say, no doubt, that the whole thing is a subterfuge of the sexual impulse. I wonder whether the shoe is not sometimes on the other foot. I wonder whether, in ages of promiscuity, many a virginity has not been lost less in obedience to Venus than in obedience to the lure of the caucus. For, of course, when promiscuity is the fashion, the chaste are outsiders. They are ignorant of something that other people know. They are uninitiated. And as for lighter matters, the number who first smoked or first got drunk for a similar reason is probably very large.

—from "The Inner Ring" *(The Weight of Glory)*

A Permanent Mainspring of Human Action

My main purpose in this address is simply to convince you that this desire is one of the great permanent mainsprings of human action. It is one of the factors which go to make up the world as we know it—this whole pell-mell of struggle, competition, confusion, graft, disappointment, and advertisement, and if it is one of the permanent main springs, then you may be quite sure of this. Unless you take measures to prevent it, this desire is going to be one of the chief motives of your life, from the first day on which you enter your profession until the day when you are too old to care. That will be the natural thing—the life that will come to you of its own accord. Any other kind of life, if you lead it, will be the result of conscious and continuous effort. If you do nothing about it, if you drift with the stream, you will in fact be an "inner ringer." I don't say you'll be a successful one; that's as may be. But whether by pining and moping outside Rings that you can never enter, or by passing triumphantly further and further in—one way or the other you will be that kind of man.

—from "The Inner Ring" *(The Weight of Glory)*

Why Avoid Becoming an "Inner Ringer"?

To nine out of ten of you the choice which could lead to scoundrelism will come, when it does come, in no very dramatic colours. Obviously bad men, obviously threatening or bribing, will almost certainly not appear. Over a drink or a cup of coffee, disguised as a triviality and sandwiched between two jokes, from the lips of a man, or woman, whom you have recently been getting to know rather better and whom you hope to know better still—just at the moment when you are most anxious not to appear crude, or naïf or a prig—the hint will come. It will be the hint of something which is not quite in accordance with the technical rules of fair play; something which the public, the ignorant, romantic public, would never understand; something which even the outsiders in your own profession are apt to make a fuss about, but something, says your new friend, which "we"—and at the word "we" you try not to blush for mere pleasure—something "we always do." And you will be drawn in, if you are drawn in, not by desire for gain or ease, but simply because at that moment, when the cup was so near your lips, you cannot bear to be thrust back again into the cold outer world. It would be so terrible to see the other man's face—that genial, confidential, delightfully sophisticated face—turn suddenly cold and contemptuous, to know that you had been tried for the Inner Ring and rejected. And then, if you are drawn in, next week it will be something a little further from the rules, and next year something further still, but all in the jolliest, friendliest spirit. It may end in a crash, a scandal, and penal servitude; it may end in millions, a peerage, and giving the prizes at your old school. But you will be a scoundrel.

. . . . Of all passions the passion for the Inner Ring is most skillful in making a man who is not yet a very bad man do very bad things.

—from "The Inner Ring" *(The Weight of Glory)*

Discovering Your Own
Ring of True Friendship

The quest of the Inner Ring will break your hearts unless you break it. But if you break it, a surprising result will follow. If in your working hours you make the work your end, you will presently find yourself all unawares inside the only circle in your profession that really matters. You will be one of the sound craftsmen, and other sound craftsmen will know it. This group of craftsmen will by no means coincide with the Inner Ring or the Important People or the People in the Know. It will not shape that professional policy or work up that professional influence which fights for the profession as a whole against the public, nor will it lead to those periodic scandals and crises which the Inner Ring produces. But it will do those things which that profession exists to do and will in the long run be responsible for all the respect which that profession in fact enjoys and which the speeches and advertisements cannot maintain. And if in your spare time you consort simply with the people you like, you will again find that you have come unawares to a real inside, that you are indeed snug and safe at the centre of something which, seen from without, would look exactly like an Inner Ring. But the difference is that its secrecy is accidental, and its exclusiveness a by-product, and no one was led thither by the lure of the esoteric, for it is only four or five people who like one another meeting to do things that they like. This is friendship. Aristotle placed it among the virtues. It causes perhaps half of all the happiness in the world, and no Inner Ringer can ever have it.

—from "The Inner Ring" *(The Weight of Glory)*

The Obstinate Tin Soldier

Did you ever think, when you were a child, what fun it would be if your toys could come to life? Well suppose you could really have brought them to life. Imagine turning a tin soldier into a real little man. It would involve turning the tin into flesh. And suppose the tin soldier did not like it. He is not interested in flesh: all he sees is that the tin is being spoilt. He thinks you are killing him. He will do everything he can to prevent you. He will not be made into a man if he can help it.

What you would have done about that tin soldier I do not know. But what God did about us was this. The Second Person in God, the Son, became human Himself: was born into the world as an actual man—a real man of a particular height, with hair of a particular colour, speaking a particular language, weighing so many stone. The Eternal Being, who knows everything and who created the whole universe, became not only a man but (before that) a baby, and before that a *foetus* inside a Woman's body. If you want to get the hang of it, think how you would like to become a slug or a crab.

—from *Mere Christianity*

One Tin Soldier Comes Alive

The result of this was that you now had one man who really was what all men were intended to be: one man in whom the created life, derived from His Mother, allowed itself to be completely and perfectly turned into the begotten life. The natural human creature in Him was taken up fully into the divine Son. Thus in one instance humanity had, so to speak, arrived: had passed into the life of Christ. And because the whole difficulty for us is that the natural life has to be, in a sense, 'killed', He chose an earthly career which involved the killing of His human desires at every turn—poverty, misunderstanding from His own family, betrayal by one of His intimate friends, being jeered at and manhandled by the Police, and execution by torture. And then, after being thus killed— killed every day in a sense—the human creature in Him, because it was united to the divine Son, came to life again. The Man in Christ rose again: not only the God. That is the whole point. For the first time we saw a real man. One tin soldier—real tin, just like the rest—had come fully and splendidly alive.

—from *Mere Christianity*

A God Distinct

The Christians are not claiming that simply 'God' was incarnate in Jesus. They are claiming that the one true God is He whom the Jews worshipped as Jahweh, and that it is He who has descended. Now the double character of Jahweh is this. On the one hand He is the God of Nature, her glad Creator. It is He who sends rain into the furrows till the valleys stand so thick with corn that they laugh and sing. The trees of the wood rejoice before Him and His voice causes the wild deer to bring forth their young. He is the God of wheat and wine and oil. In that respect He is constantly doing all the things that Nature-Gods do: He is Bacchus, Venus, Ceres all rolled into one. . . . .

On the other hand, Jahweh is clearly *not* a Nature-God. He does not die and come to life each year as a true Corn-king should. . . . . He is not the soul of Nature nor of any part of Nature. He inhabits eternity: He dwells in the high and holy place: heaven is His throne, not His vehicle, earth is His footstool, not His vesture. One day He will dismantle both and make a new heaven and earth. He is not to be identified even with the 'divine spark' in man. He is 'God and not man'. . . . .

Jahweh is neither the soul of Nature nor her enemy. . . . . She is His creature. He is not a nature-God, but the God of Nature—her inventor, maker, owner, and controller. To everyone who reads this book the conception has been familiar from childhood; we therefore easily think it is the most ordinary conception in the world. 'If people are going to believe in a God at all,' we ask, 'what other kind would they believe in?' But the answer of history is, 'Almost any other kind'.

—from *Miracles*

Think of It Like This

Let us suppose we possess parts of a novel or a symphony. Someone now brings us a newly discovered piece of manuscript and says, 'This is the missing part of the work. This is the chapter on which the whole plot of the novel really turned. This is the main theme of the symphony'. Our business would be to see whether the new passage, if admitted to the central place which the discoverer claimed for it, did actually illuminate all the parts we had already seen and 'pull them together'. Nor should we be likely to go very far wrong. The new passage, if spurious, however attractive it looked at the first glance, would become harder and harder to reconcile with the rest of the work the longer we considered the matter. But if it were genuine then at every fresh hearing of the music or every fresh reading of the book, we should find it settling down, making itself more at home and eliciting significance from all sorts of details in the whole work which we had hitherto neglected. Even though the new central chapter or main theme contained great difficulties in itself, we should still think it genuine provided that it continually removed difficulties elsewhere. Something like this we must do with the doctrine of the Incarnation. Here, instead of a symphony or a novel, we have the whole mass of our knowledge. The credibility will depend on the extent to which the doctrine, if accepted, can illuminate and integrate that whole mass. It is much less important that the doctrine itself should be fully comprehensible. We believe that the sun is in the sky at midday in summer not because we can clearly see the sun (in fact, we cannot) but because we can see everything else.

—from *Miracles*

Everywhere the Great Enters the Little

The discrepancy between a movement of atoms in an astronomer's cortex and his understanding that there must be a still unobserved planet beyond Uranus, is already so immense that the Incarnation of God Himself is, in one sense, scarcely more startling. We cannot conceive how the Divine Spirit dwelled within the created and human spirit of Jesus: but neither can we conceive how His human spirit, or that of any man, dwells within his natural organism. What we can understand, if the Christian doctrine is true, is that our own composite existence is not the sheer anomaly it might seem to be, but a faint image of the Divine Incarnation itself—the same theme in a very minor key. We can understand that if God so descends into a human spirit, and human spirit so descends into Nature, and our thoughts into our senses and passions, and if adult minds (but only the best of them) can descend into sympathy with children, and men into sympathy with beasts, then everything hangs together and the total reality, both Natural and Supernatural, in which we are living is more multifariously and subtly harmonious than we had suspected. We catch sight of a new key principle—the power of the Higher, just in so far as it is truly Higher, to come down, the power of the greater to include the less. Thus solid bodies exemplify many truths of plane geometry, but plane figures no truths of solid geometry: many inorganic propositions are true of organisms but no organic propositions are true of minerals; Montaigne became kittenish with his kitten but she never talked philosophy to him. Everywhere the great enters the little—its power to do so is almost the test of its greatness.

—from *Miracles*

God Descends to Reascend

In the Christian story God descends to reascend. He comes down; down from the heights of absolute being into time and space, down into humanity; down further still, if embryologists are right, to recapitulate in the womb ancient and pre-human phases of life; down to the very roots and seabed of the Nature He has created. But He goes down to come up again and bring the whole ruined world up with Him. One has the picture of a strong man stooping lower and lower to get himself underneath some great complicated burden. He must stoop in order to lift, he must almost disappear under the load before he incredibly straightens his back and marches off with the whole mass swaying on his shoulders. Or one may think of a diver, first reducing himself to nakedness, then glancing in mid-air, then gone with a splash, vanished, rushing down through green and warm water into black and cold water, down through increasing pressure into the death-like region of ooze and slime and old decay; then up again, back to colour and light, his lungs almost bursting, till suddenly he breaks surface again, holding in his hand the dripping, precious thing that he went down to recover. He and it are both coloured now that they have come up into the light: down below, where it lay colourless in the dark, he lost his colour too.

—from *Miracles*

1956 The announcement of Lewis's marriage to Joy Davidman Gresham appears in the *Times* (London).

The Grand Miracle

The central miracle asserted by Christians is the Incarnation. They say that God became Man. Every other miracle prepares for this, or exhibits this, or results from this. Just as every natural event is the manifestation at a particular place and moment of Nature's total character, so every particular Christian miracle manifests at a particular place and moment the character and significance of the Incarnation. There is no question in Christianity of arbitrary interferences just scattered about. It relates not a series of disconnected raids on Nature but the various steps of a strategically coherent invasion—an invasion which intends complete conquest and 'occupation'. The fitness, and therefore credibility, of the particular miracles depends on their relation to the Grand Miracle; all discussion of them in isolation from it is futile.

The fitness or credibility of the Grand Miracle itself cannot, obviously, be judged by the same standard. And let us admit at once that it is very difficult to find a standard by which it can be judged. If the thing happened, it was the central event in the history of the Earth— the very thing that the whole story has been about. .... It is easier to argue, on historical grounds, that the Incarnation actually occurred than to show, on philosophical grounds, the probability of its occurrence. The historical difficulty of giving for the life, sayings and influence of Jesus any explanation that is not harder than the Christian explanation, is very great. The discrepancy between the depth and sanity and (let me add) *shrewdness* of His moral teaching and the rampant megalomania which must lie behind His theological teaching unless He is indeed God, has never been satisfactorily got over.

—from *Miracles*

The Signature of the Soul

This signature on each soul may be a product of heredity and environment, but that only means that heredity and environment are among the instruments whereby God creates a soul. I am considering not how, but why, He makes each soul unique. If He had no use for all these differences, I do not see why He should have created more souls than one. Be sure that the ins and outs of your individuality are no mystery to Him; and one day they will no longer be a mystery to you. The mould in which a key is made would be a strange thing, if you had never seen a key: and the key itself a strange thing if you had never seen a lock. Your soul has a curious shape because it is a hollow made to fit a particular swelling in the infinite contours of the Divine substance, or a key to unlock one of the doors in the house with many mansions. For it is not humanity in the abstract that is to be saved, but you—you, the individual reader, John Stubbs or Janet Smith. Blessed and fortunate creature, your eyes shall behold Him and not another's. All that you are, sins apart, is destined, if you will let God have His good way, to utter satisfaction. The Brocken spectre 'looked to every man like his first love', because she was a cheat. But God will look to every soul like its first love because He is its first love. Your place in heaven will seem to be made for you and you alone, because you were made for it—made for it stitch by stitch as a glove is made for a hand.

—from *The Problem of Pain*

A New and Secret Name

The thing you long for summons you away from the self. Even the desire for the thing lives only if you abandon it. This is the ultimate law—the seed dies to live, the bread must be cast upon the waters, he that loses his soul will save it. But the life of the seed, the finding of the bread, the recovery of the soul, are as real as the preliminary sacrifice. Hence it is truly said of heaven 'in heaven there is no ownership. If any there took upon him to call anything his own, he would straightway be thrust out into hell and become an evil spirit.' But it is also said 'To him that overcometh I will give a white stone, and in the stone a new name written, which no man knoweth saving he that receiveth it' [Revelation 2:17]. What can be more a man's own than this new name which even in eternity remains a secret between God and him? And what shall we take this secrecy to mean? Surely, that each of the redeemed shall forever know and praise some one aspect of the Divine beauty better than any other creature can. Why else were individuals created, but that God, loving all infinitely, should love each differently? And this difference, so far from impairing, floods with meaning the love of all blessed creatures for one another, the communion of the saints. If all experienced God in the same way and returned Him an identical worship, the song of the Church triumphant would have no symphony, it would be like an orchestra in which all the instruments played the same note.

—from *The Problem of Pain*

To Drink Joy from the Fountain of Joy

When human souls have become as perfect in voluntary obedience as the inanimate creation is in its lifeless obedience, then they will put on its glory, or rather that greater glory of which Nature is only the first sketch. For you must not think that I am putting forward any heathen fancy of being absorbed into Nature. Nature is mortal; we shall outlive her. When all the suns and nebulae have passed away, each one of you will still be alive. Nature is only the image, the symbol; but it is the symbol Scripture invites me to use. We are summoned to pass in through Nature, beyond her, into that splendour which she fitfully reflects.

And in there, in beyond Nature, we shall eat of the tree of life. At present, if we are reborn in Christ, the spirit in us lives directly on God; but the mind and, still more, the body receives life from Him at a thousand removes—through our ancestors, through our food, through the elements. The faint, far-off results of those energies which God's creative rapture implanted in matter when He made the worlds are what we now call physical pleasures; and even thus filtered, they are too much for our present management. What would it be to taste at the fountainhead that stream of which even these lower reaches prove so intoxicating? Yet that, I believe, is what lies before us. The whole man is to drink joy from the fountain of joy. As St. Augustine said, the rapture of the saved soul will "flow over" into the glorified body.

—from "The Weight of Glory" *(The Weight of Glory)*

A Hymn to God's Creation

I spoke just now about the Latinity of Latin. It is more evident to us than it can have been to the Romans. The Englishness of English is audible only to those who know some other language as well. In the same way and for the same reason, only Supernaturalists really see Nature. You must go a little away from her, and then turn round, and look back. Then at last the true landscape will become visible. You must have tasted, however briefly, the pure water from beyond the world before you can be distinctly conscious of the hot, salty tang of Nature's current. To treat her as God, or as Everything, is to lose the whole pith and pleasure of her. Come out, look back, and then you will see...this astonishing cataract of bears, babies and bananas: this immoderate deluge of atoms, orchids, oranges, cancers, canaries, fleas, gases, tornadoes and toads. How could you ever have thought this was the ultimate reality? How could you ever have thought that it was merely a stage-set for the moral drama of men and women? She is herself. Offer her neither worship nor contempt. Meet her and know her. If we are immortal, and if she is doomed (as the scientists tell us) to run down and die, we shall miss this half-shy and half-flamboyant creature, this ogress, this hoyden, this incorrigible fairy, this dumb witch. But the theologians tell us that she, like ourselves, is to be redeemed. The 'vanity' to which she was subjected was her disease, not her essence. She will be cured in character: not tamed (Heaven forbid) nor sterilised. We shall still be able to recognise our old enemy, friend, playfellow and foster-mother, so perfected as to be not less, but more, herself. And that will be a merry meeting.

—from *Miracles*

Heaven's Revels

The golden apple of selfhood, thrown among the false gods, became an apple of discord because they scrambled for it. They did not know the first rule of the holy game, which is that every player must by all means touch the ball and then immediately pass it on. To be found with it in your hands is a fault: to cling to it, death. But when it flies to and fro among the players too swift for eye to follow, and the great master Himself leads the revelry, giving Himself eternally to His creatures in the generation, and back to Himself in the sacrifice, of the Word, then indeed the eternal dance 'makes heaven drowsy with the harmony'. All pains and pleasures we have known on earth are early initiations in the movements of that dance: but the dance itself is strictly incomparable with the sufferings of this present time. As we draw nearer to its uncreated rhythm, pain and pleasure sink almost out of sight. There is joy in the dance, but it does not exist for the sake of joy. It does not even exist for the sake of good, or of love. It is Love Himself, and Good Himself, and therefore happy. It does not exist for us, but we for it.

—from *The Problem of Pain*

Glory as Brightness, Splendour, Luminosity

This brings me to the other sense of glory—glory as brightness, splendour, luminosity. We are to shine as the sun, we are to be given the Morning Star. I think I begin to see what it means. In one way, of course, God has given us the Morning Star already: you can go and enjoy the gift on many fine mornings if you get up early enough. What more, you may ask, do we want? Ah, but we want so much more—something the books on aesthetics take little notice of. But the poets and the mythologies know all about it. We do not want merely to *see* beauty, though, God knows, even that is bounty enough. We want something else which can hardly be put into words—to be united with the beauty we see, to pass into it, to receive it into ourselves, to bathe in it, to become part of it. That is why we have peopled air and earth and water with gods and goddesses and nymphs and elves—that, though we cannot, yet these projections can enjoy in themselves that beauty, grace, and power of which Nature is the image. That is why the poets tell us such lovely falsehoods. They talk as if the west wind could really sweep into a human soul; but it can't. They tell us that "beauty born of murmuring sound" will pass into a human face; but it won't. Or not yet. For if we take the imagery of Scripture seriously, if we believe that God will one day *give* us the Morning Star and cause us to *put on* the splendour of the sun, then we may surmise that both the ancient myths and the modern poetry, so false as history, may be very near the truth as prophecy. At present we are on the outside of the world, the wrong side of the door. We discern the freshness and purity of morning, but they do not make us fresh and pure. We cannot mingle with the splendours we see. But all the leaves of the New Testament are rustling with the rumour that it will not always be so. Some day, God willing, we shall get *in*.

—from "The Weight of Glory" *(The Weight of Glory)*

Sources by Book

Abolition of Man
    November 5
The Great Divorce
    January 26, April 16, October 20, November 13, November 14, November 29, November 30, December 6, December 8, December 9, December 10
A Grief Observed
    March 21, April 17, April 18, April 23, July 13, July 14, July 15, July 16, August 1, August 2, August 3, August 4, August 5, August 6, September 29, September 30, October 1, October 2, October 3, October 4
Mere Christianity
    January 5, January 6, January 7, January 8, January 9, January 14, January 17, January 18, January 19, January 22, January 23, January 24, January 25, January 27, February 5, February 6, February 7, February 11, February 12, February 13, February 14, February 15, February 16, February 17, February 21, February 22, February 23, February 26, February 27, February 28, March 1, March 2, March 10, March 12, March 16, March 17, March 18, March 19, March 20, March 22, March 23, March 24, March 25, March 26, March 27, March 28, March 29, April 11, May 3, May 6, May 8, May 9, May 10, May 11, May 13, May 14, May 15, May 17, May 18, May 19, May 21, May 22, May 23, May 24, May 25, May 29, June 1, June 21, June 22, June 23, June 24, June 25, June 26, June 27, June 28, June 29, June 30, July 7, July 8, July 9, July 10, July 11, July 12, July 17, July 18, July 19, July 20, July 22, July 24, July 25, July 26, July 27, July 28, July 29, July 30, July 31, August 7, August 10, August 11, August 12, August 13, August 16, August 17, August 18, August 19, August 20, September 9, September 10, September 11, September 12, September 13, September 15, September 16, September 17, September 18, September 19, September 21, September 22, September 23, September 24, September 25, September 26, September 27, October 27, November 24, November 25, November 26, December 7, December 19, December 20

Miracles
    January 1, January 2, January 3, January 4, March 11, March 13, March 14, March 15, May 4, May 5, May 7, May 12, May 16, June 2, June 3, June 4, June 5, June 6, June 7, June 9, June 10, June 11, June 12, June 13, June 14, June 15, June 16, June 17, June 20, October 21, October 28, October 29, November 15, December 21, December 22, December 23, December 24, December 25, December 29
The Problem of Pain
    January 10, January 11, January 12, January 15, January 16, February 18, February 19, February 20, February 24, February 29, March 3, March 4, March 5, March 6, March 7, March 8, March 9, April 2, April 21, April 22, July 21, September 14, October 5, October 6, October 7, October 8, October 9, October 10, October 11, October 12, October 13, October 14, October 15, October 16, October 17, October 18, October 30, November 23, November 27, November 28, December 1, December 2, December 3, December 4, December 5, December 26, December 27, December 30
The Screwtape Letters
    January 13, January 28, February 8, February 9, February 25, March 30, March 31, April 1, April 3, April 4, April 5, April 6, April 8, April 9, April 10, April 12, April 13, April 14, April 15, April 19, April 20, April 30, May 1, May 2, May 26, May 27, May 31, June 18, June 19, July 23, August 8, August 9, August 14, August 15, August 21, August 22, August 23, August 24, August 25, August 26, August 27, September 2, September 20, September 28, October 26, October 31, November 1, November 2, November 9, November 10, December 11, December 12, December 13
The Screwtape Letters: "Screwtape Proposes a Toast"
    July 1, July 2, July 3, July 4
The Weight of Glory: "The Inner Ring"
    December 14, December 15, December 16, December 17, December 18

The *Weight of Glory:* "Is Theology Poetry?"
January 20, January 21, November 3,
November 4, November 6
The *Weight of Glory:* "Learning In War-Time"
May 30, September 3, September 4, September 5, September 6, September 7, September 8, October 22, October 23, October 24, October 25
The *Weight of Glory:* "Membership"
February 10, April 24, April 25, April 26, April 27, April 28, April 29, May 20, July 5, July 6
The *Weight of Glory;* "On Forgiveness"
August 28, August 29, August 30, August 31, September 1

The *Weight of Glory:* "A Slip of the Tongue"
January 29, January 30, January 31, February 1, February 2, February 3, February 4
The *Weight of Glory:* "Transposition"
May 28
The *Weight of Glory:* "The Weight of Glory"
April 7, June 8, November 16, November 17, November 18, November 19, November 20, November 21, November 22, December 28, December 31
The *Weight of Glory:* "Why I Am Not a Pacifist"
October 19, November 7, November 8, November 11, November 12

Sources by Day

All page numbers given are from the HarperSanFrancisco editions.

January 1	*Miracles*	150
January 2	*Miracles*	142–143
January 3	*Miracles*	143–144
January 4	*Miracles*	144–145
January 5	*Mere Christianity*	30–31
January 6	*Mere Christianity*	26–27
January 7	*Mere Christianity*	37–38
January 8	*Mere Christianity*	149–150
January 9	*Mere Christianity*	29
January 10	*The Problem of Pain*	31–32
January 11	*The Problem of Pain*	32–33
January 12	*The Problem of Pain*	39–40
January 13	*The Screwtape Letters*	100–101
January 14	*Mere Christianity*	164–165
January 15	*The Problem of Pain*	44
January 16	*The Problem of Pain*	47
January 17	*Mere Christianity*	170
January 18	*Mere Christianity*	153–154
January 19	*Mere Christianity*	154–155
January 20	*The Weight of Glory:* "Is Theology Poetry?"	128–129
January 21	*The Weight of Glory:* "Is Theology Poetry?"	129–130
January 22	*Mere Christianity*	50–51
January 23	*Mere Christianity*	61–62
January 24	*Mere Christianity*	32
January 25	*Mere Christianity*	41–42
January 26	*The Great Divorce*	VIII
January 27	*Mere Christianity*	63
January 28	*The Screwtape Letters*	45–46
January 29	*The Weight of Glory:* "A Slip of the Tongue"	184–185

Sources by Selection Title

410